THE SELECTIVE EYE

The Selective Eye

AN ANTHOLOGY OF THE BEST FROM L'ŒIL,

THE EUROPEAN ART MAGAZINE

EDITED BY GEORGES AND ROSAMOND BERNIER

WITH 48 PAGES IN COLOR

L'ŒIL   PARIS   LAUSANNE

RANDOM HOUSE   NEW YORK

All the material appearing in this book was selected from the first nine issues
(January-September 1955) of L'ŒIL. The texts were originally printed in French,
and are given here in English for the first time

Published in New York by Random House, Inc. and in Toronto by Random House of Canada, Limited
All rights reserved under International and Pan-American Copyright Conventions
Library of Congress Catalog Card Number: 55-11347

Printed in Switzerland

"Do you know why we like El Greco so much ?" von Tschudi, the great German museum director, once asked. "It is because he reminds us of Cézanne."

No wonder Kaiser Wilhelm fired the subversive von Tschudi from his Berlin post. The Kaiser was right : in 1900 a taste for such painters as Cézanne and El Greco was indeed a threat to the security of respectable convention even though one of the artists had been dead almost three hundred years.

Every mature civilization is concerned with two categories of art, its own and that of earlier periods. Between the now and the then there is a constant interaction. The eye, stimulated by the modern artist (even by reaction against him), seeks and finds a fresh past not yet worn thin and dull.

L'ŒIL — a monthly art review started in January 1955 — is such an eye. In its unhackneyed pages you will find the two pasts, the one we measure in centuries and that more recent one we call the present. L'ŒIL has explored both pasts with taste and wit, scholarship tempered by journalistic brevity and sense of timing, and above all an intention to delight as much as to inform.

Edited by a Frenchman and his American wife in Paris, and beautifully printed in Switzerland, L'ŒIL, even in its extreme youth, has won a grateful following. For those who missed its early issues, THE SELECTIVE EYE here republishes many of its admirably produced plates and, in English translation, its most valuable texts.

ALFRED H. BARR JR.
15 July 1955

CONTENTS

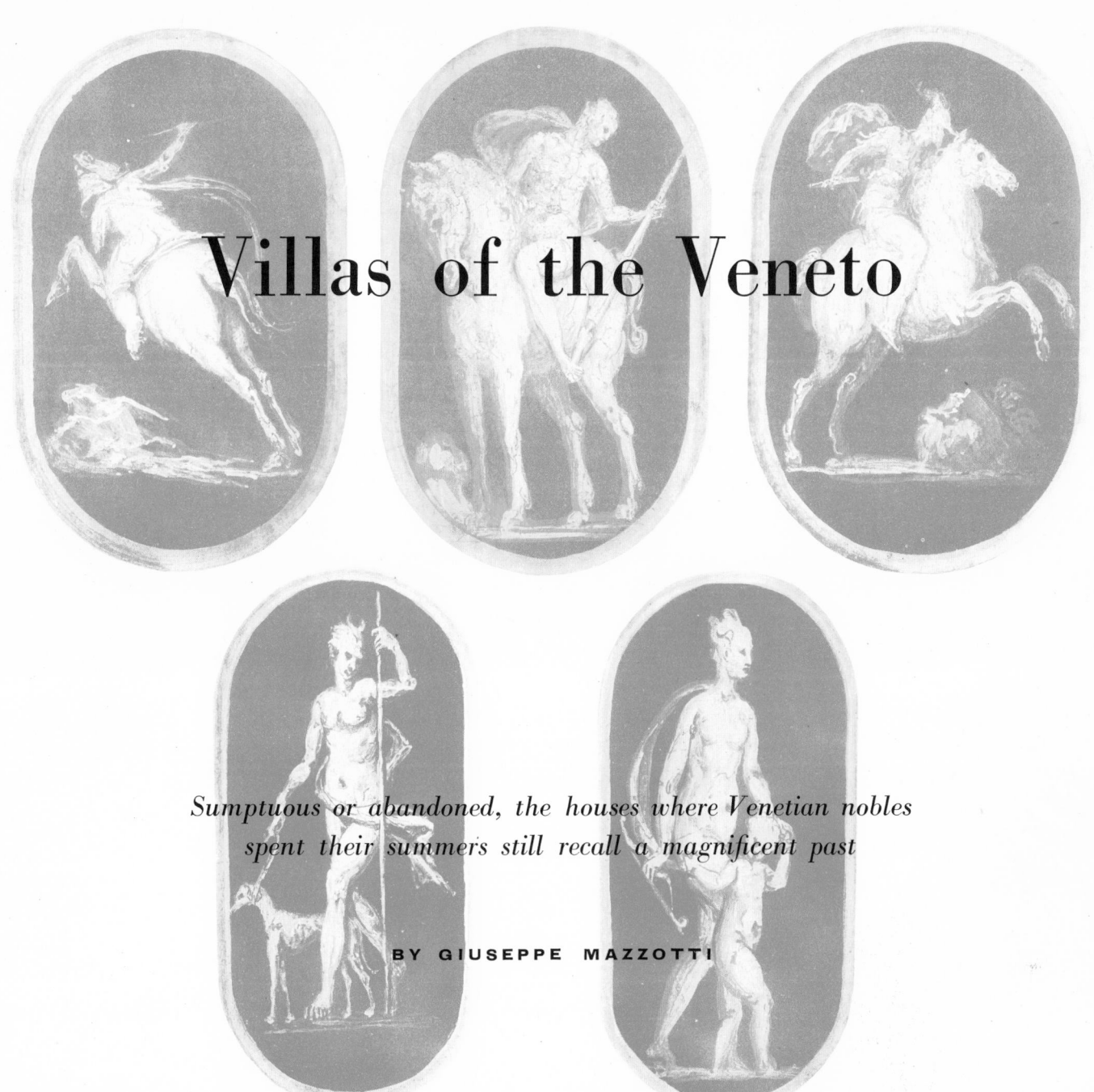

Villas of the Veneto

*Sumptuous or abandoned, the houses where Venetian nobles
spent their summers still recall a magnificent past*

BY GIUSEPPE MAZZOTTI

When Venice was one of the great powers of the world, the Venetians lived on the sea, and it was from the sea that all their riches were derived. The city was a mirror in which were reflected all the splendors of the Orient. It was decked with white marble lattice-work, spires, pinnacles and statues that seemed to soar above the buildings and dance, reflected in the dark waters of the canal This was the period of "flowering gothic".

Then came the discovery of America. New routes were opened for the sailing vessels of other nations and a chill presentiment of their future decadence made the Venetians turn their eyes back towards dry land.

In the fine print by Jacopo de' Barbari (which dates from 1500), two houses can be seen on the Giudecca built facing the garden. Until then the facades of all Venetian houses faced the water—the natural highway of Venice. In the print, these two houses have turned their backs to the sea and have a welcoming portico built facing the garden. It is the first document we have about the birth of the country house—soon to develop into the Venetian villa.

Ornamental chimney of the Della Torre villa at Fumano, built in 1558. Above: details of frescos by Veronese; Villa Barbaro, Maser

Already a century and a half before, Pietro, the son of Dante Alighieri, owned a country house at Valpolicella, above Verona, and Petrarch had retired to the quiet hills of Arqua, near Padua, to devote himself, as he said, to "agriculture and architecture". As always, the poets were the pioneers, and, long before the rich merchants, they found themselves in country house gardens talking of Plato and the beauty of the world as an expression of God. With the taste for classical antiquity had reappeared a taste for nature—particularly when it was tamed and reduced to terms of a pleasant garden. This taste may perhaps have had a literary origin; it played a determining role in the formation of that immense patrimony of houses and gardens which enriched the Veneto between the XVth and the XVIIIth centuries. The country-side, dominated by feudal castles, was up to then only sparsely covered with convents, monasteries and wretched peasant dwellings. The first villas were built in the immediate vicinity of the towns, and only timid sallies were made into the solitary countryside.

In the last ten years of the XVth century, the Venetian Republic graciously assigned, as a residence for Caterina Cornaro, the widow of Giacomo di Lusignano, King of Cyprus, "the beautiful and pleasant Castle of Asolo, built on the

Gian Battista Tiepolo owned this country villa at Zianigo, typical of the small pleasure houses built near Venice during the XVIIIth century. Tiepolo and his son Gian Domenico decorated it with charming frescos that are now in Venice at the Ca' Rezzonico.

foot-hills of the Alps, above Treviso". Here she held court for twenty years until the Republic's war against the League of Cambrai. After this, the Queen built an extraordinary edifice called "Il Barco" (The Ship).

It was a pleasure house for receptions and hunting parties, decorated with magnificent frescos traces of which can still be seen today. It is one of the few XVth century buildings, isolated in the Venetian countryside, whose structure has remained more or less intact.

There still exist—around Vicenza for instance—examples of XVth century villas with rounded porticos, surmounted by loggias and architraves, standing against an ancient tower with gothic apertures. The remarkable diversity of the architectural styles in the older villas tends to become uniform in the villas dating from the beginning of the XVIth century. Balanced in their lines, and usually ornamented with frescos, they reproduced the standard model of Venetian houses with a large hall in the center and a room at each of the four corners. This model was later repeated, with the addition of wings or "barchesse"; then enriched by classic elements, embellished with baroque forms, but it always reappeared until the end of the XVIIIth century.

The beginning of the great period for the construction of villas coincides with the end of the war of the League of Cambrai, at the beginning of the fifteen hundreds. The countryside had been pacified and security re-established in

remote localities. The first "country house parties" were given in well defended castles. Then one night the draw-bridge was left down and never raised again. Windows pierced the thick outer walls, galleries and porticos appeared, and eventually graceful frescos added the final transformation of castle into villa. However, the taste for castles persisted and walls with crenellated towers were still constructed in the guise of ornament around peaceful gardens. Naturally, not all the villas were the result of transforming ancient castles and new ones began to appear dotted all over the countryside—in particular along the "Riviera" of the Brenta, that magnificent canal lined with villas and gardens, which joins Venice to Padua and might be defined as a sort of rustic extension of the Grand Canal, and the Sile canal.

It was here that, for three hundred years, the noble families of Veneto vied with one another to construct increasingly luxurious houses. For every Venetian palace there were two, three, ten or even more villas, many of them by great architects. Princely residences were built in the foothills of Abano and Conegliano or on the Berici and examples are to be found as far away as the Verona hills and the banks of Lake Garda or on the edge of the Friulian plain.

Gian Domenico Tiepolo : fresco at the Villa Valmarana ai Nani This house was decorated in 1757 with a famous series of frescos on rustic or allegorical themes by Tiepolo; the paintings are intact.

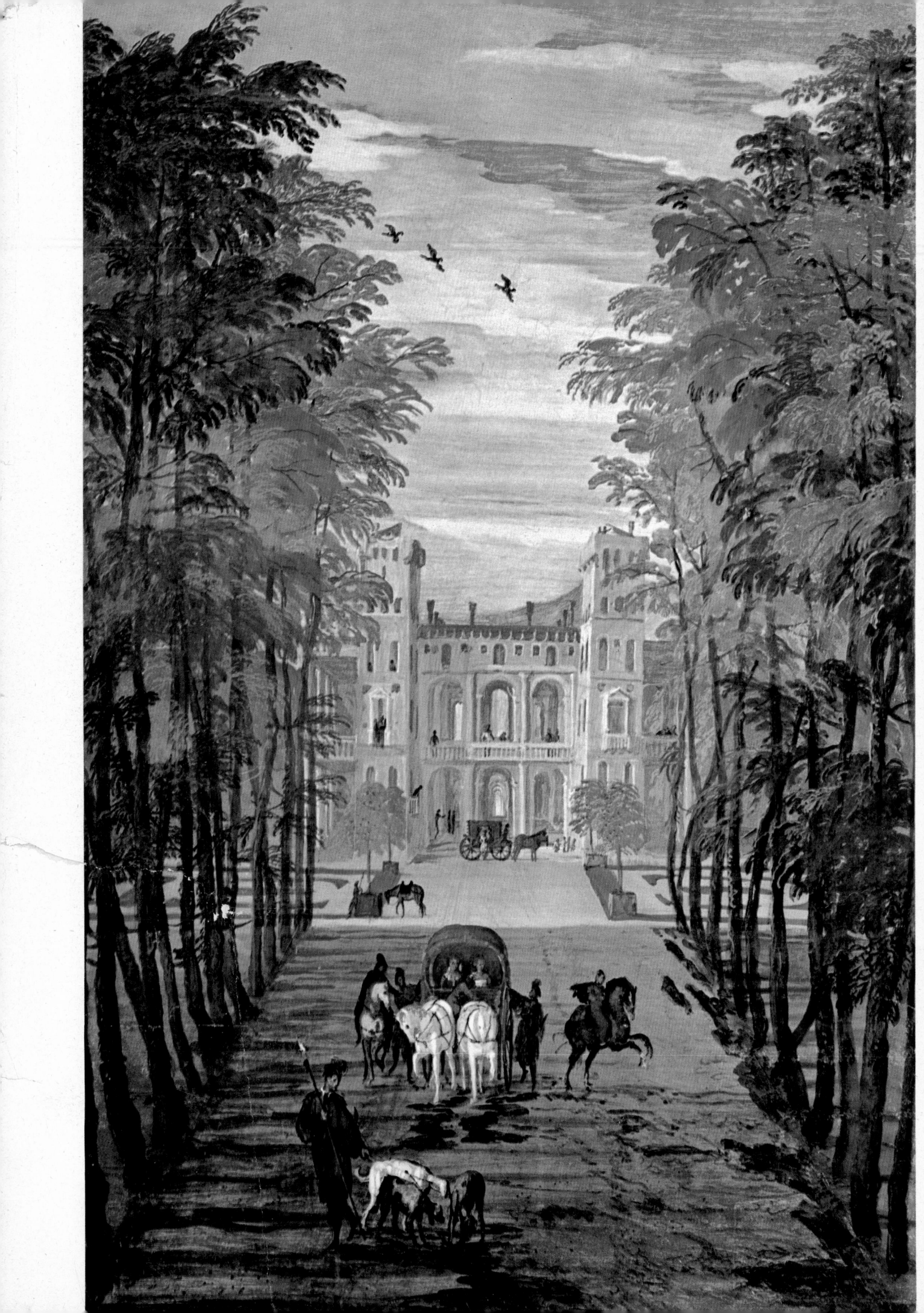

There are still some two thousand villas remaining in the Venetian country-side; built during three centuries by the patricians and wealthy merchants of the Republic. Many of these former show places have been turned into farms ; the new owners make no effort to preserve their beauty. Above : the XVIIIth century salon of a villa near Treviso, its decoration flaking, now used as a barn.

One of the most important villas, the first perhaps to be designed by a great architect, is the villa of Sansovino, built in 1527 for Luigi Garzoni at Pontecasale, in the province of Padua. Then came the "Villa dei Vescovi" built by Falconetto for Gardinal Francesco Pisani, the Bishop of Padua, at Luvigliano. Here, and particularly in the main doorway and in the separation of the arches, we can plainly see the reflection of Roman architecture which Palladio so brilliantly exploited in the middle of the XVIth century in his palaces and villas. Palladio was the creator of a form of domestic architecture which might be called the "Temple-Villa" in which vast staircases are combined with porticos wide open to greet the landscape. Palladio is to be found throughout the entire Veneto ; on the Brenta, in the imposing, melancholy "Malcontenta" built for the Foscari family, in the beautiful "Badoera", now completely abandoned, with its two "barchesse" like open arms extended to great the visitor, as well as in the highly original villa of Marcantonio Serego at Santa di Pedemonte, in the Verona foothills. Whatever aspect the villas designed by Palladio may assume, one of their most remarkable characteristics is that they

Veronese : fresco from the Villa Barbaro at Maser- a scene of patrician life in the country in the XVIth cent. Palladio built this villa in 1536 ; six rooms were decorated by Veronese.

do not simply "harmonize" with the countryside, but really merge into it as one of its natural elements.

Other important architectural experiments were being made at the same time as Palladio and even before him : Michele Sanmicheli built the grandiose villa called the "Soranza" at Treville di Castelfranco Veneto. This villa, which was entirely decorated with frescos by Paolo Veronese, was destroyed during the last century. Over a hundred large compositions including entire ceilings, were stripped off, and mostly lost. They represented his greatest cycle of frescos ; only a few vestiges remain in the sacristy of the Church of Castelfranco Veneto. There is nothing comparable to the scope of this decorative scheme except that of the Villa Barbaro, now the Villa Volpi, at Maser.

Palladio was commissioned to build the Villa Barbaro in about 1560. It is situated on the slope of a hill with a garden in the Italian manner and a fine view. Its walls and ceilings were covered with the magnificent frescos of Paolo Veronese representing divinities from Olympus, false statues, bas-reliefs framed in architectural motifs, weapons and flags disposed in the corners, strange *trompe-l'œil* effects with an extraordinary power of suggestion, and large landscapes giving the impression of windows opening onto the surrounding countryside.

The shady banks of the Brenta canal was a favorite site for Venetians who took to the country. Here Palladio built the celebrated villa La Malcontenta in 1551. With its rigorous lines and columned portico it is considered a perfect example of the architect's "temple-villa" style. Well maintained by the present owner, orange trees and willows add a nostalgic charm to its severe beauty.

The Villa Barbaro, like almost all the other villas, was built to satisfy the desire for splendor of its proprietors—a splendor intended to exact respect from the peasantry and affirm aristocratic power over the goods of this earth. But the Villa also served the purpose of resolving all the problems of country life: Palladio wrote, on this particular subject, that he had "built the Barbaro's country house, with stables, cellars and a place for making wine". There always were, in fact, either next to the main building or even joined to it, the granaries, stables, and servants quarters. The Venetians never forgot that their existence depended upon the produce of the countryside.

In the XVIIth century the taste for intellectual gatherings was replaced by a fashion for luxurious entertainment. Some of the parties, given at this time, such as the reception of the Duke and Duchess of Brunswick at the Villa Contarini at Piazzola on the Brenta, are still remembered for their incredible ostentation. But the humanist tendencies of some of these noble landlords were not entirely extinguished and their interest in the best artists of the time gave birth to several masterpieces. In the XVIth century a great deal of prestige was attached to owning a house built by Palladio and even in later times it continued to be a point of honor to employ only the very best architects. Many of these buildings particularly the smaller ones, have remained anonymous but

in the XVIIth and XVIIIth centuries we can identify works by Scamozzi, Muttoni, Longhena, Frigimelica and, at the beginning of the XIXth, by Giuseppe Jappelli, the master of neo-classical architecture.

The gardens were filled with innumerable statues by Orazio Marinali or by his pupils, the ceilings and the walls were decorated by the Tiepolos and Guarana who painted large vistas of clouds opening to reveal the luminous heavens.

The most astonishing decoration by Gian Battista Tiepolo was undoubtedly that in the villa Gaetano Soderini built at Nervesa. The main salon had two ceilings: between the two, small windows admitted the rays of the setting sun so as to give the illusion of light falling on the clouds and painted figures of the upper ceiling. There still remain intact the frescos with which he and his son decorated the Villa Valmarana ai Nani (Vicenza) and those that Gian Domenico painted in the modest country house which the two artists owned at Zianigo. They were removed from the wall and are now to be seen in the Museum of the Ca' Rezzonico in Venice. Above all there is still the magnificent ceiling of the Villa Pisani at Stra, on the Brenta, known as the "Glory of the Pisani Family", the sketches for which are in France at the Museum of Angers.

The Tiepolos were not the only painters to own a house in the Venetian coutryside. Titian built a villa in the XVIth century with a superb view of the hills of Vittorio Veneto, as payment for a triptych in the church of Castel Roganzuolo : the villa and the painting still exist, but have been extremely badly restored.

The Venetians were still building magnificent houses in last days of the Republic, even bigger and more luxurious than those of the preceding periods. Two of them are worthy of special attention : the villa that was built in 1735 according to the plans of Frigimelica and Francesco Maria Preti by Alvise Pisani, at Strá on the Brenta—the site of his family country house—and the immense Villa Manin, at Passariano, in the Friulian plain, which belonged to the last Doge of Venice. Napoleon lived in both of these villas, both have the sad and solemn splendor of abandoned palaces, particularly the Villa Manin with its enormous hexahedral porticos enclosing a vast lawn in their empty embrace, facing the main building, white, deserted and almost absurd in its utter uselessness.

From the shores of Lake Garda to the Po, from the Venetian lagoon to Friul, there are still any number of houses and villas in existence. Some are scrupulously kept up by the descendants of the people who built them ; others are deteriorating while others—unfortunately the greater part—are abandoned and falling into ruin. Sometimes the façade remains while the interior has been mutilated and ransacked by the poor of the district or by canny speculators. Frescos and statues have been sold abroad. The ceilings of the Villa Panigai at Nervesa, painted by Gian Battista Tiepolo, are in the Kaiser Friedrich Museum in Berlin. Other frescos, also by Tiepolo, are in the Musée Jacquemart-André in Paris as well as the stone lions which ornamented the entrance of the Villa Contarini. In some instances the main building has been destroyed, the statues and ornaments sold, but the outbuildings survive and so, quite often, does the chapel. Each of these villas had a chapel (often large enough to be open to the public). When the villas were demolished, it was frequently considered sacrilegious to destroy the chapels and these remained—with a statue or some vestige of a wall still standing as the only trace of their vanished houses.

Each year that passes other villas disappear because of the difficulties their owners encounter in trying to maintain them. But even today there are still many of them which

This medieval tower had been preserved when the Agazzi-Sailer villa was built around it in the XVIIIth century. The present owner, a farmer, tore it down recently to make room for his crops.

appear quite unexpectedly at the end of an avenue or at the top of a hill or are suddenly reflected in the waters of the canal. Let us hope that future generations will not be totally deprived of the possibility of enjoying one of the greatest manifestations of the art of building in which architecture is perfectly blended with its natural surroundings.

The Grimani villa at Fiesso d'Artico (XVIIIth cent. engraving).

15

Georges Braque's New "Atelier"

BY JOHN RICHARDSON

Working in stained-glass, the artist rediscovers color

Braque, as much as any XXth century artist, has constantly changed his approach to color. His earliest works were comparatively dark in tone ; then the painting of Matisse and Derain opened his eyes to the possibilities of pure color, and Braque became briefly (1906-07) a Fauve. But the Fauves were primarily concerned with the painting of light and also with decoration ; what Braque wanted was to paint space and form as well as light. So by degrees he abandoned bright hues, at first for greens and ochres and finally (in 1910) for the grays and neutral tones of Cubism. Nevertheless, while working a little later on his first

papiers collés, Braque made the important discovery, "that color acts independently of form". Color thus became for him an independent, even "abstract" element, and he felt free to treat it as he liked, regardless of the exigences of natural appearances. He has set his color harmonies in many different keys for many different purposes—sometimes because he liked a particular combination of colors, sometimes as a decorative or descriptive adjunct, sometimes to create volume and sometimes for other kindred reasons —but he has always combined them with variations in texture, translucency and opaqueness, and has integrated his use of color so completely

into the picture as a whole that it is impossible for the critic to treat it as an entirely separate element.

In his magisterial series of post-war pictures—*Ateliers* I-VI (1949-52)—Braque's attitude to color underwent a further significant change, for, after painting relatively bright works like the *Terraces* in 1948, he suddenly restricted himself to a range of grays, browns, buffs and blacks ("very rich as color," says Braque) and also to dark backgrounds which help to give an illusion of spatial depth. The main reason for this was that the problems with which Braque was concerned were of such complexity that " color would have been a distraction "; another reason is that, as Braque has himself remarked, " there is a muted quality to the light in my studio." During the last eighteen months, however, the colors which Braque banished from his palette in 1949 have returned brighter and stronger than ever—a development that occurred simultaneously with the execution of three stained glass windows for the church at Varengeville in Normandy.

In 1951 Braque spent, as usual, several months of the summer at his house at Varengeville, and while there was asked by the local *curé*, Abbé Lecoq, to assist him in choosing the design for some windows which he hoped to install in the new parish church. What the Abbé actually envisaged was that Braque should propose to design the windows himself. This the painter, with his natural good grace, did, and, while still at Varengeville, studied the problem, and finally made a pencil sketch and a large gouache. Two years then elapsed during which no more thought was apparently given to the matter ; and it was not until the autumn of 1953 that he took up the windows again. Even then it was a month or two before work started on the glass itself, for Braque, as usual, preferred to ponder

Pencil sketch dating from the summer of 1951 ; it was the first project by Braque for the Varengeville windows (11 × 6″).

At the same period Braque painted this gouache of St. Dominic. It became the theme of the central window (19½ × 11½″)

This sketch in one Georges Braque's famous notebooks was the point of departure for the large canvas The Atelier *given in color on page 20 and 21. The artist jotted down the general composition in pencil, adding vermillion and yellow. Jan. 1954 (4½ × 7″).*

deeply and at length about the project. At last, late in 1953, Braque's design was ready for Bony the *vitrier*. The firing and leading were completed in two months by Bony under the artist's active supervision, and in August 1954 the three windows, which Braque intends to complement in due course with one or two smaller ones, were inaugurated.

Many an artist might have been content to interpret one of his own paintings in terms of stained glass. Not so Braque : he has the fanatical conscientiousness of an artisan where technical matters are concerned, and so prefered to take into consideration the specific qualities as well as the limitations of stained glass. The result is that his windows are not simply beautiful patterns, but are technically apt in that they make the most of the possibilities of a time-honored craft, while at the same time representing an entirely fresh approach to that particular medium. Also we find in them that perfect accord between the subject, the "abstract" color and the material, which cha-

racterizes nearly all Braque's best works.

These windows are decorative, but it does not follow that they are merely interesting experiments on the part of a great painter in the domain of applied art. On the contrary, quite apart from their intrinsic artistic merits, they are of cardinal importance in what is to my mind a climactic period of Braque's work. For Braque's preoccupation with the luminous properties of color and with the simplification and definition of forms which the designing of stained-glass demands has been the means of changing the course of his recent painting. Various works testify to this new development, but the most impressive is the recently finished *Atelier*, a brilliantly colored picture which is probably the greatest Braque of the last twenty five years.

This luminous canvas, which is entirely different to all its sombre predecessors in conception as well as in color, though it is faithful to the original theme of the series, was begun by Braque early in 1954 soon after the

Varengeville windows were completed. The first step was a small rough drawing, heightened with color, in one of the painter's notebooks : an astonishingly bold and original composition dominated by two red forms (canvases) with a yellow

Photograph of The Atelier *after Braque had worked on it for several months (1954).*

17

Above : the Varengeville chapel ; Braque's three stained glass windows are on left. Opposite : two of the finished windows : the figure represents St. Dominic. Double color page : The Atelier, final state though still unsigned ; 1955 (51 × 76½″). Private coll. France.

one (a table top) between them, articulated almost like a screen. Braque then prepared his own canvas, as is his custom, priming it with a layer of grayish paint and by February 1954, had roughed out the basic elements, following closely the lines of the preliminary sketch. All through the spring and early summer Braque continued to work on the picture, either in Paris or in Varengeville, and with each brushstroke the orchestration of the color became more resonant ; at the same time the composition came to life, grew richer and more elaborate. In all, Braque devoted more than eighteen months of hard work and profound thought to this painting, for he was determined that this, the culminant work in the series of *Ateliers*, should sum up the discoveries of a life-time— discoveries regarding the nature of space, form, light, color, volume and texture, as well as the relationships between them. It was not until the beginning of July, 1955 that the last touches were added to what is unques-

tionably one of Braque's masterpieces.

The subject-matter of the *Ateliers* calls for a few words of elucidation. The new picture, like its predecessors, is a mirage of his own studio conjured up by the artist : an array of canvases against a neutral-colored curtain, a clutter of easels, tables piled with sketchbooks, paint-pots and palettes, odd vases, compotiers and pieces of sculpture. The objects are not, however, always painted in strictly recognizable terms, for Braque is not in the least interested in depicting things with any degree of verisimilitude. For example the white bird which appears in *Ateliers* II, III, V, VI and in the present work is neither a literary nor a mystic incarnation of the artist's inspiration, nor, as has been suggested, is it supposed to be a real bird of a recognizable species. It owes its origin to a painting of a bird (now destroyed) which existed in the artist's studio when he was working on this series ; and a " painted " bird it remains in all its different manifestations, whether it keeps to its own

pictorial background, as in *Atelier II*, whether it flies round the room or becomes a shadowy shape, as in subsequent pictures, or returns more or less to the canvas (the red rectangle) where it belongs, as in the recent work.

Successive changes have been the fate not only of the bird but of the other elements in this series of pictures, almost all of which are painted as if in a state of metamorphosis or deliquescence. Here we have to contend with a phenomenon which is largely the result of Braque's conviction that "everything changes according to circumstances, and relationships are always different", and therefore no one object can be said to have one immutable identity nor even, according to Braque, be said to exist. This belief has been instrumental in liberating the artist from his traditional servitude where natural appearances are concerned, thus making virtually everything possible for him. What better proof of this claim than this great picture, which has a vitality, harmony, logic and reality all of its own ?

The Jas de Bouffan

BY DOUGLAS COOPER

*In the painters favorite residence, wall-paper has been stripped
from a forgotten early panel*

About a mile to the south-west of Aix-en-Provence lies the property known as Le Jas de Bouffan—a Provençal expression meaning roughly 'habitation of the winds'—whose house and park were immortalized in several pictures by Paul Cézanne. The Jas was not, however, an age-old family home of the Cézannes, for it was only acquired by Louis-Auguste Cézanne, father of the painter, in 1859 and was sold exactly forty years later by his son. Louis-Auguste amassed a considerable fortune during thirty years of business dealings in Aix, first as a fashionable hatter on the Cours Mirabeau, then as a successful banker, so that by the time he reached the age of sixty he was able to afford to buy a country estate to which he and his family could retire for several months each year and escape from the bustle and the heat of the town. The purchase of the Jas de Bouffan was by no means a modest gesture. The house is quite large and with it went, in those days, some seven acres of land, cultivated partly as a farm and partly as vineyards ; the price paid was about eighty thousands francs. Externally the Jas, which was built towards the end of the reign of Louis XIV as a residence for the Maréchal de Villars, is simple, well-proportioned and rectangular in shape with yellow stucco walls and a low-pitched roof of red tiles. It is certainly an elegant building, though because it is undecorated it appears somewhat severe. Its charm which is undeniable depends largely on its setting, formed by an extensive and well laid out formal garden and park, with fountains, an ornamental pool, and two magnificent avenues of chestnut trees.

Cézanne's temperament was such that he never lived in any one place for long, but he spent more time at the Jas than anywhere else. This was the place which he looked on as his home, as the permanent background to his life, and undoubtedly it was his favourite haunt for working. Indeed one of the saddest moments of his life came when he was obliged to sell the property in 1899 after his mother's death, not only because he had become very attached to it, but also because he was thereby deprived of a studio in the countryside. So far as his work was concerned, Cézanne was essentially a conservative and timid character who needed to be in direct contact with nature and was only happy if he could go on painting the same *motifs* until, through familiarity, he was able to realize his vision of them more completely.

From the day his father took possession of the Jas, Paul Cézanne seems to have adopted it as his spiritual home. Whenever it was possible he would escape there to think and work in peace, either in the studio which he made for himself beside his bedroom on the third floor, or in the park and surrounding countryside. Hence the large number of paintings and watercolors, executed at widely differing dates, in which one finds the house itself, the avenues of chestnut trees, the farm buildings to the east of the house, the pool with its trees and ornamental sculpture, the low wall surrounding the property and even glimpses of the landscape beyond. Yet it is a noteworthy fact that Cézanne never referred to the Jas in any of the long letters which he wrote to his closest friend, Emile Zola, after he had left Aix for Paris. Nor apparently during

An unexpected Cézanne reproduced for the first time : *this* Landscape with Fishermen *(oil mural, about 1860) had been covered with wallpaper. Right : the salon today, with a mural fragment on the left wall opposite the landscape on the right*

A recent photograph of the Jas de Bouffan. Cézanne often painted this house, the reflecting pool and the alleys of trees.

all the years that he continued to work there was he ever inspired to say anything about it in letters to other friends. The Jas was always referred to as "*la maison de mon père*", even long after his father was dead, and for that reason Cézanne looked upon it as a sanctum from which virtually everyone could be excluded. We know that, on occasion, he was visited there by the painters Antoine Guillemet, Achille Emperaire and Francisco Oller, by Georges Rivière who became his biographer, by the poet

Joachim Gasquet, and of course by the dealer Ambroise Vollard. But, apart from Zola, who probably never returned there after 1880, the only great man among Cézanne's close friends who seems to have been received at the Jas was Renoir, who stayed there for a short while in January 1888 with his wife and children.

When Louis-Auguste bought the Jas, the house was not in good repair, nevertheless he had little inclination to spend money on elaborate furnishings

and decoration. This afforded an opportunity for his son Paul, then aged twenty, to display his gifts and prove to his uncomprehending father not only that painting was his true vocation but also that he had a real talent. Cézanne's first gesture was to paint for his father's study a large screen elaborately decorated in an XVIIIth century manner with figures in a landscape. This he completed probably in the summer of 1859. Next he turned his attention to the bare walls of a large and handsome salon on the ground floor—"a vast, almost unfurnished room" Gasquet calls it—which his parents did not use as a sitting-room and therefore they gave over to him as an additional studio. Two walls of this salon have big windows looking out on to the park and garden, the third wall is divided by a large fireplace and the wall at its northern end terminated in a semi-circular alcove. The surface of the walls is divided up into tall panels of different sizes by decorative plasterwork. Cézanne began by filling four panels in the alcove—each over nine feet high—with allegorical figures representing *The Seasons* : *Spring* and *Summer* on the left side, *Winter* and *Autumn* (in that order) on the right, a central panel above a divan being left empty.

These paintings were executed in oil directly on the plaster of the wall and can be dated 1860 with comparative certainty since Zola, in a letter to Baptistin Baille of 21st September 1860, mentions among the things which he would like to see in Aix *"les panneaux de Paul"*. Had he also been told by Cézanne that, as a joke, they were signed "Ingres, 1811" ? This was hardly a compliment to the master, whose style they in no way resembled, for the figures are very elongated and awkward and the execution is inept. Nevertheless, despite their coarseness, these panels form quite a colorful and decorative ensemble which is not devoid of originality. *Spring* is symbolized by a Botticelli-like young woman in a red dress holding a long garland of flowers ; *Summer* appears as a sort of Ceres, a seated woman with a sheaf of corn in her lap and a pile of fruit at her feet ; *Autumn* wanders in a mountainous landscape with a basket of grapes and apples on her head ; while *Winter* kneels on the ground, warming her hands before a fire, under a starlit night sky with fleecy clouds.

We know nothing definite about Cézanne's plan for decorating this salon. We cannot even be sure about the order in which his various paintings were executed, nor about their dates. So we must reconstruct their history from the stylistic evidence available. On this basis it would seem that Cézanne next attacked

Top photograph, the alley of trees as it looks now on an autumn day. Beneath it, Cézanne's wintry version of the scene, the Minneapolis Art Institute (28½ × 36½", 1871). Left : Cézanne's painting of his house seen from the S-E (9 × 11", 1871).

The house and park of the Jas remain very much as they were in Cézanne's day, although the town is reaching their surrounding wall. The artist has placed the Mont Sainte-Victoire behind the trees, above ; in reality it cannot be seen from here.

the two long walls of the salon, each of which offered two large panels some twelve feet high by ten feet broad. On the two nearest the alcove he painted conventional picturesque landscapes, derived no doubt from some romantic prints which he had seen or perhaps from an illustrated book. For Cézanne continually sought inspiration in such publications during the first ten years of his artistic career and Gasquet, repeating what he had no doubt often heard from the painter himself, tells us that at this time "in the evening, one of his passions was to sit beneath a lamp and thumb through illustrated papers or

The Four Seasons *used to be in the curved alcove of the salon (see photograph page 23). They were executed in about 1860, and signed "Ingres" as a joke; the last panel on the right,* Winter, *was even dated 1811. The murals were transferred to canvas when the Jas was sold; they are in the Petit Palais, Paris (height 118½", width 38" and 39½").*

even fashion magazines... and to re-create or to compose from these photographs of towns, landscapes and houses and from the movements and gestures made by all kinds of people, immense canvases which he could never paint but which consumed him with desire from head to foot."

This is the kind of picture with which he seems to have experimented on the walls of the salon at the Jas, but unfortunately only one example has survived intact, a *Landscape with Fishermen*, hitherto unpublished and here reproduced in color. This can still be seen on the wall to the left of the fireplace in the salon; originally *Autumn* filled the adjoining panel. On the wall immediately opposite this fishing scene was a rocky landscape with two cedars, a waterfall and a house on top of a hill, into which, at some later date, Cézanne painted a male nude seen from behind which was quite disparate in scale and bore a striking resemblance to the principal figure in *The Bathers* by Courbet (Montpellier Museum). The execution of these landscapes is certainly less inept than that of *The Seasons*, but they are still the work of an unskilled hand and are undeniably pastiches. So it would seem that they must have been painted some time between the summer of 1860 and November 1862 when Cézanne was finally allowed by his father to leave Aix to pursue his artistic studies in Paris.

This journey interrupted the progress of his decorative scheme and in consequence it was destined never to be completed. For the remaining panels had

not been executed when he left and by the time Cézanne returned to Aix, in the summer of 1864, he had begun to paint in another manner and had quite different stylistic ideas. However, he seems to have been free to paint more or less what he liked in this salon, and to have greatly enjoyed doing so. As a result, each time he came back to his beloved Provençal home—and from 1864 till 1869 he divided his time irregularly between Paris and Aix—Cézanne left some trace of his development on its walls. Thus, judging by other pictures which are dated, it must have been in 1864-65 that he added the *Nude* to the picturesque landscape, the conception of which by then appeared to him outmoded.

At about the same time too Cézanne painted a life-size portrait of his father to fill the empty panel in the alcove. "It's papa! he said to me abruptly with gruff tenderness when he pushed me, for the first time, in front of that moving portrait", Gasquet records in his memoirs. "The good man, wearing a cap, was seated in a familiar pose between the four allegories, reading a newspaper. His rather purple complexion, his taut flesh, his shoulders, bespoke, despite his age, the robust and healthy being whom his son had looked at so lovingly." Some time after this, that is to say in 1865-66, Cézanne executed, with no apparent decorative intent, a curious double painting on the empty panel on the same wall as the *Landscape with a Nude Man*. The left half of this (seemingly slightly earlier than the right) consisted of a rough and somewhat dramatized inter-

pretation of a painting by Sebastian del Piombo, *Christ in Limbo*, in the Prado, a painting which Cézanne can only have known through the engraving published by Charles Blanc. The right half consisted of a large kneeling figure, either prostrate with grief or lost in meditation—hence its present title *Sorrow*. There seems to be no logical explanation for these two overlapping compositions, which are widely different in scale, except that Cézanne was experimenting with free copies after works by old masters. This hypothesis seems to be borne out by another large painting on the opposite wall, an interpretation of Lancret's *Hide and Seek*, also done after a print. Vigorously painted in light colors and with heavy impasto, this picture seems to date from 1866-67. Here too Cézanne clearly had no decorative intention, for he took no account of the dimensions of the wall panel and selected a horizontal composition. Thus, although there was a comparatively formal decoration at one end of the salon, the other end had no unity at all. The subjects of the pictures differed greatly as did the way in which they were painted. And the thesis that, after 1862, Cézanne lost interest in his first decorative project is further supported by the fact that, also in 1866, he casually painted a small portrait head of Achille Emperaire underneath his version of the Lancret.

When Cézanne sold the Jas de Bouffan, Monsieur Louis Granel, the purchaser, inherited these paintings as well as a few others abandoned in the studio. But, unlike Louis-Auguste, he promptly began to make a number of changes in the park and even to remodel the interior of the house. However, rather than destroy or obliterate Cézanne's wall-paintings, he generously offered, in 1907, the year after Cézanne's death, to remove them from the walls of the salon and present them to the National Museums. Accordingly Monsieur Léonce Bénédite, then Curator of the Luxembourg Museum, was sent to Aix to inspect them, but it is not surprising to discover that he felt it his duty to advise against accepting "empty and banal productions which Cézanne himself does not appear to have taken seriously." So it was that Monsieur Granel saw no alternative but to accept a tempting offer (said to have been as much as one hundred thousand francs) from the dealer Josse Hessel to take away those which interested him. The following were thereupon transferred to canvas and removed: the four *Seasons*, the *Portrait of Louis-Auguste Cézanne*, the figure of the *Nude*, which was cut out of its landscape leaving the top half in place on the wall, as well as *Christ in Limbo* and *Sorrow*, which were so impossible to divide that the kneeling figure had to be deprived of part of its robe, and this still appears in the bottom right corner of the *Christ*. Today this group of pictures is widely scattered. The four *Seasons* were recently acquired by the City of Paris and now can be seen at the Petit Palais, while *Sorrow* has been added to the Louvre collection ; the *Portrait of Louis-Auguste Cézanne* hangs in the Pennsylvania Museum in Philadelphia ; *Christ in Limbo* was acquired some forty years ago for the Pellerin collection, and the *Nude* now belongs to a dealer in New York. The others, after being covered with wallpaper for some years, can now be seen again on the walls of the salon at the Jas thanks to the initiative of the present owner, Dr. Corsy, who is the grandson of Monsieur Granel.

I have written at length about this curious group of early wall-painting by Cézanne because they are seldom intelligibly described in the literature. and because confusion exists with regard to their dating. Yet if they are examined separately they provide us with quite a lot of evidence concerning Cézanne's stylistic evolution ; then it will be found that their dates can be determined by comparison with other paintings and by our knowledge of the dates at which Cézanne was in Aix. I do not want to suggest, however, that they are by any means the most important or the most interesting works painted by Cézanne at the Jas. It is only necessary to

The father of the artist, Lecomte collection, Paris. This is another version of the portrait which was once in the salon of the Jas. The Jas portrait belongs to the Pittcairn collection and is now on loan at the Philadelphia Museum of Art.

In about 1865-66 Cézanne painted a rough version of Sebastian del Piombo's Christ in Limbo *(of the Prado) as part of a double panel in the salon. It is now in the Pellerin coll.*

remember that, for forty years, this property provided a large part of the background to his life. There in the salon he painted, in 1866, those two magisterial portraits of Achille Emperaire and his father in high-backed armchairs—"the tones are tawny and the general impression magnificent, the father would look like a Pope on his throne, were it not for the fact that he is reading '*Le Siècle*'", said Guillemet in a letter to Zola. There too on the third floor he painted many a wonderful still-life or self-portrait, in that studio which Vollard describes as follows : "I can still see the studio, with those reproductions pinned to the wall bearing witness to the painter's love for the old masters : Luca Signorelli, El Greco, Tintoretto, Titian and, nearer our time, Delacroix, Courbet and finally, Forain. Poor reproductions, bought for a song, but they sufficed for him to recreate the atmosphere of the Museums." And there, as Gasquet tells us, he also painted his great series of the *Card Players*. "One

of the projects which haunted him longest and which he only realized after making an infinite number of sketches and studies was to paint a group of peasants playing cards, seated on rustic chairs around a bottle beneath the mantlepiece of one of the farms of the Jas—being waited upon and watched by a young girl..." Every corner of the park too speaks to us of Cézanne and one cannot fail to recognize many of the *motifs* which he painted, even if the buildings of the town have encroached more and more on the landscape until now they have almost reached the surrounding wall of the Jas. But the park still displays that same beauty which Cézanne discovered, and those who need proof of the exactness with which he saw and recorded the shapes, the colors and the effects of light in the Provençal landscape cannot do better than request the privilege of being allowed to visit his erstwhile home, where they will recognize a painting by Cézanne at every turn.

Altdorfer

1480-1538

BY FRANZ ROH

Albrecht Altdorfer is the contemporary of Cranach, Dürer, Grünewald and the younger Holbein. But his vision of the world is not demoniac like Grünewald's, nor is it austere and reserved like Dürer's, nor elegant like Holbein's. He is nearer to Cranach (who, in about 1500, created the Danube School with the Swabian painter Jörg Breu) and closely resembles him in the imaginative ease with which he treats landscapes.

In fact, it is Albrecht Altdorfer who, with the painter Wolf Huber, brought the "Danube style" to its culmination. By this, we mean the discovery, made at the end of the Middle Ages, of the meaning of landscape in painting. Blue mountains, rocks, flowing water, exuberant vegetation, all this is suddenly presented in a broad, animated rhythm which betrays a feeling for the universe very close to the concept of life that a Paracelsus might have imagined. This style might almost be said to be the harbinger of pantheistic German romanticism: nature as it is presented here is already "infinite".

Like most of the Renaissance masters, Altdorfer is a universal artist. He paints, draws, makes wood-cuts, engravings,

etchings, frescos and is also an architect. Born about 1480 in Amberg, a remote Bavarian village, in 1505 he became a citizen of Ratisbon, an episcopal town on the Danube originally founded by the Romans. It is there that he passed the remainder of his life, though he undertook various journeys in northern Tyrol and in Bavaria, in the course of which he continued to discover ever new forms of landscape. In 1511 he went down the Danube as far as the monasteries of Melk and Krems. Then he married and founded a studio from which an enormous number of works of art were to appear. Soon he was in a position to buy two houses. In 1518, he made another trip down the Danube: this time it was in order to execute altar paintings for the monastery of Saint-Florian in Upper Austria. In 1519, he was elected a member of the Privy Council of Ratisbon. He participated, as an architect, in the construction of the pilgrims' church known as *Zur schönen Marie*; a model in wood of this curious building in late Gothic style still exists today. He was also responsible for the plans of a large building in Ratisbon which contained the slaughter house and the wine cellars of the city.

Perhaps Altdorfer may have visited Italy; but the only indications of this are the charming face of the Virgin, in the *Rest during the Flight Into Egypt* in the Berlin Museum, so like the Italian Renaissance Madonnas, or the architecture of that period, depicted in a number of his paintings, particularly in his *Susanna and the Elders*. In spite of any possible Italian influence, it is astonishing to see how far Altdorfer's vision of landscape remained personal and nordic.

His wife's death left him in solitude and, shortly before his own demise, which was to take place in 1538, he became the protector of the nearby monastery of the Augustinians. In 1535, Ratisbon sent him as ambassador to the court of King Ferdinand of Austria in Vienna. His mission consisted of bringing about a mutual reconciliation, for Ratisbon had fallen into disgrace for political and religious reasons.

The attitude of the great painters towards the spiritual and religious upheavals of the period was very varied. It seems that Grünewald took sides with the "radicals", in other words, with the Anabaptists, and, for

The Battle of Alexander, *1529* (62×47½"). *Munich Art Muse*

ALEXANDER M DARIVM VLT: SVPERAT
CÆSIS IN ACIE PERSAR: PEDIT: CM. EQVIT
VERO A. M INTERFECTIS. MATRE QVOQVE
CONIVGE. LIBERIS DARII REGCVM M. HAVD
AMPLIVS EQVITIB: FVGA DILAPSI. CAPTIS.

this reason, had to flee western Germany and settle in Halle—very reminiscent of events during the past decades. Dürer belonged to the Reform party, and supported Luther: he even went so far as to ask Erasmus to protect Luther, and the masterpiece of his old age, *The Apostle*, is a profession of Lutheran faith. Altdorfer is also Lutheran, but of a rather more conciliatory temperament. He continues to paint the Virgin Mary, although Lutherans no longer attached any importance to Her veneration. However, he participated in persecutions against the Jews and, in particular, it is known that after a disturbance near a miraculous statue, he notified the Jewish community, as representative of the Council, that they would be immediately expelled from the two synagogues of the town which were to be razed to the ground. Curiously enough, Altdorfer made several etchings which have preserved the memory of these two buildings.

In spite of a very full public life, the artist and his studio produced a prodigeous quantity of pictorial art. He also developed a very special technique for drawings, which he regarded not as studies or sketches for other compositions, but as complete works in themselves. The drawing in these works is always very free: the lines are drawn with such impetus that they almost seem to break into song like a chorus of Bavarian yodellers. The sinuous movement that gives them their life is admirably enhanced by the color of the paper he used, sometimes brown and sometimes green. Altdorfer carefully signed and dated all these drawings, so it is obvious that they were conceived as complete works on the same basis as a painting, and sold or offered as such. Artists of the period often exchanged their drawings. It was in this way that Dürer gave Altdorfer a

pencil portrait of himself. Emperor Maximilian asked the Bavarian painter to collaborate on the illustrations for his prayer book. It was also Altdorfer who designed the Arch of Triumph for the Imperial procession which the Emperor himself had commissioned. Finally the Bavarian painted frescos and did the mural decorations for the Imperial baths in the Episcopal Palace near the Ratisbon Cathedral. Unfortunately nothing remains now of these frescos but minute fragments. They represent gay bathing scenes in which amorous couples, courtiers and buffoons are shown against a Renaissance background, in rich and brilliant colors.

Taking in all of Altdorfer's work at a glance, we can distinguish three periods. At the beginning his painting is exuberant and the forms are very close to nature. The size of his canvases is small but there is abundant detail. Into small paintings such as *The Beheading of Saint Catherine* (21 × 14 ins., Museum of Vienna) or *Saint Francis Receiving the Stigmata* (9½ × 8 ins., Museum of Berlin), Altdorfer manages to concentrate all the tragedy and passion that other artists can only express in monumental works. Here it is already possible to perceive one of the essential features of his art, the bond uniting nature and human events. The tragedy of man's destiny is expressed by flames from Heaven, by sparks that fill the air and by trees bending to the whirlwind. Walls swell like sails, contours disappear, human forms seem deprived of their skeletons. Man becomes part of vegetable life and plants appear human. In *The Woodsman's Family*, in the Berlin Museum, Altdorfer is depicting a microcosm in which Canterbury bells, lilies of the valley and wild orchids flower in profusion in the exuberant forests; rays of light flame across the green or golden-brown background. The

human beings he introduces might be characters in either or both the Christian legend and folk-tales of the German people.

Next, Altdorfer painted much larger canvases peopled with highly animated figures. The *Saint Jerome* of 1510 (Wallraf-Richartz Museum, Cologne) and even more so *The Two Saint Johns* (Saint Catherine's Hospital, Ratisbon)

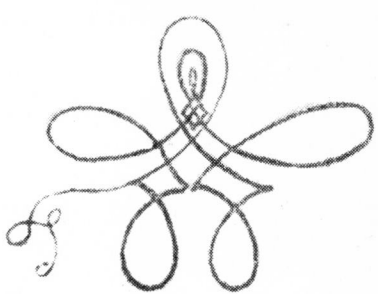

indicate the transition to a new phase in which the macrocosm replaces the microcosm, and in which the forms become monumental, the flowers gigantic and the space majestic. Never was Albrecht Altdorfer closer to Cranach than in these paintings. To the same period belongs the *Birth of Christ* which has, as part of a most peculiar background, a house in ruins, like one in woodcuts by Dürer, against a sky where dawn and dusk vie with one another and where angels appear surrounded by streamers of light.

The master work of this period is the altar piece of Saint Florian, representing the Passion of Christ and the martyrdom of Saint Sebastian. It is remarkable both for the brilliance of its pure colors, scarlet, emerald green and blue, and because the gold of the background is no longer purely symbolic but represents the fire of the setting sun or the brilliance of midday.

With advancing age, Altdorfer returned to a concept of painting that gave increasing importance to detail and was rather more concerned with "prettiness". His *Susanna and the Elders* is a magnificent example of architectural painting and can be said to forecast the baroque. The superb palace with its open halls and galleries is the central theme of the painting. Interest in architecture, at the beginning, only seemed to be a caprice of Altdorfer's, but became an increasing pictorial necessity and corresponds to an affirmation on his part of the profane to

...anna at the Bath, *1526* (29½ × 24"). *Munich Art Museum.*

the detriment of religious spirituality. Moreover it was in 1526 that Altdorfer became the official architect of the city of Ratisbon.

The principal works of the painter's last period, particularly *The Battle of Alexander*, which marks the zenith of his art, attain a power of expression of almost cosmic proportions.

This war scene is one of the marvels of the painter's art. All the best qualities of Altdorfer, somewhat sparingly used in the rest of his work, are united here. Unusual contrasts blend into a mysterious unity. Painted on wood, it only measures $62\frac{1}{4} \times 47\frac{1}{4}$ inches, and yet it has the scope of a cosmic epic poem. It gives the impression of a miniature : everything is reduced and fragmented to the utmost degree and the human figures have the appearance of ants dwarfed by a vast universe. Devotees of painting are often to be seen standing for hours, magnifying glass in hand, in front of this work. It can be pored over like a book for days on end and endless new details can be discovered. It would be fascinating to analyse it in a book containing at least fifty reproductions. Each page would be devoted to detailed consideration of new and complete landscapes—landscapes that would give the impression of never having been seen before. In the whole history of art no painting has ever portrayed so much. Despite the fact that the entire work gives a general effect of complete unity, full of intensity and life, there is no trace of any general composition.

The plain extends to infinity, the mountain chains soar above the valleys, rivers roll through their winding beds, lakes glitter and, in the distance, shines the island-studded Aegean sea. Winds howl, clouds glow and, crowning the whole scene, a brilliant blue dawn rises up to meet the clouds. The cold nocturnal crescent of the moon makes its appearance while the fiery disk of the sun still shows above the horizon. At the top of the painting, giving an almost surrealist effect, is suspended a heavy stone tablet with the following inscription in Latin : "Alexander the Great finally defeats Darius after having killed about 100,000 foot soldiers and 10,000 horsemen, and having captured Darius' mother, wife and children, who were fleeing in disorder with 10,000 horsemen." The famous battle of Issus is also represented—the battle described

by Q. Certius Rufus in the third book of the "Exploits of Alexander".

From the point of view of form, the painting is a marvel. Almost every color, shape, and reflection are to be found in it. It is a veritable catalogue of the possibilities of painting, both in terms of the microscopic and the monumental. It is remarkable that inspiration has in no instance failed the painter : in the entire work there is not a single particle that is not endowed with expression and life. When we compare this picture with others of the same period in which other masters have represented battles of antiquity, there is absolutely no doubt that Altdorfer made the most prodigal use of forms that had ever been seen in painting. In reality, it is the perfect example of profane art examining the universe with the inward contemplation and the intensity of religious art.

Wilhelm V, Duke of Bavaria, had

ordered a series of battle scenes from antiquity to decorate the country seat he had just built. As well as Altdorfer, the painters Burgkmair, Feselen, Refinger and Heller took part in decorating this house. When Altdorfer received the Duke's commission, he was just about to be elected Burgermeister of Ratisbon. But he refused the municipal honor he was offered as though his instinct warned him that he should proceed with this work in which he was going to be able to display, to the fullest scope, his fantastic vision of landscape : a grandiose vision of the same magnitude as the decisive struggle which took place at Issus between the West and the East and which was finally decided by that battle.

Altdorfer's painting intrigued so much Napoleon that he seized it from the Gallery of Munich, where he happened to be after his victory over Bavaria in 1800. The picture remained in Paris until 1815. The Emperor hung it, for a while, in his bathroom at Saint-Cloud —probably the only room in which he found time to meditate. Let us hope that, while taking his bath, he was not interested solely in studying the technical details of the battle. These are represented in the painting in terms of the naive ideas of the Middle Ages, as if the battle had been fought in medieval times.

Finally it is worth noting that the German writer Frederick Schlegel praised this work in his "Descriptions of Paintings in Paris and in Holland in the Years 1802-1804." This tribute, from a romantic, is not at all surprising. For Altdorfer's very varied art finds its unity in its immediate contact with life. His painting goes beyond the medieval distinction between spirit and matter and is, essentially, a search for the meaning of the palpable world and a study of the vital and spiritual forces which his contemporaries believed to be at work in all the manifestations of the universe.

Opposite : The Birth of Christ ($14 \times 10''$). Berlin Museum. Page 34 : a drawing of 1508 representing a country flirtation. Page 35 : The Burial of Saint Florian, detail of the Saint Florian altar-piece ($32 \times 25\frac{1}{2}''$). Nurenberg Museum. The drawings on the text pages were selected from the illustrations, on parchment in colored ink, made about 1515 for the Prayer Book of Emperor Maximilian.

36   The Burial of Saint Sebastian, *one of the wings of the Saint Florian altar-piece*; *1518* (44 ½ × 37″).

Altdorfer as seen by Picasso

Picasso is much addicted to exercises in style which consist of copying and interpreting works by painters of the past. In 1949 he did several drawings and lithographs after Cranach. Recently he completed a whole series of paintings based on his memory of Delacroix's Women of Algiers in the Louvre, a picture he has not seen for fifteen years.

It is not generally known that Altdorfer has also attracted his attention. In 1953, he executed the three drawings in the manner of Altdorfer reproduced here for the first time. Daniel-Henry Kahnweiler, who for the last thirty years has made notes of all his conversations with Picasso, tells how his friend got to know the Bavarian painter's work:

"In the autumn of 1953, when calling on Picasso one day, I had Benesch's book on Altdorfer under my arm. Picasso, whose curiosity is always aroused by anything to do with art, asked me to let him see it. He became very enthusiastic and I gave him the book. Here is the conversation with him which I noted down a few days later: '18/11/53. 29 bis Rue d'Astorg, 5 p.m.—Picasso came to sign some lithographs. Afterwards we talked for a while. Beaudin arrived. He asked Picasso if he had been working. Picasso said no.

"Some lithographs at any rate!" I interposed.

"I've done some Altdorfers", he said. "Copies of a few things. How very good he is, Altdorfer! There's everything there: a little leaf on the ground, a broken brick; not at all like the others. There's a painting with a sort of small enclosed balcony—a cupboard I call it. Every detail is integrated. It's beautiful. All that was lost later. Painting went as far as Matisse—color! Perhaps it's a step forward but it's something quite different. We ought to copy things, as they did in the past. But I know very well, it wouldn't be understood."

Picasso amused himself by signing *Altdorfer* in Gothic letters to the drawings inspired by a detail of the painting on the opposite page. 37

38 Above, detail of the painting reproduced on page 36. Opposite the interpretation of this painting by Picasso $(17 \times 12\frac{1}{2}'')$

Rustic Fare for the Spanish Court

BY GEORGES DE LASTIC SAINT-JAL

Luis Menéndez painted sober plenitude on the walls of an ornate palace

About fifty still-lives painted during the last half of the XVIIIth century most of which are in Spain, a few in the United States, one in the Louvre and one in the Bonn Museum, constitute, at the present moment, almost all the known works of Menéndez, one of the most interesting Spanish painters of his time who has been—erroneously—described as the "Spanish Chardin".

Grandson, son, nephew and brother of painters from Oviedo, Luis Menéndez was born in Naples in 1716. A long series of vicissitudes led his father, who had worked in numerous Italian cities and who was finally compelled to combine the career of a soldier with his work as a

Still-life with oranges and boxes of fruits paste; (18½ × 13½"), *The Prado, Madrid*

painter, to settle in that city, where he married a respectable farmer's widow from the Neapolitan countryside.

A year after the birth of their son, Luis Eugénio, the Menéndez family arrived in Madrid, though not before they had been through a storm at sea which put them in serious danger and which almost deprived Spain of a family of excellent artists and of one of its best painters.

Francisco Antonio Menéndez, who was famous at the Court for his "miniature" portraits of the great, tried to persuade the King to found a Royal Academy of painting, sculpture and architecture, on the same model as the Academy in Paris and, in 1726, he published a brochure in which he demonstrated the advantages which the Spanish Kingdom would derive from such an undertaking. Unfortunately, it was necessary to wait twenty-five years before the Academy of Saint Ferdinand was formed, but, in 1744, Menéndez opened a studio in his house in Madrid which it would be slightly pompous to call an Academy but where he taught young artists the principles of drawing and painting. His daughter Ana and two of his sons, Luis and José Augustín were among his pupils. The only one of interest here is the elder of the sons : Luis Eugénio.

His self-portrait now in Paris in the Louvre was painted in 1746. Menéndez was thirty at the time. He probably worked on it in his father's studio and this supposition is largely confirmed by the study of a male nude, curiously painted

in *trompe-l'œil* which is prominently displayed. Luis Menéndez presents himself elegantly dressed, despite the fact that his hair is carelessly bound with a blue and white striped kerchief, and the painting suggests one of the portraits then presented on admission to the French Royal Academy which were so often a mixture of solemnity and nonchalance. The bronzed face, with its accentuated and virile features and black eyes with their velvet luster betray his Spanish origin, while the attitude and the draperies, which are conventional despite their subdued tones, disclose the influence of Jean Ranc and Louis-Michel Van Loo, two French painters at the Court of Spain.

Luis Menéndez was sent to Italy by his father where he lived first in Rome and then in his native city. The future Charles III of Spain was ruling over Naples at the time under the name of Charles VII. Menéndez presented him with two paintings, gained his confidence and was nominated painter of the King's chamber. On his return to Madrid, he was commissioned by Ferdinand VI to do the illuminations for the psalters of the royal chapel.

Who was responsible for his undertaking the series of forty-four still-lives which he painted between 1760 and 1772 to be set in the *boiseries* of one of the rooms at Aranjuez, the palace built for Philip II and completely transformed by the Spanish Bourbons ? Was it the painter himself, who wished to continue the Spanish tradition of *bodegones* ? Or

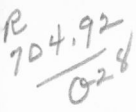

Still-life with a white pitcher; (13½×18½"), *The Prado*.

was it his master Charles III, the easy-going monarch, inconsolable widower and enemy of etiquette who, in the middle of the desert where Aranjuez was built, and in the palace with its rococo *décor*, tried to stimulate his jaded palate in the contemplation of these ambrosial canvases ? In any case it is pleasant to imagine Charles III, who took refuge at the Palace of Aranjuez for several months during the disturbances directed against his Minister of Finance, Esquilache, contemplating these rustic collations with delight.

They were probably not the first still-lives of this style that Menéndez painted, but the success of the *bodegones* of Aranjuez is demonstrated by the fact that just after they were finished another series was ordered, apparently on a smaller scale, for the *Casita del Principe*, built by the Prince of the Asturias, the future Charles IV, in the park of the Escorial.

Seven years later, Don Luis Menéndez de Rivera was no more. We know practically nothing at all about his private life except that the practice of his art did not enrich him.

We shall now try to analyze some of the constituent elements of Menéndez's *bodegones*, the sources of his art and what he owes to heredity, to tradition, to the period in which he lived and to foreign influences.

The painting of still-lives, which originated in the "Xenia" of antiquity was developed in Italy and in Flanders, and had reached one of its highest peaks in XVIIth century Spain. The great names of this period were Cotan, Zurbaran and Velasquez.

Neapolitan by birth, but Spanish by breeding, Menéndez is more in the tradition of his own country than of Italy. He re-discovered the painters of the Spanish golden age, abandoning the decorative manner of XVIIth and early XVIIIth century artists he adopted the themes of his distinguished predecessors. Some of his still-lives, composed of fruit, enormous melons cut in half, pears, figs, grapes and half-opened pomegranates, closely resemble Neapolitan painting which liked to represent piles of fruit in brilliant colors, placed directly on the ground and silhouetted against an evening sky. If Menéndez had only produced paintings like that, he would soon have been forgotten.

41

Still-life with a melon and pears ; (15¾×20″), *Boston Museum*.

Menéndez : Self-portrait. *Dated 1746,* ▶ *this work is signed "Luis Meléndez", a spelling later abandoned by the artist. It first belonged to the Infante Don Sebastian of Bourbon, grandson of Charles III, then to his daughter the Duchess of Marchena. After entering the collections of Paul Mantz and Paul Cosson, it came to the Louvre in 1926* (38 ½ × 10″). *Pages 44 and 45 :* Still-life with fish, *1772* (16½×24¼″). *The Prado Museum.*

Menéndez's *bodegones* are generally situated on a rough, uneven, wooden table. The background is a sombre gray or brown, almost black and semi-abstract, in the middle of which are to be seen—bathed in a crude, irrational light—objects which might have been painted a century earlier by Cotan or Velasquez.

What did Menéndez actually place on the canvases lining the royal chamber at Aranjuez ? Luxurious objects ? Very few. A tray, a golden platter, a silver fork, a crystal goblet or a valuable piece of porcelain are rare exceptions. His choice is purposely rustic : pots, jars, glazed earthenware pitchers, cauldrons, beaten copper basins and saucepans, coarsely woven baskets, thick, almost black bottles with vivid high-lights, wine coolers from which emerge the broken neck of a bottle, heavy bronze mortars, stiff rough linen. And near all these commonplace objects, fruit, vegetables of all kinds—everything, in fact, to make a tasty soup— we find fresh or smoked meat, game, fish, eggs, cheese and bread, basic but delicious food which Menéndez particularly relished—round, golden loaves with thin crusts, smooth and mat like the skin of the loveliest of Spanish women.

With the choice of subject the resemblance to Chardin ends, particularly in that the French painter is infinitely less prolix and usually satisfied with a very limited number of objects. But where Chardin arranges them with almost musical rhythm, full of metre and half-tones, Menéndez disposes them in pyramidal compositions, where the confused planes of the objects are contrasted to the verticals and horizontals, the spherical or cubic forms, in an intentional geometric design which leads one to think that the painter must have meditated on the *Discurso sobre la figura cubica* by Juan de Herrera, and at the

Still-life with a pitcher, ham and eggs ; (19¼×14″) *The Prado Museum, Madrid*

same time been influenced by the baroque, imported into Spain in the XVIIIth century by the Italians. Many aspects of his painting make him dissimilar to Chardin without putting him into exactly the same category as the Spanish painters of the preceding century whose sober and monumental compositions were always severely classical in concept.

All the objects that Chardin treats so tenderly, giving them a silent, vibrant existence in a soft and changing light, are plunged, by the Spanish painter, into the brilliant light of day leaving no detail in shadow. He presents them to our eyes as through a magnifying glass, accentuating their forms, their colors and their flavor and making them palpable with a strange and unexpected definition which transforms each one of them into an unknown world full of promise and danger. The earthenware, the porcelain which shines with a tactile and transparent glaze, are worn out from use, sometimes even broken. The bread burst open by the heat of the oven is on the point of becoming stale. The skins of the figs, pears and peaches are punctured by invisible insects. Putrefaction lies in wait for all these inanimate objects—one can almost feel it. But this is never even suggested in a painting by Chardin. In this respect, where Luis Menéndez most resembles the painters of his own race, he is entirely different from Chardin. The pleasure which we find in the latter is intellectual, with the former it is emotional and sensuous.

But there is still a great difference between the rustic *nature mortes* of Luis Menéndez and the strange expressionism of Goya's still-lives. A genuine product of Spanish soil, Menéndez forms a kind of bridge between the votive, mystical still-lives of Cotan and Zurbaran and the raw meat with which Goya was soon to startle the world.

A Painter's Philosophy

A RECORDED INTERVIEW BETWEEN JEAN BAZAINE AND GEORGES BERNIER

One of the most representative of the post-Picasso generation of French painters, Bazaine had his first one-man show in 1949. In 1952 he was invited to Pittsburgh as European member of the Carnegie International Jury.

Georges Bernier. / *If I'm not mistaken, you studied simultaneously at the Beaux-Arts and at the Sorbonne for a Master's degree in Literature ?*

Jean Bazaine. / For a degree in Philosophy.

G. B./ *Before going any further, I'd like to clear up a point that has always intrigued me. I read, in a biographical note about you, that you knew Proust's work at a very early date and that he was a friend of your family's ?*

J. B./ That's quite true. When my father was young he knew Proust well. I often heard stories about «Marcel», but I never met him for, as you know, he was very ill.

G. B./ *What did your father do ?*

J. B./ He was in aviation in the pioneer days. I spent almost all my childhood on the aerodromes at Issy-les-Moulineaux and Villacoublay near Paris. I was absolutely fascinated by flying ; not from the mechanical point of view, but in terms of conquering space. And sometimes I think I haven't changed.

G. B./ *You studied painting at the Beaux-Arts ; with whom ?*

J. B./ I started to be a sculptor, I had sculpted since the age of ten. Later, at the Beaux-Arts, I worked with Landowski who was extremely nice to me; at the same time, I began painting. Ever since I was ten or twelve years old, I had gone every Thursday to the Louvre on my own.

G. B./ *When you were at the Beaux-Arts were you already familiar with the work of the great painters of the period immediately preceding your own ?*

J. B./ Yes, of course, but I can't say that they attracted me very much or that I knew much about them.

G. B./ *About what date was this ?*

J. B./ About 1925. I was eighteen or twenty. It was then that I realized, having painted all summer long from nature, that sculpture was not my medium. I left Landowski and went to the Académie Jullian.

G. B./ *Did you learn much ?*

J. B./ I didn't learn anything, but I copied a great deal from the old masters.

G. B./ *Who aroused your interest in the works of men like Braque and Picasso ?*

J. B./ I think it was Diaghilev. One evening I went to the *Ballets Russes* and I was swept off my feet. I went back every evening and saw everything there was to be seen : décors by Picasso, Rouault, and Braque's ballet "Les Fâcheux"...

G. B./ *Were you interested in Klee's work as well as in Braque's and Picasso's ?*

J. B./ I got to know Klee much later and it is really only now that he has begun being important to me.

G. B./ *Who would you say was a particularly strong influence at the time ?*

J. B./ Bonnard. I had, and still have, a very special admiration for him. I wrote to him when I had my first exhibition in 1932. He came to see it. That astounded me. I didn't see him again until much later, a

Ucello and Cézanne are particularly important to Bazaine. He has these reproductions pinned to the wall of his studio: left, a detail of Ucello's Battle of San Egidio; right, Cezanne's Les grandes Baigneuses.

...aine: **The Flame and the Diver,** 1953 (76 ¾ x 51 ¼").

Banks of the Loire drawing, 1948

few years before his death. He always showed an interest in my work. I knew, for instance, that pinned to the wall in his room he had a bad color reproduction—horrible in fact—of a small painting of mine. He said to me one day : "You're on the right path."

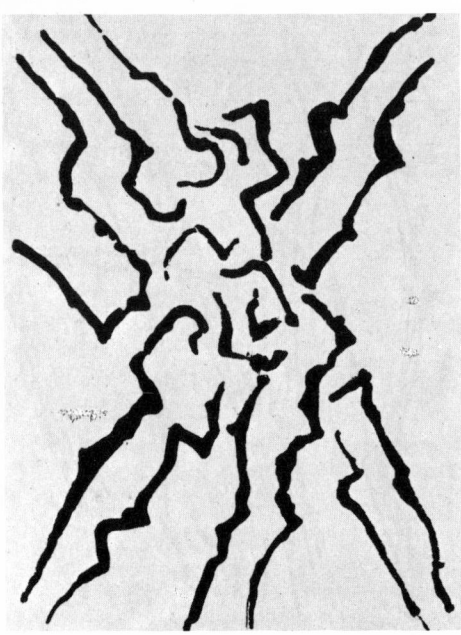

The Dancers drawing, 1952

G. B./ *But isn't it also true that Cézanne's work was very important to you ?*

J. B./ I haven't mentioned it because it's so obvious. Cézanne has always been a god to me. Everything that we have seen in the course of this century springs from him. The Cubists, naturally, but so do we.

G. B./ *Could you explain that a little more ?*

J. B./ What I mean is that one of the most important discoveries of the Cubists was the animation of space by the breaking up of objects. But it seems to me that the object still remains, thrust back upon itself and without any outside affinities—and it strives only to reconstruct itself.

The Wrestlers drawing, 1952

This "multiple space" was already being used by Cézanne. He went far beyond the concept of the fixed plane. At the end of his life, he really seems to live and breathe the concept of space in a way that obsesses me more and more and which is the basis of all *observation*. The sky is no longer a screen against which completely separate objects are silhouetted. In a landscape like the *Rocks of Bibemus*, the

structure of the rocks is exactly that of the clouds and the structure of the tree mingles with that of the rocks. In the water-colors that he did during his last years, Cézanne literally conquered space and opened the world to us on a vast scale.

G. B./ *But let's get back to the beginning of your career. After the years of conventional schooling and your personal experiments, you reached the conclusion that you could no longer continue to paint in the same way you had been painting.*

J. B./ I reached that point gradually without there being any abrupt difference between one canvas and the next.

I never stopped working from nature. I always make an enormous number of drawings, not in any way a preparation for a specific painting, but simply a means of self-enrichment ; some from this summer are extremely important to me. What I saw when I was making them created other dimensions which I have not so far succeeded in expressing. It was really nature that showed them to me. It is because I continue to look at the world, to immerse myself in it, that I go on developing. It amuses me that what the public or the critics call a greater degree of abstraction in my work is really the result of a more profound contact with the world.

G. B./ *The water-colors I see over there— where did you do them ?*

J. B./ On the beach in the region of Bordeaux, Gironde, at Meschers, in a countryside with very fine spatial effects and great sweeping movements of sea and sky.

I've been working on that canvas over there ever since I came back... Let's call it *After the Storm* if you like. It's very difficult to give it a title.

G. B./ *How do you chose your titles ?*

J. B./ I don't like using literary or poetic titles because that falsifies the problem. For me, a painting is always built around a theme. For exemple, over there is a canvas I painted after two trips to Spain. When I came back I did—not really a series of paintings—but all the same four big canvases which for me coincided with very vivid memories of old Castille, with certain landscape formations, certain conditions of light and finally with the whole physical feel of the country. All that is lying dormant.But it needs time to bring it out : I only did that series at least a year after I had been in Spain... I had to "digest".

G. B./ *You "digest" slowly, don't you ?*

J. B./ Ten years sometimes. I'll tell you a story which is fairly typical because it deals with a subconscious process. In one of my last exhibitions, I showed a painting called *Winter*. One of my friends, who works very much as I do, looked at this canvas and said : "Well, that's strange, this reminds me of certain landscapes in Lorraine, look, there are some clipped willows and over here some small streams"... and so on. I got angry and said to him : "No, that's not what it is, it's just winter and nothing else." But it stuck in my mind all the same and suddenly I discovered in that canvas, which dates from 1948, the very same themes that I had drawn during the winter of 1939-1940 in Lorraine. The drawings had been burned in a fire and I had completely forgotten them for ten years. Nevertheless they had reappeared in a painting which might be considered completely abstract but which for my friend could not have been more concrete.

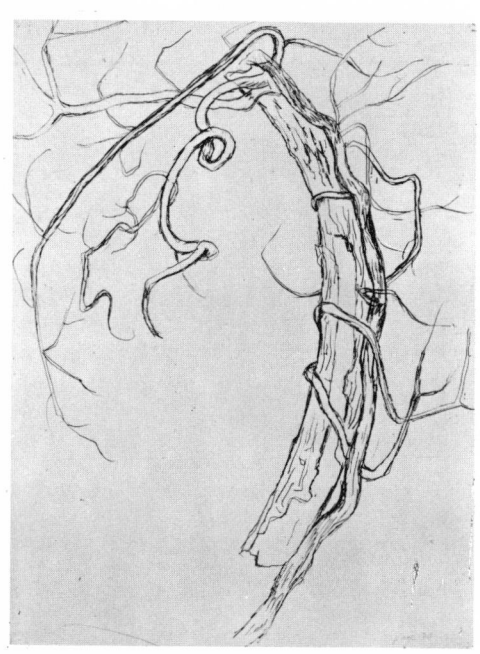

Branch drawing, 1951

G. B./ *But things like that can reappear in your work sooner, can't they ? Last year you did some paintings inspired by the visit you had made to the United States only a few months before.*

J. B./ Yes, but when I look at them again, I say to myself : "Maybe they came a bit too soon." It's the shock that America gives you ; when you see America you

Early every morning Bazaine leaves his Paris home for his studio at Vanves, a nearby Suburb. He works in solitude often listening to records of XVIIth and XVIIIth century music

immediately want to say the effect it has had on you. I think my visit taught me a lot and will teach me still more about breaking up light and also in terms of a tremendous change of scale...

G.B ./ *What particularly struck you about the cities you saw in America ?*

J. B./ I found New York miraculously beautiful. None of the other towns I saw can compare with it. Chicago also has a kind of heavy, terrible beauty. I tried to do some drawing in Chicago but I couldn't do a single one in New York.

G. B./ *Of course you noticed the extraordinary interest for abstract painting in America. What do you think about it ?*

J. B./ You know that I went there as a member of a jury ; and therefore I saw a tremendous amount of painting. American painting is very young. I don't want to say anything disparaging about it ; on the whole, it seems to me to represent a sort of animated protoplasm which so far has not developed any definite form. But it has real vitality and a blind, prolific kind of enthusiasm. The light there is very strange, cold, abstract and very difficult to catch. The color of the landscape, beautiful though it is, also has something abstract about it. Young painters often oscillate between an

abstractionism and a realism that are equally absolute, and which basically come to the same thing. German Expressionism—which corresponds much more to the real American temperament than does French painting—seems to me to have a very great influence there.

G. B./ *We have just used the word "abstraction" several times, but what exactly do we mean by abstract painting ?*

J. B./ Nowadays so many of the words we use have lost their proper meaning. In one sense, all painting is, of necessity, an abstraction. I think it's all a question of race and climate. The French are hardly abstract in the meaning of the word today. They keep contact with the soil, and this has been the source of greatness for French art for centuries. But on the other hand people like Kandinsky, like Klee, even like Mondrian never rejected the exterior world. The term "representational" isn't much more satisfactory than "abstraction".

G. B./ *Did the experiments of the Italian Futurists or of Marcel Duchamp in trying to represent movement by breaking it up interest you ?*

J. B./ I knew about them quite early and they opened certain perspectives for me ; I soon realized their limits and I rediscovered them later from a different angle.

Earth and Sky 1950 (76 ¾ x 51 ¼")
Right: Rocky Hill 1952 (21 ¾ x 18")

For me the movement of a painting has nothing to do, for example, with the materialized movement of someone walking; its an internal movement. I don't try to paint canvases full of movement, but in my paintings there is a very strict, yet invisible structure, a structure which evokes perpetual motion and which obeys an interior rhythm.

G. B./ *In other words, one of the main objects of painting, to your mind, is to express this rhythm of the elements presented to you by the exterior world?*

J. B./ If you like, it's a need to go farther than simply expressing the world... through a kind of identification.

G. B./ *Was it on the level of identification that the work of the primitives struck you so much?*

J. B./ Very early, I was interested, fascinated even, by African art. Nowadays I still like it, but I am more touched by medieval statues, or by Hindu, Chinese or primitive Greek sculpture. I find a feeling of interior experience in medieval works; their religious aspect overwhelms me even more than the magic aspect of African art.

G. B./ *Since you mentioned religious art of the Middle Ages, I'd like to ask you how you first came to work in the church at Assy and then at Audincourt.*

J. B./ I was brought up a Christian and Christianity is very important to me. Then I've always been interested in the art of stained-glass. I made my first stained-glass window just before the war at Hébert-Stevens' at the same time as Gromaire and Rouault. I made some more in 1943 with Huré where I learned the technique and then, in 1947, I did the *King David* which is, I think, the best of my windows at Assy. It was Father Couturier, whom I liked very much, who encouraged me to work at Audincourt. It was a thrilling experience for me.

G. B./ *Why?*

J. B./ First of all on the human level: you know that the church was built by workmen out of their savings. Some of them asked to have a mosaic. Father Couturier took the risk; he asked Fernand Léger to do the stained-glass, and he commissioned me to do a mosaic. When? I took a sketch of it one winter evening to these country farmers who had never seen painting like mine, it was an extraordinary experience: they got extremely excited and I had the marvellous feeling of really working for and in a joint enterprise. I would never have done it without their support for I would never have wished to impose something they did not like on these people who had put their trust in me.

G. B./ *Are you working a great deal at the moment?*

J. B./ More and more, particularly because I get slower and slower and find that I paint fewer and fewer canvases each year—between ten and fifteen counting the small ones, which give me an almost equal amount of trouble. But usually I do fairly big canvases.

Below: Spain 1954 (45 ½ x 32")

Detail of the façade in mosaic designed by Bazaine for the church at Audincourt

G. B./ *Do you always work on several paintings at the same time?*

J. B./ Yes. You don't always have something to add to the same canvas every day. But a moment arrives when one of them becomes the most important.

G. B./ *But when you're surrounded with the paintings you are working on—what exactly are you looking for?*

J. B./ I'm looking for what we are all looking for, the something that is beyond painting. But it takes fifty years of hard work to—sometimes—achieve it. Jacques Villon whom I like and admire said to me recently, with a smile, "I'm looking for the philosopher's stone." Nothing moves me more than the incessant and passionate search pursued by these men. Braque, for instance, is really on a quest for the essential. I'm profoundly struck by the way Braque continues to want to excel himself in all his most recent canvases. I absolutely agree with him when he says: "It isn't color in itself which interests me." For my part, I never think of doing a painting in terms of beautiful colors or because it has "pleasant tones". But I go back fifty times to get an effect which seems to me to express a truth, or a more accurate and more profound aspect of reality.

G. B./ *Who amongst the old masters seems to you best to express this quest for what lies beyond painting?*

J. B./ A man like Rembrandt. The more I look at his work the more Rembrandt's real mystery astounds me. In the Frick collection in New York there is a canvas called *The Polish Cavalier...* It goes far beyond the realm of painting. Rembrandt has achieved in it a kind of metaphysical knowledge. I think this is something that painters feel more and more as they advance in painting—or rather in life. I have a reproduction of Cézanne's *Grandes Baigneuses*: he took seven years, I think, to paint it. It reaches far beyond reality —far beyond everything. We can see in it how far this famous reality is always something mysterious and unknown. I also own a detail of the *Battle of San Egidio* by Paolo Ucello... if abstract painting really has a meaning, it is to be found in Ucello, Van Eyck and Vermeer.

The Italian "Manner"

BY ANDRÉ CHASTEL

Mannerist art, popularized by engravings, spread from XVIth century Italy through all of Europe

It was customary, during the XVIth century, to grace by the term "manner" the inevitable affectation of artists who believed that they could formulate the 'ideal style' by copying great masterpieces. The term assumed a disparaging sense when the more vigorous generations of the next century decided to oppose "nature" to this somewhat decadent "mannerism". The period was one of lassitude which felt the need for subtlety and amusement. These, by making art less direct and sincere, led to a blending of styles and, eventually, to eclecticism. Later these tendencies gave rise to the dream of the "ideal picture". "To really portray Adam and

Parmigianino strove more for elegance than realism. Left, Girl With The Turban, *also called* The Turkish Slave, *1530 (26½ × 21"), Parma. Above:* An Evangelist *by Pontormo, 1526. Sta. Felicitá, Florence.*

Eve, the drawing would have to be entrusted to Michael-Angelo, the brushwork to Titian, the proportions and the correct expression to Raphael and the colors to Antonio da Correggio. This would produce the greatest painting in the world", wrote Lomazzo of Milan in 1590 in his *"Idea del Tempio della Pittura"*.

This recipe was the result of endless learned discussions in the Academies. In 1541, the Grand Duke of Tuscany founded the Florentine Academy of Letters where, in 1546, Varchi commented on a sonnet by Michael-Angelo on the subject of the artist's ideal; in 1562 the Duke created an Academy of Drawing. Similar institutions soon sprang up all over Italy with the aim of codifying art as well as all other forms of expression. Violent rivalries inevitably arose as typified by the incidents surrounding Michael-Angelo's funeral in 1564. His body was secretly transported

to Florence, where the Grand Duke entrusted the recently founded Academy of Drawing with the arrangements for a magnificent ceremony; the committee included Vasari and Bronzino, Cellini and Ammannati. To all intents and purposes Cellini was pushed aside, and as a result conceived a violent hatred for Vasari which is expressed in no uncertain terms in the sculptor's "Memoirs"; one of the reasons for this was the predominance given, in the allegorical figures of the catafalque, to Painting (placed on the right) over Sculpture (placed on the left) in front of Architecture and Poetry. This gives some idea of the atmosphere of the court with its official ceremonies, its academic rivalries and its artificialities.

The middle of the century is dominated by Vasari's powerful work (published in 1550 and reprinted, after an immense success, in 1568) which gave the first

Pietro Barbino : a fountain in the Boboli Gardens, Florence.

left a collection of three hundred and forty one. Giulio Clovio, the miniaturist and collector, "an excellent painter of small objects" according to Vasari, brought off the brilliant feat of reducing the most famous compositions by Raphael and Michael-Angelo to ridiculously small proportions.

Despite the seeming rigidity of the Counter-Reformation and of court life, there was nevertheless a profound "Mannerist" emancipation of sensibility and imagination. One of the most remarkable consequences was the new interest in still-life and landscape painting, in which Italian taste was stimulated by influences from the North as well as by its own spontaneous feelings. We know, from a subsequent copy, a vase of flowers with large lemons and a small lizard by Giovanni da Udine, Raphael's collaborator, dating from 1538. A generation later the representation of fruit and flowers is already familiar enough to be treated as an amusing and paradoxical "fantasy" in the famous and over-rated compositions by Arcimboldi. The same is true of landscape painting. Two other pupils of Raphael's, Maturino Fiorentino and Polidoro di Caravaggio, produced several lively examples, about 1540, for the

general history of art. His theory of genius and of the essential harmony between nature and art to be discovered through the study of the great masters, his doctrine of the superiority of drawing over color, and finally his definition of the "modern manner" born with Giotto, developed by Masaccio, formulated by Leonardo and perfected by Michael-Angelo, are the culminating point of all Florentine criticism. The first discordant note was struck by Ludovico Dolce's treatise, in the "dialogue" entitled *L'Aretino*, in which Raphael is placed above Michael-Angelo in the field of drawing, and Titian above both for color. Vasari commented on this Venetian reaction in his second edition (1568).

The fashion for fables from antiquity is no longer limited to the glowing compositions by Raphael and Titian : it also embraces scientific works. These supplied the humanist culture of the second half of the century with an abstruse form of symbolism and gave rise to a decorative art overburdened with literary allusions, allegories and emblems, stressing the obscure and the unexpected.

This burdening of artistic culture corresponded to the introduction of a solemn and formal protocol at court, never known in Italy before the Spanish occupation. Court life was a decisive

factor in Mannerist art ; it provided the subjects painted with a conventional and refined exterior. The term "Mannerist" is all the more apt in that it defines, in the literature of the period, an elegant and studied deportment, often in association with the adjectives *pellegrino* (foreign, in other words rare, distinguished) and *affettato* (elegant, "chic").

The evocation of the heroic age through decoration and stylized behavior became, in the course of time, pure affectation. This official and excessively contrived art engendered a compensatory desire to escape to rustic life, to popular characters and to fantasies as far removed from etiquette as possible. Hence the success of all the strange inventions and imaginative flights, often bizarre to the point of buffoonery and even—in an artist such as Rosso—to a kind of provocative satanism. Among these paradoxes, the fashion for paintings of very small dimensions and minute portraits is typical of the 'Mannerist' taste : twenty-four miniatures by Bronzino were in a cabinet in the Palazzo Vecchio and Catherine de Medici is said to have

Agostino de' Musi : The Carcass, *engraving after Raphael (12×64"), about 1525 ; Lessing Rosenwald coll. Page 55, top : astrological medallions painted for one of the halls of the Palazzo del Té in Mantua.*

church of San Sylvestro del Quirinale, and from that time on landscape painting developed steadily from Dosso Dossi through Niccolò dell'Abbate to the Bassani. One of the most interesting features of the period is the tendency "to realism of detail within a basic unreality of the whole" (G. Briganti, *Il Manierismo*).

The invention of the "rustic" style, begun in Mantua, is no less revealing with its intentional heaviness and its grottos, its surprises, its vast humorous fantasies extending throughout every park. In short, this period can be characterized by the dissociation of the elements of form and content which, at moments of strength and certainty, are always automatically attuned. The middle of the XVIth century witnesses the exaggeration of formalism in artificial works executed in already established style, and of intellectualism endowing paintings, ornamentation and even architecture with increasingly complex symbolic values.

It would be impossible to explain all these phenomena except in terms of the revolution that took place at the beginning of the century due to the spread of engraving. The technique of reproduction by engraving, begun by Mant-

egna and the Florentines, was perfected by Marc'antonio Raimondi (1475-1534). He first spent considerable time reproducing Dürer, then entered Raphael's service in about 1510 and began disseminating the latter's works throughout all Europe. Later on a Dutchman, Cornelius Cort, was given a kind of monopoly for reproducing Titian's work (1566). Between these two dates, the rhythm of artistic life had been profoundly changed by this new method; discoveries made by painters were now spread as

rapidly as the ideas contained in books, and were subjected, in exactly the same way, to imitation or to immediate condemnation. An engraved plate is both more easily handled, quicker to distribute and more elaborate than a drawing, which accounts for the artists' insistence on controlling their execution.

Without engravings, the overwhelming imprint of the great masters and the parallel development of the various schools would have been inconceivable

—particularly the assimilation of Northern art and the familiarity with Dürer who, between 1515 and 1520, had a strong influence on such diverse painters as Luini, Lotto and Pontormo. The over-elaboration of the mannerists was aggravated by the easy availability of these prints : they furnished ever-increasing numbers of motifs to artists who were already inclined to complicate their work. Certain exaggerations of the period were definitely due to this phenomenon, but it was also responsible for the formula becoming international : between 1540 and 1550, Italian Mannerism was present throughout all Europe.

It had begun twenty or twenty-five years earlier in Florence, Rome and Mantua. By 1520, the Florentine world had reached a point where medieval candor and unadulterated confidence in the human race and its possibilities were equally shaken. A disturbed and highly contradictory art, imbued with Leonardo's doubts and Michael-Angelo's agonies of mind, was now irresistibly coming into being, using the classic forms in a way that was, to a certain extent, self-defeating. Every master was a model for a particular distortion, full of capricious and subjective effects, often still showing repressed "Gothic" tendencies, and in which the very new alliance with the confused but intense art of the German states was visible.

Jacopo Carucci, known as Pontormo, freed himself from the tender and veiled classicism of Andrea del Sarto and Fra Bartolomeo, to which he had first adhered, by turning to the clear and sharply defined painting of Michael-Angelo. Through Cardinal Ottaviano's patronage he was given the task of decorating the main hall of Poggio at Cajano, still unfinished at the time of Lorenzo the Magnificent's death. Pontormo directed all the decorative work and personally undertook the lateral lunettes framing enormous "oculi". He only had time to paint one, on the east wall, illustrating the legend of *Vertumnus and Pomona*—an exquisite rustic scene, whose line, carried to its utmost degree of intensity, is qualified by the use of almost toneless grays and yellows (1519-1521).

In the main cloister of the monastery at Galuzzo, Pontormo painted a *Cycle of the Passion*, much deteriorated today, in which his dense crowds, his elongated, tense figures, are directly inspired by Dürer engravings. Vasari actually accuses him of having abandoned the Tuscan style in favor of the German, and the modern for the Gothic. In the

admirable *Descent From the Cross* in the Church of Santa Felicità (1536), with its thin, cold tones in mauve, pink and green, forms undulate in a sinuous composition blocked out in tiers. In his portraits Pontormo is observant, light and penetrating, with the same combination of withdrawal and excitement displayed four centuries later in Modigliani.

The other anxiety-ridden artist, less inspired than Pontormo, who makes the orientation of Florentine Mannerism extremely clear, is Giambattista di Jacopo, known as Rosso (1496-1540). A born revolutionary, he went through every Florentine studio without conviction and, in defiance of the delicacy of Andrea del Sarto and Fra Bartolomeo, painted large draped figures with haggard faces in strident, uniform colors. Rosso often silhouetted his subjects against a curious light. His *Madonna With Four Saints* (1518, Uffizi) was refused by his patron. The huge, complicated and strange *Descent From The Cross* (1521, Volterra) attests his fidelity to XVth century composition, like Filippino's for example ; and the picture of *Moses Defending Jethro's Daughters* (about 1523, Uffizi) demonstrates — by its cool, clear tonality, the scale of its animated construction, by the avalanche of bodies in the foreground—the attraction of Michael-Angelo. His stay in Rome from 1523 to 1527, where he failed to work creatively, proved to be a disturbing experience for his neurotic talent. But on reaching France (1530)

Rosso was triumphantly successful in his decoration of François I's gallery at Fontainebleau. *The Pietà* (1537-1540, Louvre) with its watered tones, over-elegant figures, and crowded composition, is the final masterpiece of a form of art that is both capricious and dynamic.

With the second generation, Florentine painting abandons its note of troubled sensitivity and adapts itself to its formal and demanding surroundings. It develops, in fact, into Court painting with the appearance of Pontormo's pupil, Bronzino (1507-1572). Dry and displeasing in his *Pietà* (Berlin) and in his decoration for the Chapel of Eleonora of Toledo in the Palazzo Vecchio (1555-1564), he achieved success as a portrait painter, thanks to his intentional impassivity. In his double portrait of *Eleonora of Toledo and Don Garcia* (Turin), the striped curtains painted with impeccable but excessive realism, create a perfect setting for the dress, the hands and the regal bearing of the noble lady. In another portrait (Uffizi) a brocade dress has become the center of the painting and in his *Lucrezia Pucci* a violet robe is the point of focus. This attention to costume reminds one of Flemish devotion to detail, but the effect is concentrated on the fixity of attitude, the ivory tones of the flesh, and the transparency of the unreal surroundings onto which the figures are projected with the intention of creating an atmosphere of "grandeur". He puts more character into the small portrait of *Maria de' Medici* (Uffizi) and into his paintings of various artists.

Bronzino : Allegory of Love, about 1546, National Gallery, London. Right: drawing of a skeleton, Alessandro Allori, Department of Drawings, the Louvre. Far right: Pontormo, drawing for a fresco at Cajano. Department of Drawings, the Louvre.

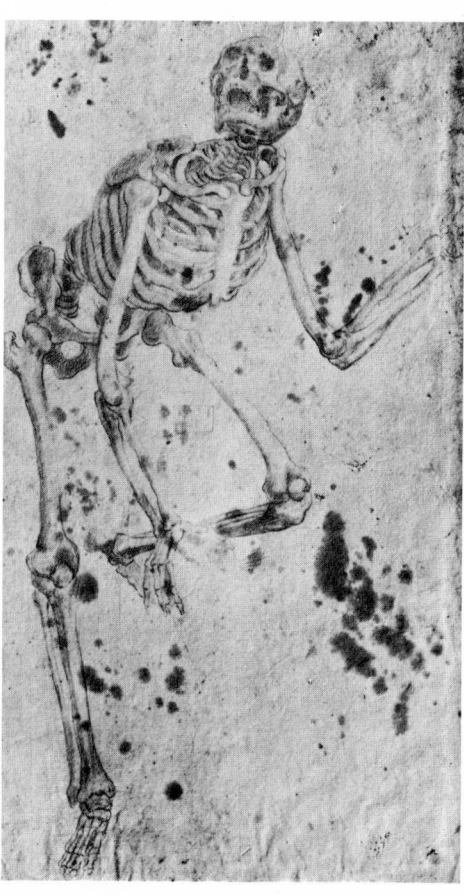

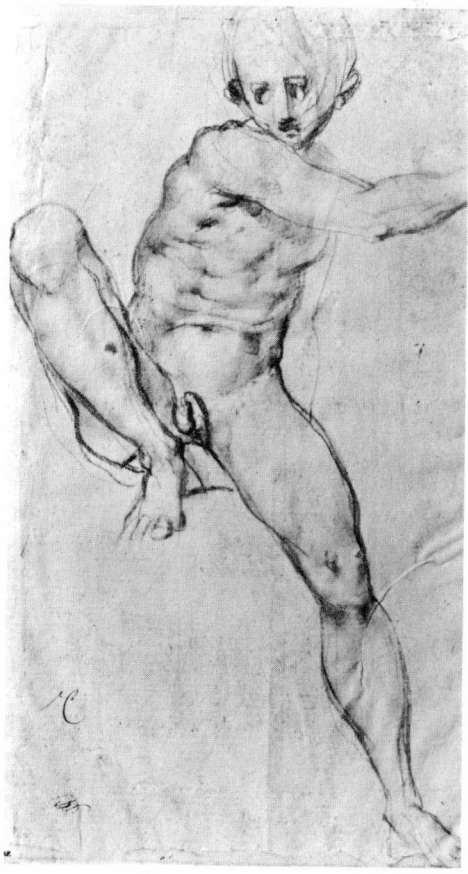

Pontormo: Descent from the Cross, *fresco at the Charterhouse of Galuzzo, about 1525.*

The primary function of Mannerist sculpture in Florence was to provide monuments. In the Piazza della Signoria is Ammanati's *Fountain of Neptune* with the white marble giant or "biancone" in the center (too directly inspired by Michael-Angelo's David) and, radiating around him, the voluptuous naiads and fauns by Tacca and Giovanni Bologna. It is the height of capriciousness to have placed it in this austere square. Such compositions on several levels, with statues grouped around pools of water, are more appropriate to the parks of princely palaces. Most of the sculptors who decorated these pleasure gardens collaborated with the inventive engineer of the Grand ducal household, Nicolò Pericoli, called Tribolo (1485-1550). About 1540, at the villa of Castello, he constructed a series of terraces on the side of a hill, with niches and grottos to hold bronze animals by Bologna, and lower down a terrace for the fountain of Hercules and Cacus and various other statues also by Bologna.

The Boboli Gardens, laid out on the slopes behind the Palazzo Pitti, were comprised entirely of ilexes, laurels and cypresses. They are joined to the Palace by a large amphitheatre, rebuilt in the XVIIIth century. The general design, by Tribolo (1550), is an interplay of perspectives and inclines, leading from grove to grove and giving the impression of flowing from one room to another. Each of these verdant rooms accomodated a statue. At the entry to the gardens, Buontalenti arranged a vast grotto for the *Venus* by Giovanni Bologna and another with facetious paintings by the Menaboni : strangely grimacing figures and erotic scenes against a background of nature in its most complacent mood.

The other source of "Mannerism" is no longer Michael-Angelo, but Raphael, creator of the "Loggias" of the Palazzo Madama and of the Farnesina. His highly productive studio which was dispersed by the master's premature death in 1520 and finally broken up by the appalling sack of Rome (1527), spread the seeds of intellectual art whose purpose was to decorate and enliven everything with pictures. One of the key buildings of the period was the Palazzo del Tè at Mantua. It was built with amazing rapidity by Giulio Pippi, known as Giulio Romano, (about 1499-1527) who after having finished the "Stanzas" of Raphael went to work for Frederigo Gonzaga. The latter, a son of Isabella d'Este, had been raised in 1530 to the rank of Duke by Charles V and was anxious to demonstrate his magnificence.

The palace is a kind of recapitulation of dynamic classicism as defined by Alberti and the Roman masters : but all the elements are brought to a new pitch of tension by the exaggeration of width, the introduction of gigantic reliefs and the large-scale use of rustic themes permitting violent contrasts, heightened still further by the use of vivid colors, in particular in the metopes.

The rooms were decorated from floor to ceiling ; carpets covered the flagstones, the doors were enriched with marquetry and above the marble cornices were frescos covering the entire arch. There are two quite separate series : one on the north in the "Hall of Psyche" (1527-1581) where everything is devoted to the praise of pleasure and one, on the south, in the wing built around the "Hall of Giants", consecrated to the themes of triumph and power (1530-1535). These two symmetric groups carry out, with an impressive degree of virtuosity and feeling, the two main themes of the decoration : eroticism and the most outspoken love scenes—*Venus and Adonis, Psyche...* a voluptuous paganism which would have delighted Ingres, with an interplay of foreshortening and ceiling effects combined into a continuous decoration. At the other end, gigantic battles and overwhelming cataclysms, apparently complementing the rugged landscapes of the rustic themes, cover the room with huge rocks rolling over hideous giants. Illusion is heightened by the disposition of the fire-place, arranged in such a way that the fire burns at the exact place where the Cyclops roll into the crater of Etna.

The palace was held to be a "veritable model of the architecture and painting of our time" ; some of the buildings in Vicenza were inspired by it and Palladio retained certain aspects of its planning.

But the vigorous Romano was not unique : the most remarkable of the "Mannerists" of the province of Emilia was that somewhat decadent disciple of Correggio and Raphael, Francesco Mazzola known as Il Parmigianino (1503-1540). While Giulio Romano was developing a decoration with an excessive degree of vitality and paradox

Portrait of a Sculptor, *about 1550, by the Florentine Court painter Bronzino. (43 ¾ × 35 ¾") Louvre Museum, Paris.*

in the Palazzo del Tè, Correggio's gifted pupil was attempting to achieve the quintessence of grace and charm by eliminating every trace of realism from both figures and composition. His style *(maniera)* was "imitated by any number of painters, because he has discovered a deliciously graceful way of representing light..." (Vasari). With Parmigianino, painting attempts, far more radically than it did with Raphael, to capture the "something" that comes from the inward image, cleverly fused with natural forms. This "Mannerist" attitude was to influence the entire personality of this elegant, nervous, unstable painter. From 1522 to 1524 he installed himself in Correggio's studio, then, so as to see the works of the great masters, suddenly left for Rome where his youth and beauty caused a great sensation. Driven out by the German occupation, he went to live in Bologna and returned to Parma after the death of Correggio, whom he survived by only ten years. So charming and brilliant that "it might have been said that Raphael's soul had passed into his body", Parmigianino had a taste for the strange and the mystic which is expressed in his convex, foreshortened portrait (1524, Vienna) and, still more, in his interest in alchemy. He spent his strength by the study of this occult science to the point of becoming, just before his death, "strange and melancholy"

Left : Parmigianino, Madonna With The Long Neck *(84 × 52 ⅓") Pitti Palace, Florence. This page :* Christ in Limbo, *Bronzino, details. Santa Croce, Florence.*

The tender and vivacious talent of the painter is to be seen in the two series of frescos which date from his first period in Parma : two chapels of Saint John the Evangelist (1522) with large vibrant figures under the diffuse light of enormous niches, and the *History of Acteon* on a ceiling in the castle of Fontanellato (1523).

Admirable drawings of all his works, full of emphasis and elliptical invention, are still in existence and allow us to appreciate the subtle elaboration of the painter's three masterpieces, the *Vision of Saint Jerome* (1527, London), the *Madonna With the Rose* (1530, Dresden) and the *Madonna With The Long Neck* (about 1535, Pitti), where every detail is brought to the point of perfection : the refinement of expression in the figure of the Virgin, her lowered eyes, charming coiffure and too elongated hands and feet create all the allure of a great lady. The elaboration of the "serpentine figure", conceived in the form of an S, imprints its dominant theme on the composition. The illusion of space created by the horizontal and vertical planes in the background give a feeling of incredible depth enhanced by a thin film of color.

An admirable portraitist, the artist was able to represent a whole generation in a manner that delighted it : *Portrait Of A Man With Ancient Relief* (Strafford Collection), *Young Prelate* (Borghese), *Malatesta Baglioni* (Vienna), *Bearded Man In A Cap*—perhaps a self-portrait (Uffizi) and some delicious feminine figures, *The Turkish Slave* or rather *The Girl With The Turban* (Parma), *Antea* (Naples) reach the perfection and sophistication of forms desired by the artist. Parmigianino was admired and understood from Venice to Naples, thanks to engravings which familiarized an entire century with his compositions and figures. It is therefore difficult to exaggerate his importance. Coming after the voluptuous Coreggio and adding an intellectual coldness and abstraction to his master's work that had never been seen before, he gives the impression that he created a new form of beauty and that, without him "Mannerism" would neither have been aware of itself nor developed to such a height of elaboration.

Paseo de Gracia, 48

BY ROSAMOND BERNIER

*In Barcelona, Picasso's sister keeps unknown paintings by "Uncle Pablo"
among her family treasures*

"Come in, we are so very glad to see you!"

I was very glad to be there, but in truth could see very little. Two young people had opened the door and ushered me into a small hallway, barely lit. "I don't know what happens to the electric bulbs around here, they are broken all the time", the girl explained cheerfully, "and besides, the fuses blow—just like that—for nothing." "I am Pablín", the man introduced himself, "and this is Lolita. Mother is waiting for you over there."

Picasso had said we could photograph the collection of his paintings owned by his sister Lola, Señora de Vilato, in Barcelona; this was my first visit to the family. The surprises had begun when I telephoned for a rendez-vous; a friendly, insistant voice had urged me to come that very day, or rather, that very night. Since I had heard that Señora de Vilato, who is a little younger than Picasso, was a semi-invalid, I was a bit startled at the hour fixed for the meeting: eleven at night. And the prosperous apartment house on Barcelona's main residential avenue, the Paseo de Gracia, with its smooth-running elevator, was unexpected after Picasso's crowded Left Bank quarters and the narrow, leg-breaking staircase that leads to them. But once inside the Vilato door, the conformities of the

Picasso's sister Lola, wrapped in blankets, and her children Lolita, Jaime and Pablin, photographed during an impromptu flamenco session in their Barcelona home. On the wall, an early Picasso: The First Communion (1896), posed for by the painter's sister and father.

bourgeois world appeared to break down under the impact of the collective family personality.

Señora de Vilato was seated in an armchair, her round body rising out of a heavy cocoon of blankets. Only one part of one of the two lamps in this little room functioned; I made out an old, round face lit by a pair of remarkably dark eyes, Picasso eyes. They made it possible to remember that their owner was once a great beauty. Doña Lola welcomed me warmly, and showered me with questions as she accepted the flowers I had brought her: "And how is Pablo? And Javier (a son who lives in Paris)? And did you know that Fin (another son who lives in Paris) came back to Barcelona for the first time in eight years and immediately caught a fever? Lolita, we must have a vase somewhere, we used to have a vase, take the flowers." Lolita, her very pretty daughter, scuttled out on her high heels and came back with a kind of copper coal bucket, the tall flowers stuck in at a perilous angle, the string still around their stalks. "That's the way it is in this house," she said proudly, "it's not like anywhere else!" She was right.

Everyone seemed to be talking at once. Besides Doña Lola there were her sons Pablín and Jaime, and Lolita; we sat around in a circle in Spanish style, wedged between the walls and an old upright piano. Doña Lola had caught Maltese fever during the Spanish War and had not been properly taken care of; she was left with acute rheumatism, and spends most of her time in bed. The family keeps her company

at night — they all seem to stay up until six in the morning—but it is not hushed conversation around the invalid's bed, I gathered. All the children play the guitar and sing and dance, and Doña Lola likes nothing better than a good flamenco, so the hours pass gaily, accompanied by little glasses of sweet Malaga wine.

Often the old lady interrupted her children, correcting an error, or adding a bit of information. Pablo had never seen this apartment; they were still living on the Calle de la Merced when he last came in 1936, that was the year of his exhibition in Barcelona at the Salon Esteve—his first exhibition in Spain since 1902—"here, he has not been appreciated. When we first came to Barcelona from Coruña," continued Doña Lola, "Pablo was fourteen (1895). Our father (José Ruiz Blasco) taught at the School of Fine Arts, but he did not like Catalonia. He felt lonely without his Andalusian friends. (Picasso has said of this period of his father's life: "*Ni Malaga, ni taureaux, ni amis, ni rien.*")

"That first year in Barcelona Pablo painted the big picture over the piano." Lola's glance was directed through the semi-gloom to the opposite wall where I could dimly see a huge dark canvas of a woman dying in bed, accompanied by a nun and a doctor (*Science and Charity*, 1896). "And he painted this with me posing in a first communion dress—I didn't want to pose, but he insisted. It was not my dress, we borrowed it from a friend's daughter, and Papa posed too, there he is on the left—". The tall, thin figure of Picasso's

father (who also posed for the doctor in the *Science and Charity* picture) was clearly recognizable (1896).

"What is the earliest picture you have by Picasso?" I asked. (It was well past midnight but the rapid fire conversation showed no sign of letting up, and it seemed difficult to suggest interrupting it to see the paintings.) "The portrait of an old man in Coruña," answered Jaime, Tío Pablo must have been thirteen (1893), he painted very dark, realistic portraits, very Spanish."

"And the drawing of Tío Pablo's father in my room was done the next year (1894)", added Lola. "Then there is the portrait of Tía Juana (1896)" reminded Doña Lola. "She was very old and a bit crazy, and we knew she wouldn't live very long. She was always hard to handle and we couldn't persuade her to pose, but we wanted a remembrance of her. Suddenly one day she was in a peaceful mood, for once, and Pablo thought it would be the right moment. He went to her house with his paints and worked so quietly she hardly noticed what was going on. The portrait was finished in an hour. She died a few days afterwards.

A little later he did a portrait of me," reminisced Doña Lola. "He has it—I haven't seen it in years. And at the same time he made a drawing

Left: The Waiter, *1917* (39½ × 29"). *The hand in* trompe l'œil *is a departure from the artist's usual Cubist style. Below*: Bowl of Fruit, *1917* (15 × 11"). *Right*: The Balcony, *1917* (15¼ × 13"), *a gay summer view of the Barcelona harbor.*

of me (1899)." Lolita went out to get a reproduction of the drawing, the original being in the Barcelona Museum of Modern Art. "There was an exhibition here of Pablo's paintings about then." (Actually the exhibition was in 1897; the artist was sixteen.)

Unlike his father, Picasso, the young "Andalou", flourished in the creative bustle of turn-of-the-century Barcelona, a prosperous sea-port receptive to the currents of new ideas flowing in from other countries. He met with a regular group of Catalan intellectuals—writers and painters—at the café "*El 4 Gats*" (The Four Cats). One of his close friends of that period was the painter Sebastian Junyer. When Picasso looked at our photographs he was delighted to come across his own portrait by Junyer and said that at the same time he had painted Junyer's portrait in exchange, but that he did not know where this portrait was now. I was able to tell him Junyer still has it in his Barcelona house.

Picasso first left for Paris in 1900, and after that lived most of the time in France in spite of repeated visits, some of them extended, back to Spain. "The other paintings we have of Pablo all date from the summer of 1917" explained Doña Lola, "because that is when he came to Barcelona with the ballets." Cocteau had convinced Picasso to join Diaghilev's *Ballets Russes* company which had arrived in Rome in

February 1917. It must have taken all of Cocteau's inventive persuasion to get Picasso to go to Italy—he dislikes travel except when driven by unavoidable circumstances; he had shown no previous interest in designing directly for the theatre in spite of his series of Harlequins and circus performers. In Rome he made the sketches for the décor and costumes of *Parade*, to be given later with Satie's music and Cocteau's libretto, an event of considerable and revolutionary artistic importance. The company came on to Barcelona, Picasso with it. But when the company left, Picasso stayed on, having abducted one of the dancers from the troupe, Olga Koklova, who eventually became his wife.

By then Lola had married Juan Vilato Gomez, a distinguished psychiatrist who was to become director of Barcelona's Psychiatric Clinic. " Pablo was with Olga, so he did not live with us, he stayed at a hotel, a hotel that does not exist any more, the Rancini, down by the Christopher Columbus Column next to the port, " said his sister. " That is where he did the little painting we have called *The Balcony* (Picasso claims this view was not painted from his hotel window, as the family thinks, but from the window of a friend who lent him a studio). " Tío Pablo left us a whole group of pictures made during his few weeks here in 1917, " Pablín explained, " all different from each other, all different we are told from what he did in Paris at the time."

This was too much of a temptation, and kind Señora de Vilato felt it herself. " Take her to see the pictures if she would like it, " she ordered. I followed her children back into the hall, then into a much larger living-room, also extremly dimly lit, where there was very dark Spanish furniture, an uncomfortable looking stiff high-backed sofa, and book cases filled with what appeared to be surgical instruments. There were pictures hung on the walls, propped against shelves; others were on the floor, leaning against the wall. " You can't see much, can you—those bulbs, I really must buy some new ones, " Lolita obligingly lit a match and held it close to a picture so I could make out a little more. " Perhaps it might be possible, " I suggested, "to come here in the day time ?" This seemed to arouse real consternation " In the day time, well, let's see. No one's up in the morning, then we have breakfast... well, come tomorrow afternoon at six. "

At six I was back. This time there was sufficient light in the hall to see the Spanish dancer we later photographed in color; it hung unframed to the right of the door. The features are carefully modelled, and the left arm and lower body merely suggested. Against the realistically treated figure and stretching beyond it on both sides are brightly colored little dots, perhaps the last example (1917) of Picasso's pointillist treatment which he started combining with his Cubist style in

Lola as a young girl, *Barcelona Museum of Modern Art, 1899* (19¼ × 11½")

1914, when he showed a renewal of interest in color. (Unlike Seurat however, Picasso's intention in using these dots was not to produce an optical illusion—pure blue and yellow spots to suggest green to the eye of the viewer—, his purpose in spreading confetti like spots was simply to enrich the color values.) One of the nephews mentioned that the subject of this painting was Olga, but he probably confused it with another portrait of the same year of Olga wearing a white mantilla which belonged to the family but seems to have disappeared. Picasso said a girl he knew posed for the pointillist dancer whose real name he could not remember, but who was called " *La Saucisse* ".

Also hanging in the hall are the portrait of the old man from Coruña, a Picasso copy of the Velasquez portrait of Philip IV, a portrait of Picasso's father by the Spanish painter Ponce, a plate decorated by young Pablo with the head and shoulders of an Indian, and a print of the famous *The Frugal*

Picasso has not seen his sister for twenty years. When shown her photograph, right, he exclaimed "She looks wonderful! Like a bullfighter's mother—or a Roman Empress." The Virgin, left, was originally a Venus. Picasso's father added drapery and painted the face, making "a collage before the letter" according to his son.

black. The curved outlines and the addition of a calligraphic red line suggesting a nose and eyes evoke the figure of a woman. The paint is spread very thinly, almost transparently, so that at places the canvas can be felt through the colors, giving a chalky effect. This picture is totally unlike any other Picasso of these years. Picasso himself agrees that it is " *hors série* ", unrelated to his *œuvre* of the period, and a kind of anticipation of later preoccupations.

The Vilatos brought out a large unframed picture that was gathering dust beside the sofa : a typically Cubist-constructed figure in planes of black, red and white, but with the unexpected addition of a hand appearing to poke right through the flat painted surface in a surprising *trompe-l'œil*. The hand holds a knife and fork, while another hand—not treated realistically—clasps a bowl of fruit. At first the subject appeared to be a person seated at a table, but as Lolita pointed out, it is a waiter setting a table, hence the knife and fork held in the same hand.

The same bowl with fruit appears in another painting, the bowl and its shadow breaking into concentric curves of white and black, the fruit bright yellow and green. " *The Balcony* "

Two dancers painted by Picasso in 1917 : right, in the realistic manner with pointillist touches of color (46½ × 35"); *left, in the Cubist style with flat surfaces of subdued brown, gray and green,* (28¾ × 18½")

Right : Cubist construction in red, black, gray and brown, more closely resembling ▶ Picasso's Paris work of 1917 than the other paintings of the collection. (42½ × 23¾").

Repast engraving of 1904. (When shown a photograph of this hall with its white tile floor and heavy furniture, Picasso commented with amusement : " Ha, they live much better than I do. And look at that etching, it's worth a fortune now ! I didn't remember that they had it. " Obviously Picasso was referring to his crowded Paris studio and not to the fine villa acquired recently in the south of France.)

The large room seen tantalizingly by match light the night before turned out to be a reception room used by Jaime and Pablín who are both doctors— hence the case with medical instruments. (I wondered, considering the very spe-

cial Vilato hours, when patients were received...) Here were some fascinating paintings, lying around negligently with the casualness of the much-loved and the much lived-with. The most striking element of most of these 1917 paintings was their contrast in color and conception with works of the same period executed in Paris. They proved how exceptionally sensitive Picasso is to his surroundings, the light, the season, the materials at hand. In the brilliance of a Barcelona summer he had chosen a new palette for the large Cubist composition we reproduce in color. It is built up with flat surfaces of pink, mauve, almond green, bright red and

One of the painter's nephews, Jaime, whom Picasso has not seen since he was a small child. When shown this photograph the uncle exclaimed "He looks like the Comte de Paris!" Left of Jaime: an early portrait of Picasso by his friend Junyer.

described by Doña Lola hangs as a pair to this still life: a gay synthesis of holiday impressions with the red and yellow Spanish flag in the foreground, that famous landmark of Barcelona, the Christopher Columbus Column, rising out of a clump of palm trees, a suggestion of sea and masts, and the dazzling Catalan summer sky treated almost in a Fauve manner with quick brushstrokes in blue, yellow and red.

Over the medical cases, next to a group of plaster casts of deformed feet (Pablín's speciality) is another painting of a dancer, so totally unlike the pointillist dancer that only the extraordinary diversity of Picasso's styles makes it possible to believe that the two canvases were painted at approximately the same period (an example of the way Picasso plays back and forth between his "realistic" style and Cubism). Here the figure is flattened

Picasso says of this 1917 canvas that it is "hors série", quite unlike his work of that period. There is no other example of his use of these colors. (36 × 27½").

into a characteristically Cubist play of sharply defined surfaces, the long curved arm and the indented skirt suggest the whirl of motion; the head is seen simultaneously from the front and in profile. The colors are strikingly like those used by Juan Gris: slate blue, blue green, gray, black, brown and white. (Were you thinking of the ballets when you painted these dancers? I asked Picasso later. "Not at all," he answered, "I used to go to Barcelona music halls.")

The Vilatos very kindly allowed me to come back several times to see their paintings, and thanks to them and to Tío Pablo we were able to photograph most of them. The only place we could find any natural light for the color pictures was in the exterior staircase, where we propped up the pictures on a machine used for measuring Jaime's patients and prayed that the elevator would not arrive during the exposure.

Before my departure the family loaded me down with recommendations—for Pablo, for Javier, for my health, for the

voyage: "how difficult it must be, a woman travelling alone"—with presents to take to Paris. I knew that the two heavy boxes for Javier contained *membrillo*—an aggressively gelatinous brand of fruit paste that only Spanish birth makes palatable, but I wondered what could be in the bulging shoe box intended for Pablo.

When he opened the package in his Paris studio, out came a penny bank in the form of a pottery cock painted in loud colors; it rattled, they had put in a few coins for good luck. Then a paper bag bearing the trade mark of a butcher shop, containing outsize Jordan almonds; "*c'est bien l'Espagne*", said Picasso, "*les bonbons s'achètent chez le charcutier.*" And lastly, carefully rolled in tissue paper, a handful of cotton seeds, perhaps intended for the south. Picasso looked around at his studio heaped with canvases, old papers, books, portfolios, magazines, sculpture, parts of a stove and the extraordinary conglomeration of objects he collects, and said happily: "They are just what I need, we will plant them right here."

French Gothic Illuminations

BY JEAN PORCHER

*Leaving stylization behind them, miniature painters show life
and landscape for the first time*

It was in the XIIIth century that France first took over the artistic leadership of the West and created a style which, modified and varied by constant contributions from without, was soon to be adopted all over Europe. Never, since the days of the Carolingians, had France manifested such originality, not only in the domain of painting but in other fields. The country, in fact, changed from the receiver that it had been in the Romanesque period (this did not exclude either brilliance or even creative talent) into a transmitter. Under what conditions was this change brought about, what elements played a role and what influences were brought to bear ? What part did the Paris of Saint Louis play in this bursting of ancient bonds ? It is difficult to define all this precisely but it is possible to formulate a general concept.

Two magnificent volumes still in existence provide valuable evidence about manuscript illumination in the first half of the XIIIth century : the *Psalter of Blanche of Castille*, completed before 1223, (Blanche was not yet Queen when it was made for her) now in the Bibliothèque de l'Arsenal in Paris, and the *Psalter of Queen Ingeborg*, (the wife of Philip-Augustus who died in 1236) now in the Musée Condé in Chantilly. Both works are still essentially Romanesque in terms of their component elements ; in this respect they resemble the great Bibles made in France during the last decades of the XIIth century. The iconography of these Bibles reveals contacts with English art ; an example of this is the copy executed in Paris by Manerius, a scribe from Canterbury, now in the Bibliothèque Sainte-Geneviève in Paris. There is no doubt that the contacts established in the North of France, during the XIth and XIIth centuries, between the art of England and that of the continent were still very strong at the beginning of the Gothic period. The figures are more intensely alive, there is a flexibility of attitude which had not been seen before and, above all, the composition of the paintings and the actual details of the drawing and coloring reveal very strong resemblances to the stained-glass windows that illuminated cathedral and church naves. An admirable illustrated Bible of about 1250 is ornamented, like these windows, with scenes framed in medallions, ablaze with color, raised on a golden background which bathes them in light like sunshine through a pane of glass. Like the psalters of Blanche and of Ingeborg, all the copies of this Bible (one of them is in the Paris Bibliothèque Nationale) were painted by artists in the royal entourage.

This is also true of the *Psalter of Saint Louis*, executed between 1253 and 1270 for the King, that marks the real beginning of Gothic painting in France. Compared to the manuscripts which preceded it, even if only by a short time, the illumination of the psalter is striking in the novelty of its conception and particularly in the importance given to architecture—when the subjects chosen in no way dictated such a treatment. The painter took pleasure in copying directly what he saw of the Sainte-Chapelle, then being built by Saint Louis, instead of using traditional themes. What is remarkable both here and in the gospels commissioned for the Sainte-Chapelle is the extreme delicacy—in contrast to the final examples of French Romanesque art—of the drawing in which the expression of the faces is rendered almost entirely by line. There is also an attempt to achieve a kind of canon, expressed by an intentional grace and an atmosphere of youthful gaiety which already anticipates the exquisite figures to be seen in Parisian painting of the following centuries. This method of treating facial expressions finds an

The Master of Jouvenel des Ursins : History of the Gracchi, illumination from the Mer des histoires by Giovanni Colonna. 1449.
All the illustrations for this article come from the Bibliothèque Nationale of Paris.

Cy commencent les paraboles Salomon
en françois sur la bible et hystoire.

Les paraboles Salomon le filz
de dauid roy disrael a sauoir
sapience et discipline a en
tre parolles et prudence a
receuoir enseignemens
et doctrine et iustice et iu
gement et loyaulte et droiture que sens
soit donnes aux petis cest adire a humbles
ignorans et que science soit donnee et eu
tendement a ceulx qui en ont mestier les
sages seruir plus sages en sera et cellui
qui entent mieur en saura soy et autruy
gouuerner et appertenir paraboles et i

terpretacions et les figures et les parole;
des sages. La parolle de nostreseigneur est co
mencement de sapience les fos despisent
sapience et doctrine mon filz oye la disci
pline de ton pere et ne laisse mie la loy de
ta mere que grace soit adioustee ansi
sur ton chief et fermail dor a ton col mon
filz se les pecheurs taleschent ne les croy mie
Cest adire se les losengiers te losengent
ne les croy mie que ilz ne te deçoiuent se
ilz te dient bien a nous mettons aguies
pour occire repitons contre iustice po
lui prendre. Englouticons les comme
enfers tous vis et tous entiers comme
descendens en la fosse nous trouuerons

exact counterpart in the drawings of an architect of the period, Villard de Honnecourt. Thus architecture which so passionately interested Saint Louis influenced the psalter designed for him, and the illuminations ornamenting the manuscript inevitably remind us of architectural drawings. The great Parisian artist of the XIIIth century was perhaps King Louis himself : of course he was only part of a general movement, but he epitomized it so well that he left an indelible mark upon the age.

Most of the works of the period are anonymous, but the fact that illuminations are, by definition, linked to a text, allows them to be dated with a certain degree of accuracy. Also, in the case of liturgical books destined for a specific church, their geographic origin can be traced. At long intervals, some rare name appears to throw a ray of light into the darkness, but it is generally extremely difficult—and will always remain so—to establish any definite connection between these names and the works themselves. Happily this is not the case with the two Parisian artists whom we know both through documents from contemporary archives and also thanks to an incredible piece of luck, from actual signatures. One of these signatures is to be found in a list of Parisian taxes of 1292 and on a royal account of 1296. The artist concerned was called Honoré and there is every reason for attributing to him a breviary executed for Philippe le Bel (Paris, Bibliothèque Nationale) : this attribution seems all the more legitimate in that a copy of the *Décret de Gratien*, today in the Library of Tours, bears an inscription to the effect that it was bought in Paris in 1288 at Master Honoré's studio. The other, Jean Pucelle, together with two of his assistants, signed a Bible called, after the name of the copyist, the Bible of Billyng. This book was completed on April 30, 1327. Pucelle made a note of the sums paid to his collaborators in a breviary of the Belleville family. He also designed the seal for the Brotherhood of Saint-Jacques-aux-Pélerins in Paris (an account for the years 1319-1324 attests to this) and painted a "very small prayer book" for Queen Jeanne d'Evreux, third wife (1325) of Charles IV, who died in 1328. This book has been most authentically identified with an admirable small volume ornamented with *grisailles*. It is one of the marvels of French medieval art and has recently been added to the collection of the Cloisters Museum in New York.

Honoré and Pucelle are two great artists : and their names are, therefore, doubly precious to us : the name of Pucelle, in particular, for he was an innovator and, in his day, seems to have enjoyed real fame, more than justified by his open-mindedness, his originality and his curiosity (the first connections between French art and Italian art were established by him). The breviary executed for the Belleville family contains a series of illustrations that must have been conceived by a learned theologian anxious to emphasize, in a particular way, the points of agreement between the Old and New Testaments. Until the beginning of the XVth century most of the artists in the royal household who illustrated psalters or Books of Hours took their inspiration from this breviary.

But if Pucelle is certainly the most remarkable painter of the XIVth century, he is far from being the only one. There are documents from the reigns of Jean Le Bon and Charles V that give us many names to whom unfortunately we can attribute no specific work except in the most problematic manner. One of these is Jean Lenoir, the painter who first worked for the Comtesse de Bar, then for Yolande of Flanders, and then for the Regent of France (the future Charles V). He finally joined the household of Jean de Berry where we hear of him between 1372 and 1375. The abundance of painters accounts for the very great variety of styles which are so difficult to classify. Books on profane subjects begin to assume an increasing importance : novels in prose or verse (these enjoyed a great vogue in the second half of the XIIIth century and their burgher origin is reflected by simple but racy vignettes), translations of Latin texts, many of which were commissioned by Charles V, and world histories or chronicles of France.

The illustration of the period is divided into pictorial groups of varying merit ; but two in particular are worthy of our attention. The first group is mainly represented by two manuscripts of poetic and musical works by Guillaume de Machaut (Paris, Bibliothèque Nationale), by the *Décades de Tite-Live* (Paris, Bibliothèque Sainte-Geneviève), by the *Bible historiée de Charles VI* (Paris, Bibliothèque de l'Arsenal) and by the *Grandes Chroniques* in the Bibliothèque Nationale. This group, very characteristic of the reigns of Jean le Bon, Charles V and Charles VI, contains animated and amusing scenes peopled with gesticulating and slightly caricatural figures which the art historian Henri Martin has classified under the designation of work from the "Studio of the Master of the Copses", so-called because of the shrubs and bushes of a particular shape which seem to have been characteristic of his work-shop. Despite the obvious relationship between these paintings, Henri Martin hesitated, with some reason, to recognize the hand of a single artist. Nevertheless their vigor and liveliness bear the personal imprint of an original and inspired painter : we know of no one who anticipates him and he has no followers.

No work reveals the characteristics of the second group better than the famous copy of the *Miracles de Notre-Dame* of Gautier de Coincy, called de Soissons. This group has a long tradition of Parisian elegance behind it—an elegance that is sometimes rather facile—the first manifestations of which are to be found in the *Psalter of Saint Louis* and again in Pucelle. Those marvellous artists, the de Limbourg brothers, did not escape from this essentially Parisian tradition, despite their foreign origin and their powerful personalities. Several artists collaborated on the *Miracles de Notre-Dame*: the frontispiece, a Triumph of the Virgin, derives from Pucelle's art even more than do the rest of the illustrations. In these one almost recognizes, in some of the female faces, which seem suffused with beatific serenity, the incomparable Madonnas of the *Belles Heures de Jean de Berry*. The extremely marked characteristics of the Paris tradition were possibly even accented, but not exaggerated, by fertile influences from the North of France, from Flanders and from Holland, mingled with but not diluting them, and to these was later added the Italian influence which has continued since Pucelle's time until the present day.

France, at the beginning of the XVth century, and Paris in particular, were the crucible in which the most diverse influences were fused. Charles V already had in his service a Flemish painter, Jean de Bandol, or de Bruges, who executed for him an excellent copy of the Bible translated in 1371 by Jean de Vaudetar—now to be found in The Hague. But it was his brother, Jean de Berry, who patronized the most illustrious painters of the North and commissioned their most remarkable works. Between 1385-1390 he asked André Beauneveu, a celebrated sculptor and architect, the designer of several royal tombs in the Cathedral at Saint-Denis, to paint heads of Prophets and Apostles in the Psalter preserved in the Bibliothèque Nationale and mentioned specifically in the inventory made in 1402 of the de Berry library. The same inventory attributes to Jacquemart de Hesdin the *Très Belles Heures de Notre-Dame* which up to now has been identified as a manuscript belonging to the Royal Library in Brussels, even though there is no absolute proof of this.

But it is to the three brothers Pol, Hermann and Jeannequin de Limbourg, whose real name was perhaps Malouel (they were nephews of Jean Malouel, Philippe le Hardi's court Painter) that we owe the most magnificent of the works commissioned by Jean de Berry. They entered his service about 1410, probably after the death of Jacquemart de Hesdin, and went to work immediately. It is between that date and 1413 that the *Belles Heures*, recently acquired by the Cloisters Museum of New York, was completed. This work, which is of the utmost importance in French art, combines the influences of the Parisian tradition, the Flemish tradition (already established in Paris for many years as we have seen in discussing Jean de Bruges) and finally of the Italian tradition whose influence reached its culminating point with the Limbourgs. It was from Italy that they acquired their sense of masses, of mobility and of balance in general composition. Their landscapes, which alternate with traditional decorative backgrounds, are still composed in tiers but they flatten out in the *Très Riches Heures* which the death of Jean de Berry in 1416 prevented them from finishing. This manuscript is the prize possession of the Musée Condé in Chantilly.

Before describing another very important work from their studio, we must mention, among other artists who were active in Paris between 1400 and 1415, the painter, possibly an Italian, who worked for Christine de Pisan and illustrated some of the poetic works which this woman writer dedicated to personalities at the Court. There is nothing to equal the animation and spirit with which these small compositions are treated; the painter was perhaps a Lombard and the predecessor of Giovanni de'Grassi and of Pisanello. We must also mention the master known by the name of Boucicaut, whose fine Book of Hours, preserved in the Musée Jacquemart-André in Paris, displays both originality and talent; his pupil and imitator, the so-called Master of Bedford, who worked for Jean the Regent of France between 1422 and 1435, is responsible for a Book of Hours (in the British Museum), a breviary (in the Library at Châteauroux) as well as the decoration of several other manuscripts.

Jean de Berry was a great art patron whose enthusiasm often led him to harry his artists. We have every reason to believe that the de Limbourg brothers began an illustrated Bible for him which was to have more than three thousand illustrations. Until well on into the XVth century many artists strove to complete this Bible which is now in the Bibliothèque Nationale. It would take too long to explain why it seems probable that one of their pupils figured among the artists who continued the work and how this pupil, who for a long time was identified as Fouquet—a young Fouquet—can, without too great a degree of improbability, pass as being, if not the artist of the portrait of the *Man with a glass of wine* in the Louvre and of the *Young Man* of 1456 in the Liechtenstein collection, at least as

Jean Colombe: The Rape of Helen, *illustration for the* History of the Destruction of Troy. *About 1*

Following pages : enlarged detail of this miniature.

pres ces choses comme dit
vertus livre ou premier
livre de la seconde bataille pu
nique furent avec consaltz
queuls fervilius z bapus fla
mineus. Et hambal au comman
cement du prin temps print so
chemin vers tostane. mais ainsi

quil passoit le mont apennin
temps scha tone a uelle tempeste
pleine de plusieurs vens et greffes
Pourquoy par ce quelz veuent
quil estoit necessaire de tendre
les tentes il se arresterent le cul
dune faire mais il ne pouvoit
faire tenir riens ferme z ce qui

being one of his friends. This pupil, who will later appear as a great painter, if this theory is correct, is in any event the author of some excellent illuminations. The most important of these are in Geneva (in a volume of Boccaccio) and in the Paris Bibliothèque Nationale, in a *Mer des Histoires* decorated for the Chancellor Guillaume Jouvenel des Ursins between 1444 and 1449. This last connection leads me to suggest the name of "Master of Jouvenel" for him. This master only worked in the region of the Loire, between Tours and Nantes.

The Loire valley is also the country of Fouquet, Colombe and Bourdichon. Fouquet is too well known to be discussed in detail here. Everyone interested in painting knows of the forty illuminations taken from the *Heures d'Etienne Chevalier* to be seen in the Musée Condé at Chantilly. We know that this book was broken up a long time ago and that many leaves are still missing; Paris has three (in the Louvre and the Bibliothèque Nationale) and London two. Two more were discovered a few years ago in London, in a private collection whose owner had no idea what they were worth and who was greatly surprised at the large price they fetched. They are now in America. We are quite certain about the paintings we attribute to Fouquet: he stands so much above his contemporary artists that any error is avoidable (but not always avoided); but this certainty is due only to chance. It was the most extraordinary piece of luck for us that François Robertet, son of the recorder of the *Ordre de Saint-Michel* and secretary of Pierre II de Bourbon, for whom Fouquet had worked, thought of making a note at the end of the copy of *Antiquités judaïques* belonging to his master, to the effect that some of the paintings had been executed "by the hand of the good painter and illuminator of King Louis XI, Jean Fouquet, a native of Tours". If these lines had not come down to us, we would have been reduced to conjectures about the work of the French painter who was rated by his contemporaries among the greatest. Because of them it is possible to state with absolute certainty that the illustrations in the *Heures d'Etienne Chevalier* and the illustrations for a manuscript of the *Grandes Chroniques*, the origin of which is unknown, are by his hand.

We can identify Fouquet by these few lines of writing. This is also true, thanks to an equally extraordinary chance, of Jean Bourdichon, who was his most brilliant pupil and perhaps his last. By a warrant issued on March 14, 1508, Anne of Brittany decreed that he should be paid six hundred golden crowns to recompense him because—as the Queen says—"he sumptuously illustrated and illuminated a Book of Hours for our use and service, into which work he put a very great deal of his time". But there the resemblance to Fouquet ends, for it would be impossible to imagine a pupil more different from his master. Bourdichon was born about 1457 and died about 1521 at Tours; he was a painter without equal in his particular field—the prototype of the academic artist with the most scrupulous professional conscience: he was the Bouguereau of the XVth century. He carried Fouquet's technique to perfection without preserving any of his secret magic and he was able to profit from Jean Colombe's boldness by stripping it of every element of violence. All his painting is filled with an atmosphere of harmonious sweetness where nothing shocks and where, equally, nothing is really arresting. The technical perfection of his work, the richness of his coloring, as well as the luxury and variety of presentation assured his success among many rich patrons. In these respects his ingenuity is very great, even if he did not achieve the virtuosity of the school of Ghent and Bruges from which he took his inspiration. The Christ and Virgin from the *Heures de Charles VIII*, framed in a fillet of gold in the Bourdichon manner, stand out against a background of gilded tapestry covered by an airy tracery surrounding the figures. The *Grandes Heures d'Anne de Bretagne* (Bibliothèque Nationale) is celebrated for its borders ornamented in flowers, fruits and insects, but it is lacking in life and its illustrations are only first-rate copies which strive in vain to create an illusion.

The spirited Jean Colombe of Bourges, a contemporary of Bourdichon, is as unequal and mercurial in his work as the latter is self-controlled. He is not unknown although he is infinitely less famous. Fouquet's rival in certain aspects, he has sometimes been confounded with the great *Tourangeau* (in the *Heures de Louis de Laval* in the Bibliothèque Nationale, for example) and there may even be grounds for re-examining certain attributions. He partly inspired Bourdichon, though sharper and more vigorous. He died in the middle of the reign of François I, and could be described as the artistic forerunner of the School of Fontainebleau, to the extent that this School followed the French tradition and combined with it influences from Italy. His curiosity about antiquity, a legendary antiquity heavily encumbered with medieval trappings—explains the trend which runs through the entire XVIth century and which ends with Antoine Caron and his followers. Here, we are very far from the Middle Ages and even from the Renaissance: the influence of Gothic illuminations was to last well into the first years of Louis XIV's reign.

Colombe: Hannibal's Army stopped by snow, illumination for Romuleon *by Robert della Porta. About 1490.*

Catalan Polychrome Sculpture

BY JUAN AINAUD

Though the work of XIIth century Catalan painters is relatively well known it is not widely realized that apart from the apses and pediments they adorned with frescos, they also applied their art to the decoration of wooden sculpture, leaving behind them some remarkable polychrome works.

The museums of Barcelona, Vich and Gerona, as well as certain private collections, have preserved precious examples. But many of these sculptures continue to serve as objects of worship for the faithful in the very same places where they were carved and painted.

To be able to imagine the countryside and surroundings in which these works were conceived, we must completely ignore the frontiers invented by XVIIth century diplomacy. At that particular period, the region consisted of several groups of counties governed by closely allied dynasties and, side by side with them, bishops and large monasteries whose authority and culture extended far and wide. The influence of these monasteries over broad areas explains inter-relationships which at first sight seem hard to understand.

The monastery of Ripoll is undoubtedly the most famous : it owned land throughout the whole country from Tossa, on that section of the Catalan coast known as the " Costa Brava ", to the borders of Aragon. Its abbots were advisers to the Kings of Navarre and its monks were given episcopal thrones

in far distant parts of the country. Besides Elna, Gerona and Barcelona, the most important of its bishoprics were at that time Urgel, which controlled a vast territory in the Pyrenees extending from the Conflent to the Ribagorce, and the diocese of Vich, which included a large part of the land re-conquered from the Moors in the central region of Catalonia. The monasteries of Ripoll and Montserrat were situated within the confines of the diocese of Vich, the former at the extreme north and the latter on the southern frontier.

The county dynasties played an important role in the development of artistic efforts of the period. Members of the ruling family often assumed the patronage of churches or monasteries, swelling their treasury by donations often derived from territories conquered from the Moors. The women of these great families were no less zealous to make offerings than their lords. This accounts for the portrait of the Countess of Pallars among the mural paintings at Bourgal and the effigy of the Countess Guislaine on the golden altar-piece in the cathedral at Gerona. Sometimes, they worked gifts with their own hands, as did Elisava whose signature is to be found on an embroidered standard in the cathedral of Seo de Urgel.

From the end of the IXth century, almost all the Catalan counties were united in the hands of a single family

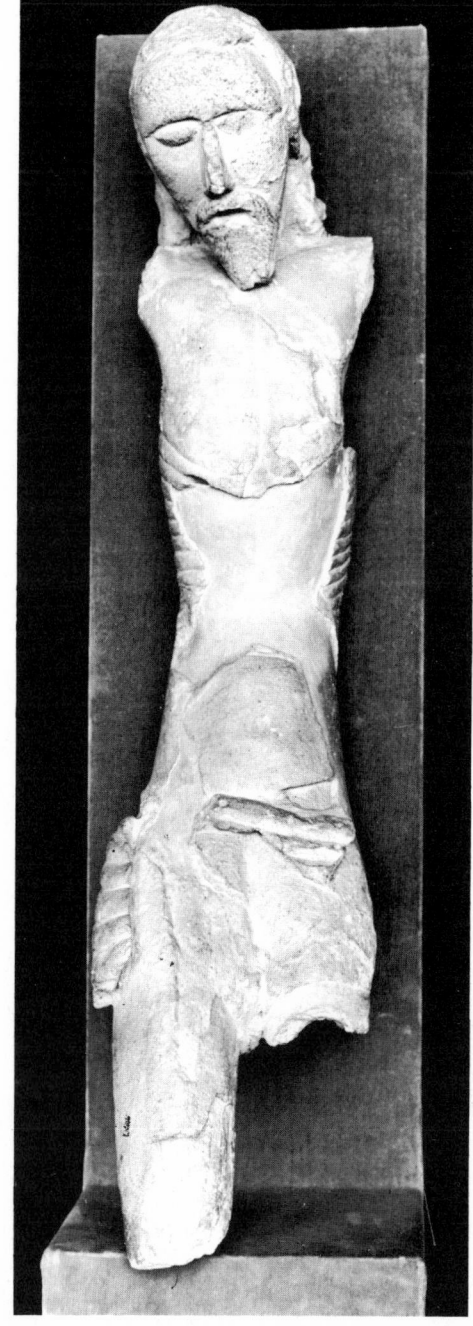

On the left : a XIIth century Catalan crucifixion. This important example of Romanesque sculpture is in the Marés Museum of Barcelona and is part of a rich collection.

On the right : torso of a mutilated Christ from the beginning of the XIIIth century. One of the few sculptures in plaster of this period; Museum of Catalan Art, Barcelona

Two Virgins with child (above), in poly-chromed wood; Marés Museum. The first, XIIIth century, has peasant features. The second, XIIIth century, is more refined.

The Virgin (below) has the straight back, and elongated profile typical of Catalan Romanesque. The figure was decked wit robes for feast days. Marés Museum.

which first governed the territory of the Conflent and then, starting from Cerdagne, succeeded in establishing its capital in Barcelona. On the other hand, certain western territories at the extremity of the country and certain valleys in the Pyrenees, with which communications were not so easy, remained independent. This was the case with the Bohi valley, a patrimony of the Barons of Erill, not finally incorporated into the diocese of Urgel until 1140, and with the valley of Aran, a halting-place for artists who were crossing the Pyrenees by the valleys of the Garonne and the Noguera Pallaresa.

The isolation of these regions, their particularism, and the fact that until the XXth century they were but little touched by the spirit of progress, contributed to the preservation of works of art exceptional in both number and quality.

Several figures, remarkable for their simplicity of style and intensity of expression, come from the valley of Bohi. The Descent from the Cross was a subject which often inspired local artists. The largest and most precious group is that of Erill la Vall, now, unfortunately, divided between the museums of Vich and Barcelona. The latter also possesses some figures of a group from Tahull and the admirable Virgin

of Durro, which is the only vestige that has reached us of a similar sculptural group. The Fogg Museum possesses another separate figure, detached from the Tahull group. The same stylized qualities are found in pieces of smaller dimensions, such as the figures of Our Lord and the Apostles,

which were part of the altar-piece of the Church of Our Saviour of Castaner de Noals (Museum of Catalan Art, in Barcelona) and also the figures on a Crucifix from Santa-Maria of Tahull.

All these works must have originated about the year 1123, the date of the frescos in the churches of Tahull from which some of them came and with which they possess certain obvious points of contact, as, for example, the unusual coiffure of the Holy Virgin. Other sculptures, also of the XIIth century, are typical of a more backward stage in technique. Among these, the most outstanding are the altar-piece of Santa-Maria of Tahull (Barcelona, Museum of Catalan Art) and that of Buira, in the Museum of the Seminary at Lerida.

If a traveller today goes up the valley of Bohi, around the string of mountain lakes and down through the valley of Aran, he can still find magnificent Romanesque sculpture in certain churches —figures of rare quality and richness of coloring. At Sardalou there is a Christ with an admirable, serene expression ; his Cross—and, in particular, the figure of an angel which ornaments it— very visibly preserves considerable traces of the primitive polychrome. Even more characteristic is the mutilated body of the Christ of Mig d'Aran. If the sculptures from Bohi recall the Far East, the Christ of Sardalou might well be said to suggest certain works from Mesopotamia. It must have been part of a Descent from the Cross : the hand of Joseph of Aramathea or of Nicodemus, carved out of the same block as the body, is there to prove it. It is because of this third hand that the statue was formerly known as the *Christ de les tres mans.* Another Christ belonging to this school is the one in the Museum of Barcelona inside which relics were discovered, wrapped in Hispano-Arabian silks, and a parchment commemorating its consecration in 1147 ; this provided precious information for determining the chronology of the series.

If we go from the west to the center of Catalonia, we find two important groups of Romanesque sculpture in wood. One, which is very varied in style, represents the seated figure of the Holy Virgin ; the other, far more homogeneous, represents Christ on the

XIIth century Virgin (opposite) departs from the traditional manner to carry the mark of an individual artist. Covered with green-gold polychrome. Marés Museum.

Cross, clad in a long tunic. These figures of Jesus are known as "Majestats".

Scattered throughout the region of the Segre river valley, are several Christs of this sort of which one wears a crown re-gilded and re-silvered in the XIVth century. However the most beautiful and the most characteristic come from the Cerdagne and the surrounding regions. The best known of all, called "Majestat Batlló" after the name of its donor, is in the Museum of Barcelona. Its polychrome is almost intact, as can be seen by the rich red and blue of the tunic. The "Majestats" of San Boi of Llucanes and of Santa-Maria of Lluça, both in the Museum of Vich, bear a very strong resemblance to this Christ.

Some fine examples of these "Majestats" from the French Cerdagne and the Conflent have recently been the subject of a study by Durliat. One of them, the "Majestat" of Llagonne, still has a good part of the original decoration on the Cross, with figures of the Holy Virgin and of Saint John. It seems to date from the last part of the XIIth century. It is comparable to a Christ from the Cerdagne which is naked and without a tunic (Amatller Collection, Barcelona).

Some of these sculptures are solemnly religious in a way which must not be confused with archaism. The devotional approach is deliberate and expresses a desire not to wander too far from Italian prototypes such as the "Volto Santo" of Lucca. The work which most closely approaches the Italian models, both in the vestments of the Christ and in its dimensions — although the style is different — is the famous "Majestat" of Caldès de Montbuy near Barcelona, which continues to be an object of particular veneration. Though the body has had to be restored, the admirable head has remained in perfect condition. Its force of expression, the perfection and richness of the modelling of the features, beard and hair, make it a masterpiece of its kind.

In the region of Ripoll, the great Romanesque tradition of preceding centuries explains the survival of this style until the middle of the XIIIth century. The Museum in Barcelona possesses a perfect example : the Christ from the Church of San Pedro, near the monastery of Ripoll. The body is delicate, slender and very human, the feet are pierced with a single nail ; it begins to show the spirit of Gothic art, but the sculptor obviously did not wish to depart from his Romanesque

This celebrated Descent from the Cross, of the XIIth century, comes from Erill la Vall. Its stylization recalls Chinese sculpture. The group was originally comprised of numerous figures ; it is now divided between the Museum of Vich and the Museum of Catalan Art in Barcelona. Opposite: the magnificent polychrome Christ in Majesty, the "Majestat Batllo" ; Museum of Catalan Art.

models. The Descent from the Cross known as the "Santissim Mistari", now restored to its place in the apse in the reconstructed monastery of Sant Joan de las Abadesses (Saint John of the Abbesses), is another important example of this style. The sculptures were consecrated in 1251; their size and quality make them one of the main attractions of the Church, extremely interesting in itself on account of both its architecture and its decoration in carved stone and alabaster.

Also from Ripoll comes an altar screen of the XIIth century (to be seen in the Museum at Vich) of which the polychrome was restored fifty years later. The artist worked in round relief; one of the Apostles is presented with a very stylized twisting movement in complete contrast to the hieratic form of the figures carved by the other sculptors.

It is interesting that although it is possible to find a few works representing Saint Martin or some other bishop among the sculptures of the period, yet, on the whole, figures of Saints are extremely rare.

There are two very interesting works dating from the end of the XIIth and the beginning of the XIIIth century in which sculpture and painting are combined. The first consists of several panels from the Church of Sant Marti Sarroca (Saint Martin of Sarroca); one of the faces is covered with a painting representing Saint Peter and Saint Paul; the other is carved to represent one of the Wise Kings and a Holy Woman. The second work comes from the Bosch i Catarineu collection. It is comprised of several panels showing the carved heads of the three Wise Men and a Holy Woman; their bodies are quite simply painted on the panels as a prolongation of the heads. The panels from Saint Martin of Sarocca, as well as those from the Bosch i Catarineu collection, are only fragments of a large group — altars or reredos representing the adoration of the Magi — in which there must have been a statue

The carving of this Virgin (above) imitates the goldsmith's art; the mantle falling in folds at the knees is characteristic of the Pyrenean style. Marés Museum.

of the Virgin or of the Child Jesus. In Asturia, a similar combination was used for a Calvary in the "Camara Santa" of the Cathedral of Oviedo. The bodies of Christ, the Holy Virgin and Saint John are painted as frescos and their heads are carved in the stone of the walls.

There remain the images of the Virgin Mary with the Child Jesus.

This is the most usual manner of representing the Virgin in Romanesque sculpture, and also the form in which the greatest number of examples has reached us. The forms are infinitely varied and so are their qualities. The veneration of the faithful for many of these Virgins has created and nourished the most extraordinary legends about them.

Several of these sculptures are extremely impressive : particularly those of Nuria and Bell-lloc (now at Dorrès) whose strength and expressive ruggedness remind one of African sculpture. There are also those in the Cathedral of Gerona or in the Cornellà at Conflent which have a classic grandeur derived directly from Italian Romanesque art. Some of these still preserve their brilliant polychrome in all its original splendor. This is also true of the figure in the Soler i Palet Museum in Tarrasa, in which the Virgin is represented as clad in a magnificent silken mantle ornamented with birds, and also of the Virgin in the Museum in Barcelona whose blue mantle is strewn with white lilies and whose large expressive eyes are painted simply in black. Like the group of the "Santissim Mistari", the famous Virgin of Montserrat combines a stylized delicacy with a profoundly human expression.

The masterpieces of Catalan Romanesque—sculptures, paintings on wood and frescos—not only played a highly important role in the European art of their period but also correspond profoundly to the sensibilities of both artists and public of today.

◄ A XIIth century Virgin in a fleur-de-lys covered robe still preserves the brilliance of its original polychrome. A prize piece from the Museum of Catalan Art.

*An angel, a saint and a Virgin of the ►
XIIIth century. It is not known if these polychrome figures once belonged to a single group. Museum of Catalan Art.*

Alberto

Two figures of women. Height 22″. 1954

Stampa is a village in the easternmost canton of Switzerland, the Grisons. It is a very small place. The surrounding mountains are very large. In such a landscape the diminutiveness of man in relation to nature becomes emphatic to the extreme. A human figure appears precarious and incomprehensible before such a manifestation of immutable matter.

At the same time, however, his confrontation with it intensifies the urgency and the dignity of the human need to impose the affirmation of a human presence upon the overpowering presence of nature.

Alberto Giacometti was born at Stampa in 1901, the eldest child of Giovanni Giacometti, a painter. The father was one of the first impressionist painters of Switzerland; works by him are to be seen in most of the Swiss museums. He was able to earn a good living for himself and his family, though, of course, in the little village of Stampa, with one café and no hotel, life before the First World War must have been simple and inexpensive.

Alberto grew up in an atmosphere not only condusive to some form of artistic expression but also free from any constraint to express himself in one way or another. His father's studio was in the house. At a very early age he began to paint and draw. He illustrated the books he read and copied paintings and sculptures from reproductions. He drew and painted directly from nature. His father helped him. Even then the vocation must have been plain. Giovanni Giacometti never had done, and never did any sculpture, but at the age of thirteen Alberto made his first busts from nature. He had not been away from Stampa then, yet these early works situate themselves as authoritatively in time as do the later. Certainly he could not have been very familiar with the sculptures of Despiau,

Giacometti, Sculptor and Painter

BY JAMES LORD

particularly if one reflects that the diffusion of reproductions and photographs of contemporary works in 1914 must have been insignificant. Yet these early works are reminiscent of Despiau, they remind one of the post-Periclean Greeks, with their graceful force, subtlety of movement and refinement of texture. The early paintings are somewhat pointillist in manner, but they have a vividness and an authority quite extraordinary for an artist so young. Nothing in Giacometti's youthful work suggests the uniqueness of his mature style. Its value is simply that it has quality. The young man had a talent. What more he might have he would have to see and situate for himself. There was nothing more then that others could do to help him.

At the age of eighteen he went to the School of Fine Arts in Geneva.

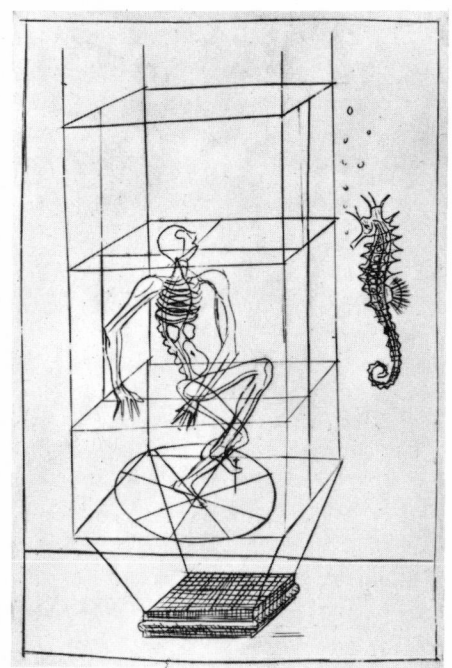

Engraving from his Surrealist period : for Crevel's "Les pieds dans le plat". 1933.

He stayed for three days : that was an affirmation. Afterwards he went to the School of Arts and Crafts to study sculpture. The element of craftsmanship is very pronounced in Giacometti's art. He would stress it more, and more formally than the formal element of art. He works in a state of constant and intimate excitement with his materials. His powerful and nervous hands alone seem to effect the transformation of clay from its condition as formless matter into a condition of perceptible vitality. It is not a deliberate effect of a will, but rather a mutation of natural elements as immediate as a geological metamorphosis.

Giacometti remains obstinately subservient to his work. His personal expression manifestly serves it. The strictures of time, place and action imposed upon the artist's expression, as distinct from self-expression, cannot but impair the results. The elements of personal drama are valid only inasmuch as they vivify an effective, resultant work of art. Despair is a luxury available to everyone. As a serviceable material, however, it is the exclusive property of the artist, whose absolute need is to equate his creative existence absolutely with nothing that has ever existed, or been created before. Giacometti himself expresses this. In his studio, small and stark, lighted with one powerful, naked electric bulb, he moves abruptly back and forth. The floor is strewn with the dust and fragments of any number of figures he has destroyed. Outside in the passage the early evening is gray, heavy. He lights cigarette after cigarette. He murmurs a phrase, a question, some secret between himself and his work. He submits to the inevitability of his use of himself.

Giacometti could not remain in Stampa or in Switzerland. The artistic genius of that country has been too

Drawing copied from a detail of a Romanesque fresco. L. Broder coll. Paris.

largely acquisitive. Its insularity has been an obligation rather than an opportunity. In 1920 the place for an artist to go was Paris. It accepted everything, and what it accepted it encouraged. Giacometti went first to Italy. In Venice, he has said, he tried not to let a single Tintoretto escape him. It is easy now to imagine his intense observation of the thin, elongated figures in these paintings. In Padua the static, statuesque drama of the groups in the frescos of the Arena Chapel, in Assisi the attenuated and anguished figures of Cimabue : these also impressed him.

He stayed two years in Italy, painted figures and landscapes and began to come to grips with the inadequacy of convention. *Is the sky really blue?* He worked on two busts, and for the first time he felt lost. No way out of the plastic problem offered itself, and he could not find one. Then, suddenly, he was face to face with the urgent, appalling reality of five thousand years of sculpture behind him. And there, in Rome, in the midst of the ruins, the mosaics, the vestiges of a past offering no help, the young man reached the frontier which separates interpretive art from creative art. This is an extreme of a sort. Beyond it there are no longer any distinctions. And to pass beyond is to risk everything on the chance that there will be something beyond. This is not wholly an act of the will, to be sure. But the part of nature is inseparable from the part of will. And those who recoil from the danger of risking everything often find very soon that they have nothing left to risk.

The decline from the zenith of perfection — wherever one wishes to place it—of sculpture to present the human figure in space has been steady and incontrovertible. For Rodin the traditional *tour de force* was still feasible, though the effort is at times embarrassingly apparent and the result often a bare and cynical exploitation of classical formulae. But he did turn the trick. After him no one could ever hope to do it again. It was no longer possible to present the figure; the only way out of this dilemma was to represent the figure. Not in an idealized appearance, after the manner of the Greeks, Italians and their followers, but in an

image as real as the immediate, transitory and functional presence of the real human figure. In short, the problem confronting Giacometti was simply: Is the execution of sculpture still a plausible reality? And for more than thirty years his ceaseless preoccupation has been plausibly to solve that problem. He has not done so to his satisfaction. If he had, he would have stopped working, he says, the essence of any artist's entire work being the tentativeness of all its separate parts. More than any other artist of our time Giacometti has submitted to the tentative.

His *raison d'être* has been to explore, not to discover, the act and not the accomplishment. This is a productive compulsion. Giacometti has said, "For

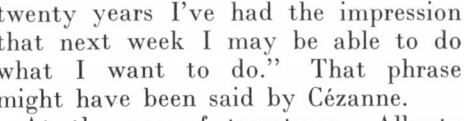

twenty years I've had the impression that next week I may be able to do what I want to do." That phrase might have been said by Cézanne.

At the age of twenty-one Alberto Giacometti was fully ready for Paris. His father sent him there. He worked at Bourdelle's studio at the Academy of the Grande Chaumière for three or

Giacometti's world is enclosed within the walls of this modest Paris studio where he has lived for over twenty years. His favorite models are his wife Annette (left) and his brother Diego. As soon as Alberto finishes a clay modelling, Diego makes a plaster cast of it in a neighboring room.

four years. There, while trying to finish his sculptures, he found himself again confronting the difficulties that had thwarted his efforts in Rome. He has said, "It was impossible to grasp the totality of a figure. We were much too near the model and if one started from any detail, from a heel or a nose, there was no hope of achieving the ensemble. But if, on the other hand, one began by analyzing the detail, the end of the nose for example, one was lost. One might have spent an entire lifetime without achieving any result. The form decomposed itself, became like specks in motion across a black, deep emptiness. The distance between one side of the nose and the other became

like the Sahara, limitless, without any fixed point, everything escaping."

For the past twenty-eight years in Paris Giacometti has occupied the same studio. By itself this is a statement of purpose ; and the stark simplicity of his physical environment complements the quality of that purpose. He shuns accumulating possessions. The superfluity of an average bourgeois interior at first contact makes him obviously ill at ease. His identity with his work is so complete that his physical needs hardly surpass its material needs : the clay, plaster, pigments, paper, canvas, wood and metals of his affective expression. The studio is very small. It is in a quarter of that very large city never visited by

anyone who has not explicit business there.

Giacometti is a stocky man. The power of his body is immediately perceptible beneath the nondescript clothes which plainly have no meaning for him other than as coverings. His head is large, set down close to the heavy shoulders. The hands are long, strong, functional, never quite clean of the contact with his work, and never still. On a café or restaurant table Giacometti's fingers will continually trace invisible drawings as he eats or drinks. The creative compulsion is as implacable as that, of an almost feverish intensity, and it imparts a rare authoritativeness of presence. Even, for example, to the

Diego by Alberto when the artist was fifteen (left), and Alberto by his father.

terrace of the Café des Deux Magots, in ironic distinction to its advertised. misnomer: the rendez-vous of the intellectual élite. Late at night anyone might have seen him sitting there, alone. At a table nearby two young girls are chattering obliviously. One is very tall, thin, the other short, fat, pale, and both are wearing discordantly colored clothes. Giacometti watches the girls, smiling slightly. His expression is *intent*, yet objective, fixed both in front of and beyond those he sees as if their presence were a prism refracting some perception of his rather than the details of their appearance and apparent relationship. But his smile is an evidence of direct, personal interest and response nevertheless. Giacometti is invariably responsive to the contact of others. He expresses himself easily and eloquently, laughs often and punctuates his talk with quick, quizzical glances of intense concentration, as if to say, "I see a great deal more than you think I see." No doubt he does. But he cordially accepts people as they present themselves. His solitude is not social. No caller is ever turned away from his studio, for instance. Both strangers and friends are accepted alike, with the same courtesy and sympathy of response. Consequently it may happen that on any day Giacometti will be more attentive to a complete stranger than to a person he has known for a long time, because the stranger's presence and perception, both for him and for Giacometti, correspond to the artist's compulsion of the moment. This might seem to be a kind of anarchy. It is not.

Giacometti's name, for all those who know him, has come to be somewhat

of a criterion of the possible sincerity and consecration of an artist. And his moral status as an individual corroborates it. In 1938, one day as he was walking in the street an automobile swerved up onto the sidewalk and crushed his foot. He was in the hospital for a very long time and to this day walks with a slight limp. The case was flagrant, but Giacometti made no effort to claim the indemnity due him, which would, in any case, have been paid through the impersonal agency of an insurance company. He felt that to make any claim would be to involve himself in a series of alien commitments from which there might ultimately be no escape. "Besides", he has said, "it's the best that could have happened to me, to be in the hopital just then." It may or may not have been, but it was there that the pharmacy wagon wheeled

through the wards gave him the initial idea for the celebrated sculpture of the woman on the chariot which he made twelve years later.

It is easy to imagine how the bombastic works of Bourdelle must have come gradually to seem unbearable to Giacometti. There was approximately the relation between their aims as between those of Cecil B. de Mille and, say, Luis Bunuel. After four years he left the Grande Chaumière. It was about 1930 that Giacometti became associated with the surrealist movement. His status in it was in keeping with his nature and his purposes. Inasmuch as it did group together for a time the artists of greatest vitality of that young post-war generation, the surrealist movement represented a state of mind to which Giacometti could not logically have remained indifferent. Of his work at this time Giacometti has said, "Since I wished to render a little of what I saw I began in desperation to work in my studio from memory. I tried to do whatever I could to save something from the catastrophe." (The catastrophe was his effective inability to produce a single sculpture that convinced him of its reality as a representation of the human figure.) "This produced objects which were the nearest I could get to my vision of reality." (He refers to these works specifically as objects, a most significant detail for his subsequent evolution.) "But I still lacked what I felt toward the ensemble, a structure, an element of sharpness I saw in it, a sort of skeleton in space. There was a further element in reality which struck me: movement. I could only make it real and effective, and I also wanted to convey the sensation of its being provoked. But all this took me away little by little from the exterior reality. I had a tendency to care only for the construction of the objects themselves. I was troubled by the reality which seemed to me to be

otherwise. The objects were without foundation and without value, to be thrown away."

In 1932 Giacometti exhibited with the surrealists at Pierre Colle's gallery in Paris. A year or two later he had a one-man show there. But the impasse was growing more and more intolerable to him. And then, as if by accident, yet with that ineluctable fatality which precipitates the evolution of art, the intuitions which had obsessed him for fifteen years, since his early days in Rome, crystallized and became a crisis. It was in 1935 that he took a model, with the notion of making some figures for a composition he had in mind. He expected these studies to take not more than weeks. He worked from the model every day after that for five years. "Nothing", he says, "was as I imagined it." Very quickly he gave up the idea of doing figures, which were too difficult, and concentrated on busts. A head seemed to him an object utterly unfamiliar and without dimensions. He was beginning again from the very beginning, as if nothing in sculpture had ever existed before. Twice a year he would start work on two heads, always the same, without ever achieving the realization of one. Finally, in order to discover what might have resulted from all this labor, he began to work again from memory. But, wishing to convey what he saw, he found—much to his terror, he says—that the sculptures became smaller and smaller. They seemed reasonable likenesses only when tiny. Yet these dimensions revolted him and tirelessly he would begin again, only to end several months later at the same point. A large figure seemed to him false and a small one unbearable. Then they sometimes became so tiny that, with a last touch of his knife, they disappeared into dust. Of nearly eight years of an incessant labor almost nothing remained. The task he had set himself must have seemed at times

—rather like that of the alchemist—insoluble. And yet the integrity and validity of the effort did exist. One is again reminded of Cézanne. The parallel, as we may see, is more than objective.

In 1945 the manifestations of Giacometti's gradual, persistent exploration began to change. He was doing a great deal of drawing, and it was this that led him to try to realize larger figures.

The constant themes of Giacometti's paintings are his wife, his studio and the objects around him. Above: Annette (36 × 25½") 1951; Maeght collection, Paris. Below, from left to right, sculpture from former periods, all bronzes: Two Figures (height 25½") 1926; A Woman (height 59") 1927; Head (height 7¼") 1934.

He did so, but to his surprise they seemed acceptable likenesses only when long and thin. This element of surprise, to Giacometti, is the guarantee of the authenticity of his work. He had already then made the unique discovery that rendered the act of sculpture possible for him.

The fundamental problem confronting Giacometti in his effort to demonstrate the continuing possibility of sculpture has been convincingly to represent the human figure in spite of the meaninglessness of the individual particularities of any such figure. It had become clear to him that a sum of the details of a figure could not represent its reality. But perhaps the total detail of one human figure might represent the totality of all such figures. This

becomes an expression of a human absolute. The great classic sculptors present us with an idealized individuality. Giacometti has devoted himself to the representation of a literal generality. Classical sculpture imposes the illusion of humanity upon the spectator. Thus the bronze or marble ultimately has more reality than the effigy it pretends to embody, because the individuality of the latter, being dependent upon the subjectivity of the individual spectator, cannot transubstantiate the generality of the former. The sculptures of Giacometti impose the illusion of humanity directly upon the concrete substance of their own reality. The aesthetic experience is no longer subject to a physical relationship between the spectator and a material mass. Giacometti's figures are established in space as arbitrarily as the real figures one sees any day at the end of an avenue or from the far side of a room. Our perception of their reality will not change if we are nearer or farther away from them, whereas in classical sculpture—because it presents a sum of details—the perception is subject to an arbitrary disposition. This is the revolutionary effect of Giacometti's discovery. By imposing an inflexible condition of perspective upon his figures he has resolved the dilemma of an apparent coherence in the multiformity of a human figure in space.

The men and women of Giacometti's sculptures are not symbols. They are not esoteric evocations conceived for "the happy few". They are as real to us as, say, the inhabitants of a country we have never visited, who exist as really as we do and in whose reality we must believe in order to remain convinced of our own.

For fifteen years Giacometti had not a single exhibition. Finally, however, it seemed to be necessary. "Mainly", he says, "because I didn't want to be thought of as sterile and incapable of achieving anything, like a dry branch." After the first exhibition, in 1948, there were others in Europe and in the United States. The public could not but respond to the originality and the quality of Giacometti's work. He had formulated the shock of recognition with an immediacy and a veracity which compelled acceptance. The exhibitions were successes. The success, however, was the public's and not Giacometti's. He had already gone on to essay other problems. It was Leonardo who stated that satisfaction is harmful to the artist.

Giacometti's discoveries and his revolution remain, for him, eternally subject to the tentativeness of his vision. It is significant that, during the period of his surrealist associations, he did a figure called $1 + 1 = 3$. So the "other problems" are always the same. However, the semblance of sameness in Giacometti's work is simply a representation of our universal sameness, as a Chinaman is like an Eskimo and a lover like a lover. There is no escape from the similarities of the human condition.

Prior to 1947 Giacometti had done relatively little painting. Between 1937 and 1947, during the period of his desperate and absolute struggle with the problems of sculpture, he had done none at all. Then he began again, this time more in earnest than ever before. And the particular problems of painting had soon become for him as imperative as those of sculpture continued to be. He was to have less difficulty in solving them, however, because the acuity of his perceptions relating to the status of sculpture were to be of great use. Furthermore, the situation of space—his ceaseless preoccupation—is less pressing a difficulty in painting, because the existence of all dimensions in painting is an illusion, and accepted as such. Thus the relationship between the spectator and the painting becomes, *per se*, an illusory relationship with an illusion. The dilemma of a work of art's immediate or relative perceptibility in relation to the subject it presumes to represent does not exist for the painter as for the sculptor.

Giacometti's sculptures constrain space to appear in reality; his paintings are remarkable organizations of illusory space. Their subject matter may at times seem secondary to this conceptual necessity. But it is not. When Giacometti establishes the space around a figure, he represents that figure as explicitly as Cézanne represented the Mont Sainte-Victoire by establishing the relation in space between it and his eye. Also like Cézanne, Giacometti has committed himself absolutely to the exigencies of his "sensation". The results, in essence, at least, are not dissimilar. Both men from the start adhered to Baudelaire's dictum of absolute sincerity as a means of originality. And this implies *ipso facto* a profound response to the human implications on any subject matter. Cézanne's apples and Giacometti's are not in the least alike, but the statement of an apple's immediacy and veracity remains indivisible. Giacometti is essentially a sculptor and there is an effect of the objective mass in his paintings which is absent in Cézanne's. However, the statement of a human reality in the portraits of Madame Cézanne is no more compelling than in the portraits of Annette Giacometti. And no fundamental distinction can be made in the statement of a material reality by a representation of bottles by the one or the other. If absolute sincerity is indeed a means of originality, then the result must also be absolute. The effects of Cézanne's researches upon contemporary art have been nearly incalculable. But, when the dust has settled, as it will, upon the works of the many who have exploited the appearances of Cézanne's innovations without bothering to emulate the conscience or the consciousness which generated them, it may seem that Giacometti has learned more from the Master of Aix than any of the others.

These speculations would strike Giacometti as being quite beside the point, and even presumptuous no doubt. The point remains his realization, in the ensemble of his work, of a reality as nearly identical as possible with his vision of reality. To this end—it is by definition a consummation—he labors incessantly. In his small, changeless studio the light will burn late night after night, regardless of season or climate, regardless of the fantasy of any human preoccupation to which his own may impart a more abiding significance. The existence of his figures will continue: those to survive and those to succumb with the same inevitability as in life, until the apparent distinctions between the one reality and the other appear to be resolved in their immediate proximity. The studio will forever exist in this context of natural flux: wars, Sunday afternoons, football games, the workmen crossing the Place Denfert-Rochereau in the rain, the boys on bicycles in the autumn and the tall, thin women standing motionless and unapproachable across the rooms behind the façades of all the buildings of all the streets of our real and illusory cities. This is the miraculous clutter and confusion of Giacometti's studio. This is the presence of it: the dust of reality covering the floor which we track out on the soles of our shoes to leave wherever we go, like the footprints of ghosts more real than we, an affirmation of our fragile rapport with our own reality, but only for the duration of our ability to endure it. These traces, however, are the significant clues to the mystery of the human condition. We can only serve them.

Giacometti's work is that of a great artist. If so, it is because *he* is a great artist. Nothing in the world is simpler or more complicated. This becomes an expression of the world itself: the nature of man and his representation of it in art honestly and inextricably bound together. So honestly and so inextricably, in fact, that they become interchangeable. The permanently variable definition of civilization is an effect of this particular interrelationship. At the surface of every era it is redefined in the creative presence of a few personalities, whose names become a condition of time, relating that era to the past and the future.

Rebirth of a Museum

BY GÜNTER AUST

Cologne's great Wallraf-Richartz collection is again on view

Everyone who has recently visited Cologne must have noticed that the Wallraf-Richartz Museum, housed in temporary premises, is showing only a small part of its treasures. The reconstruction of the Museum, on its former location near the Cathedral, is already so well advanced that, in the course of next year, all the paintings in the collection will be hung there permanently. The buildings which will house the Roman antiquities and other art objects will be completed soon after.

The Wallraf-Richartz Museum, unlike other great European galleries, did not originate from royal collections as was the case, for example, with the Museums of Berlin, Dresden and Munich. It is the exclusive creation of the town: the initial nucleus consisted of works by local artists. The foundation of the Museum and the growth of its importance were entirely due to the initiative of the people of Cologne.

The collection is based on religious painting from medieval Cologne. It is, therefore, worth while devoting a few lines to the history of the town which was, successively, a Roman province, a Frankish possession and the seat of an Archbishopric. It never became a princely capital or residence but remained a free city owing direct allegiance to the Emperor. From the time of Charlemagne, Cologne became one of the most important cultural and commercial centers in North-West Europe. Its political and economic importance, which necessitated the construction of a massive system of ramparts (the most important military architecture of the Middle Ages) was matched by an intense creative activity in the realm of art.

Cologne has always had the reputation of being a town of Romanesque churches : in the Middle Ages it had fourteen very important ones. Twelve remained until this war. With their decorations, of which only fragments have come down to us, and their famous gold and silver vessels, these churches constituted a patrimony which made a profound impression on succeeding centuries. Although, after 1248, the Romanesque Cathedral was replaced by a Gothic Cathedral, the Gothic period had little effect on the appearance of the town. The artistic activities of Cologne were principally in the field of painting on wood. There are two main sources of influence to be discerned in this domain: first, the monumental and severe form of the Romanesque frescos and then, in opposition to this style which emphasizes line, a predilection for delicate and blended colors. The most striking example of this taste is to be found in the miniaturists of about the year 1000 whose work is to be seen in the Gospel of the Abbess Hidta at Darmstadt and in the Sacramentary of Saint Gereon in the Bibliothèque Nationale in Paris. This tendency survives, in the most spectacular manner, in the panels of the Master of Saint Veronica, painted at the beginning of the XVth century.

The strength of these traditions prevented the development of XIVth and XVth century naturalism. The painting of Cologne remained impregnated with a certain religious majesty. More preoccupied with the cult they served than with the story they recounted, these paintings remained firmly " two-dimensional " and did not try to create the illusion of space. Moreover the individual expression of the faces was of little importance and, even in the later period, their characteristics remained strangely Gothic.

Unlike Southern Germany or Westphalia, Cologne received the naturalist innovations of the end of the Middle Ages with considerable reluctance and it is indicative of this obstinately medieval turn of mind that in about 1500, many Cologne painters were still painting their pictures on gold backgrounds. This conservative attitude, which undoubtedly coincided with the atmosphere of the town, is a sign of stagnation if we compare its results to the evolution in painting that was going on in the neighboring Netherlands ; but it is also the source of two centuries of cohesion and originality in Cologne painting.

Certain murals from the end of the XIIIth century — those, for example, in the Church of Saint Cecilia — and a few miniatures, constitute the oldest examples that have come down to us, of the flowering of German Gothic. There are still

Hieronymus Bosch (about 1450-1576) : Nativity (*wood, 41 ½ ×*

*Master of Cologne,
about 1430-1440 :
Wasservass Calvary
Wood 50 ½ × 69″.*

a few examples of paintings on wood from this period: among them a *Presentation at the Temple*, an *Annunciation* and a very ancient *Triptych*.

From the beginning of the XVth century the evolution of art in Cologne can be followed uninterruptedly. The period from 1400 to 1420 is particularly brilliant and paintings by the Master of Saint Veronica and his school are clearly distinguishable by their quality. In the small *Calvary* by this master we notice not only a particular care for minute detail, but also the conscious determination to preserve a two-dimensional surface. The *Calvary of the Wasserwas Family*, dating from 1430, marks the beginning of a new style, which draws directly from reality. The setting is enlarged, surrounded with buildings and animated by a series of separate incidents taking place around the Crucifixion; the figures are more thick-set, closer to the earth, and their individual characteristics are more marked. The fantastic colors of the town and of some of the horses add to the general impression of decorative splendor.

The first works by Stephan Lochner constitute a turning point. His *Last Judgment* painted about 1435 is the work of an artist who has been deeply influenced by Van Eyck and the Master of Flemalle. The dramatic movement of the composition, the realistic, almost *trompe l'œil* effect which is heightened by the use of glazes on the plants, the architecture and the implements, were entirely new to Cologne. Lochner was a native of Meersburg, a small town on the Lake of Constance in South-West Germany which was so susceptible to the new trends in art, and thus he was able to act as an innovator. Anywhere else he would have played the role of a revolutionary but in Cologne he had to restrain himself. His final works are adapted to the traditional manner of the city, while preserving, at the same time, a remarkable personal quality which can best be appreciated in contemplating his masterpiece — the ravishing *Virgin with the Rose Bush*. Lochner is the unique case in Cologne, before the XVIth century, of a painter whose name can be put to a specific work. Until that time, all painters remained anonymous.

In the second half of the XVth century, even when forms originating from the Netherlands had been totally assimilated, the paintings from Cologne preserved their stately and idealistic character. The use of gold backgrounds persists in the wing-panels of altar-pieces — for example in the works of the Master of Saint Bartholomew. The Masters of Saint Severinus and of the Legend of Saint Ursula, with the subtle atmosphere they achieve by the use of gray-brown tones, contrast, to a certain extent, with their contemporaries in Cologne.

Taking into consideration the power of the medieval religious institutions that weighed upon the town, it is hardly surprising that its artistic importance declined after the beginning of the XVIth century. Only the work of Bartolomew Bruyn, a painter who was particularly good at portraits, succeeds in carrying the art of Cologne a little beyond the confines of the Middle Ages. After him there is nothing worthy of mention. The austere and conventional atmosphere of Cologne was not encouraging to Baroque art.

This did not mean that public interest in the arts ceased. At the end of the Middle Ages and at the beginning of the XVIth century the Wasserwas, Hardenrath, Rinck and Hackenay families were outstanding art patrons: thanks to them the works of distinguished foreign artists like Roger Van der Weyden, Dirk Bouts and Joos Van Cleve became known in the city. Even later in its history, Cologne counted many supporters of contemporary artists among its citizens. Apart from the collectors of antique objects and coins, a residue from the Roman past of the town, there was also the Jabach family, particularly Everhard Jabach, a prosperous merchant who ordered a *Crucifixion of Saint Peter* from Rubens for the Church of Saint Peter in Cologne. This collector was so active that soon his native city no longer offered sufficient scope for his acquisitions and he settled in Paris in 1648. There he formed a collection that he sold to Louis XIV in 1671, when he found himself in financial difficulties. In this way the Louvre was enriched by a series of works by Titian, Correggio and Caravaggio as well as many extremely fine drawings.

In the XVIIth century the ruling classes of the town continued to display a lively interest in the great painting of Europe. In the first half of the century the Imsten brothers made a magnificent collection which later became the property of the Bishop of Olmutz. In the XVIIIth century, important collections were made by F. W. Kaas, by the Bishop von Merle and by J. A. Schaffhausen. The *Mary Magdalen* by Cranach, for instance, is in the Schaffhausen collection.

The artistic life of Cologne remained, as we can see, almost the exclusive privilege of private individuals during this period. The development of the city stopped almost completely. Dominated by its gigantic and unfinished Cathedral, Cologne lapsed into slumber. It was rudely awakened in 1794 by the entry of the French army. Many churches and convents were soon secularized or demolished and their contents dispersed. The cultural inheritance of a great past, disdained by the population, was in danger of being destroyed. It was then that Ferdinand Franz Wallraf (1748-1824), the last Rector of the University (closed in 1797), intervened.

The Boisserée brothers and Lyversberg, a prosperous banker, share the honor with Wallraf of having saved many valuable works of art by their purchases. But of the treasures which were once the glory of the churches of Cologne, very few have remained in the city: the Boisserée collection, which contains many interesting Cologne and Dutch paintings, is in the Pinakotek at Munich. The nucleus of the collection today consists of Wallraf's own selections. Assembled at the

ster of the Legend of Saint Ursula (late XVth cent.) : Apparition of the Angel to Saint Ursula (*canvas, 48½×25″*). 103

Bramantino (1460-1536) : Philemon and Baucis (23×31″).   *Opposite, Cranach (1472-1553) :* Saint Madeleine (*1525,* 19×12″).

cost of great personal sacrifice, it was intended by its owner, from the beginning, to preserve the memory of the city's past splendor. According to the Wallraf will, the collection became, after his death in 1824, the property of the municipality. Among other masterpieces, it contained three hundred and nine paintings from the Cologne School alone. Johann Heinrich Richartz, a Cologne business man, commissioned the construction of the municipal Museum which was opened in 1861, the year after his death. The Museum still bears both names.

Originally the Museum housed the entire Wallraf collection — which included many objects connected with history, bibliophily and natural history : but later it was limited to painting and also to objects from Roman Cologne. Wallraf himself had laid the foundations of a department of European painting since the Renaissance. He had acquired, among other things, the Rubens altar-piece, *Saint Francis Receiving the Stigmata* which came from the Church of the Capuchins in Cologne. This part of the collection was considerably enlarged between 1861 and 1900, by several donations, including two Rubens, the *Holy Family* and *Juno and Argus*, the *Prometheus Bound* by Jordaens, paintings by Ruysdael, Jan Steen, Terboch, Maes, Terbrugghen, Claude Lorrain, Mignard, Rigaud, David Bordone and Murillo.

Finally, in 1936, the von Castanjen collection was bought and the Museum reached its present degree of importance. Masterpieces by Rembrandt, Franz Hals and Cuyp are of outstanding interest. There are also works by Honthorst, Ruysdael, Cappell and Jan Steen. Cologne possesses a few fine examples of French XIXth century painting : Courbet's *Hunt Breakfast*, *Monsieur and Madame Renoir* by Monet, the *Bridge at Arles* by Van Gogh and a view of the Seine by Monet.

The Enigmatic School of Fontainebleau

BY CHARLES TERRASSE

*Italian artists at the French court introduced the nude
and created a style*

During the past few years, the School of Fontainebleau has been arousing a growing interest among the public. Serious studies are being made of it. A large exhibition was organized in Naples, in 1952, demonstrating how far its influence had spread beyond the borders of France. But, in actual fact, most people are far less well informed about it than its renown would suggest.

As early as the XVIth century, artists, who for one reason or another were not able to study in Italy, went instead to Fontainebleau, the " new Rome ". Later, even its creations disappeared when the Château was enlarged or restored and the School only continued to exist as a kind of legend. But it lived on, all the same, through the traditions it had established, and through the forms it had created by which whole generations of artists have been inspired. For this reason we can say that the School was the origin of XVIIIth century French art and that, for three centuries, the aesthetics of form have remained those introduced by Primaticcio.

It has almost been forgotten that the artists of the School not only created a new form of decoration at Fontainebleau, but that they also did a great deal of sculpture and of easel painting.

Today, we are trying to discover, by studying the few traces left behind, the history of the School—what were its characteristics, its principles and its spirit. It is not an easy task. The art of the XVIth century is far less familiar to us, generally speaking, than medieval art. Many riddles remain to be solved. Most of the works produced by the School, even the most beautiful, are anonymous; we only need mention the *Diana with a Stag* in the Louvre as an example. Only a short time ago it was discovered that two artists, father and son, used the same name : Jean Cousin.

What is meant today by the term : the School of Fontainebleau ? A group of artists who worked together at the Château, creating a recognizable art form in a highly cultivated atmosphere.

The beginnings of the School and its first activities are well-known. François I had been thinking, for some time, of introducing a new form of art into his kingdom. At the very beginning of his reign he had summoned to his court Leonardo da Vinci and Andrea del Sarto, both artists who were independent of the general trend of their times. In 1530, the King was thirty-five years old. He wanted to have a " home " of his own. Among the various castles he owned, Fontainebleau was the only one that could meet his wishes. It was then an ancient Gothic manor, in the midst of an immense forest providing excellent hunting. It stood on the edge of a pool, in which its pointed towers were reflected. He set about reconstructing it on a vast scale and, realizing a long-standing dream, he turned it into a veritable center for artists and for writers. In the course of the next twenty years, he installed all his collections in it, his gold and silver objects, his books. " Everything fine that the King could lay hands on ", says a contemporary writer, "was destined for his favorite castle, Fontainebleau." Finally, he started an engravers workshop for the purpose of making the outside world familiar with his collection of ancient art and everything new that was being created. Fontainebleau was more than a castle, it was a concept.

Fontainebleau's architecture was simple and spacious, in keeping with the rough sandstone of which it was built. But the King insisted upon lavish decorations for the main apartments. There were of course admirable painters in France at that moment—portrait painters like Jean Clouet, illuminators such as Jean Bourdichon, and stained-glass makers like the Pinaigriers of Paris or the Leprinces of Beauvais. But for his own decoration he had to summon artists from Italy, as well as from Flanders and France—painters, sculptors, stuccoers, and joiners. They were placed under the authority of two Italians, Rosso and Primaticcio.

Rosso, who arrived at Fontainebleau in 1531, was a Florentine. He was a man of the same age as the King, tall, red-headed as his name indicates, serious, a good musician and widely read. He had worked with Michael-Angelo. Francesco Primaticcio, from Bologna, arrived a year later. He was only twenty-eight. He had been a disciple of Giulio Romano and had worked with him on the decoration of the Palazzo del Tè in Mantua. The fate of these two masters was to be very different. Rosso, the first to arrive and the more highly esteemed of the two, was to disappear ten years later in 1541 ; Primaticcio's career was not to end until 1570, when he retired loaded with gifts and honors.

Rosso and Primaticcio each had their team of painters and sculptors, whose names have been preserved for us in the

us and Vulcan. *Oil on wood* (23¾×17″)

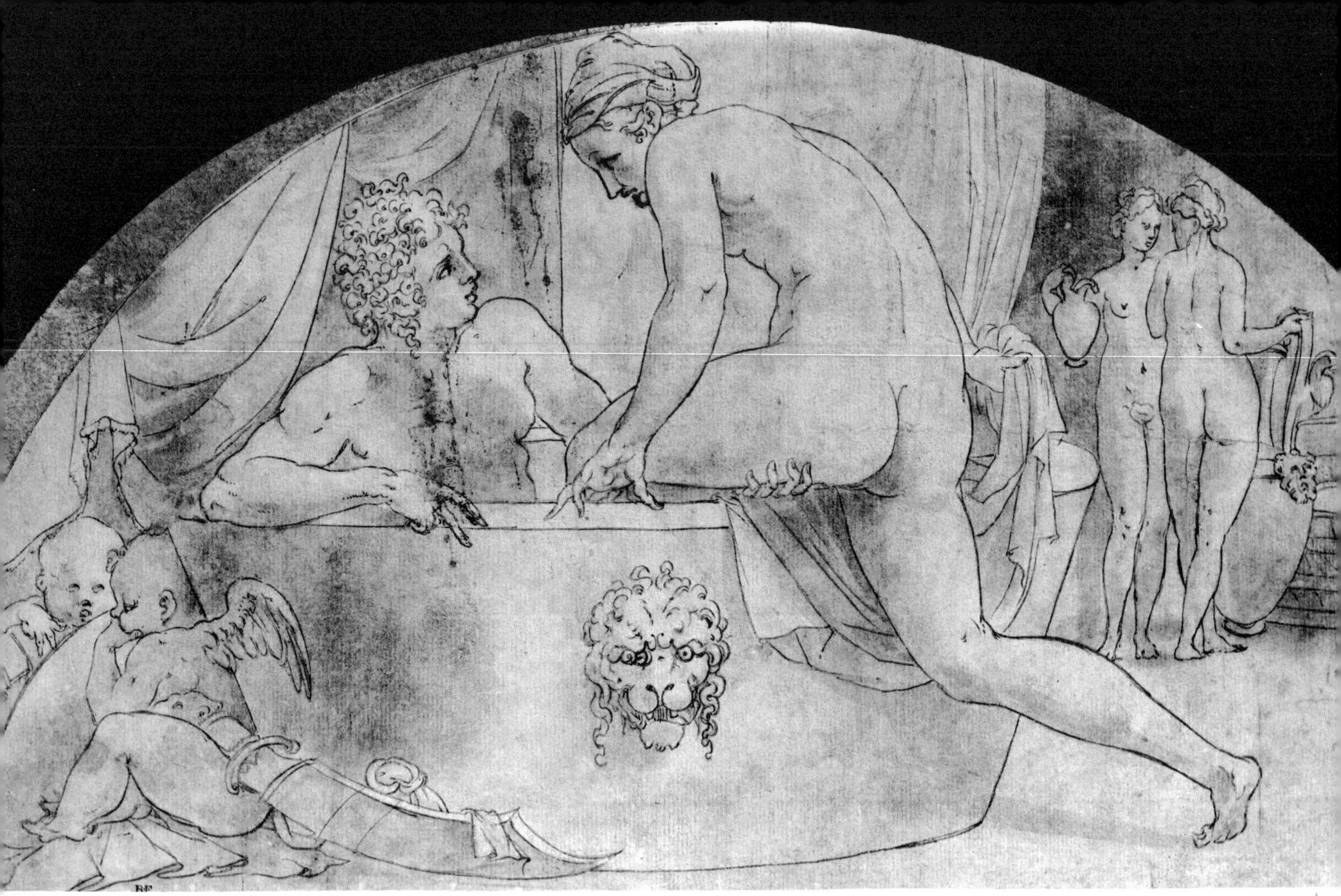

The Fontainebleau artists left many drawings, often of great beauty. very free in their choice of subject. Their attribution is most uncertain. Like all the documents shown here, this one belongs to the Louvre and has never been reproduced before.

▼

This drawing is supposedly by Primaticcio who, until his death in 1570, was the leader of the School. Invited to France by François I, he became known as Saint Martin de Boulogne, after the name of the abbey given to him by the King.

royal accounts. They provided these craftsmen with plans and sketches. Both of them were undoubtedly extremely industrious. Rosso's work consisted almost exclusively of the decoration of the gallery which ran from the keep to the main courtyard, known as the Gallery of François I. Prima-

ticcio's work, which is obviously far more extensive, included the decoration of the apartments of the King, the Queen, and the Duchess of Etampes and then, in the reign of Henri II, the ball-room and a long gallery protecting the southern wing of the courtyard, The latter was called the Ulysses Gallery because its decorations told the story of the King of Ithaca. Of all this vast undertaking all that remains today is the Gallery of François I, the ball-room and Madame d'Etampes' apartment. The rest we know only through drawings and engravings.

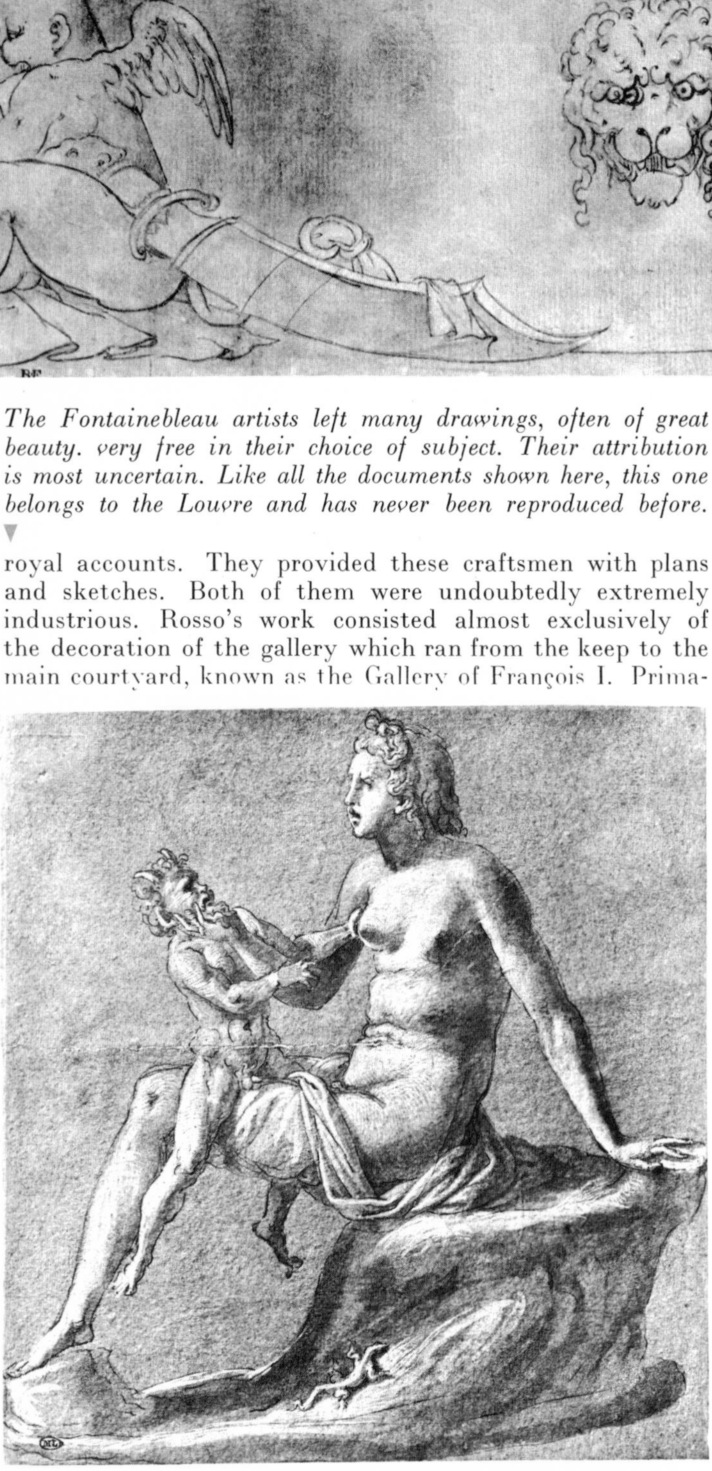

Rosso is designated in the account books as " chief of the works in stucco and painting " of the King's Gallery. The style of ornamentation that he used consisted of frescos surrounded by sculptures. This idea had been unearthed in Rome, in the baths of Titus. Raphael, in the Vatican, and Giulio Romano at Mantua had been inspired by it. But the originality of the style of Fontainebleau is mainly due to the large dimensions of the sculpture. The stuccos in fact partake as much of the art of statuary as of ornamentation. All along the Gallery, beneath these frescos and sculptures, the carpenter-sculptor, Francesco Scibecco dei Carpi, placed panelling bearing the arms and devices of the King.

The paintings are allegories about the King, and the events of his reign, the meaning of which had already been forgotten by the time of Louis XIII. The choice of subjects displays a high degree of erudition.

The stuccos have so far not been very carefully studied. They include extremely varied figures and reliefs : scenes

Primaticcio's signature is to be found on the drawing, right, but this is no real guarantee of its authenticity. The langorous nude sleeps accompanied by clusters of cherubs and horns of plenty—symbols of love and fertility in the style of the period.

from the ancient world, from Rome and Gaul, highly imaginative children's games and morality tales told in pictures. The salamander spitting flame appears everywhere, but in none of its variations does it recall the familiar native lizard as represented by the painters and sculptors of France. It is a far-fetched version of a kind of angry dachshund, ears set back, spitting and snorting—a salamander such as only Rosso had ever seen.

Primaticcio finally completed the decoration of the gallery, left unfinished by Rosso, in 1541. The *Danaë* is by him and, perhaps, the *Education of Achilles* Of the decoration which he did for different rooms, there only remain, in the Queen's chamber, a fire-place adorned with stuccos, and in Madame d'Etampes' room, figures of nymphs and children framing some frescos that represent scenes from the history of Alexander. The mythological themes in the ball-room, executed between 1552 and 1555 under his direction, by some of his pupils, of whom the most important was Niccolò dell'Abbate, still remain, but all of this decoration has been repainted numerous times.

The differences between Rosso and Primaticcio are very obvious. Rosso is full of life and warmth. He stresses movement, almost to the point of agitation, and also pathos. Primaticcio is, above all, graceful. He loves his figures balanced and calm. We can feel that he is a pupil of Raphael, whom he knew through Giulio Romano, as well as a follower of Correggio.

François I was also interested in acquiring antique statues or, failing that, casts which could provide exact copies. From Rome, where the King sent him in 1540, Primaticcio brought back marbles and also the moulds of several figures. He set up a foundry in the Château itself and produced several bronzes.

Benvenuto Cellini must also be included among the artists of Fontainebleau. Cellini, who was with the King from 1543 to 1545, executed the high relief, in bronze, of the *Nymph of Fontainebleau*; and it is from his studio that the marble *Diana with a Stag* came. Neither of these works had been placed in Fontainebleau at the time of the King's death; Diane de Poitiers made Henri II give them both to her for her Château at Anet. They are now in the Louvre.

Tapestry-workers also appeared upon the scene. The King installed a work-room in the Château where six frescos by Rosso were reproduced. These tapestries are now in the Vienna Museum. They indicate the original state of the frescos and the harmony of their colors.

Rosso and Primaticcio worked not only at Fontainebleau and for the King. They produced designs and plans for various ceremonies, such as the entry of Charles V into

Top right: anonymous decoration, School of Fontainebleau.

109

The Bath. *Detail. Drawing Department of the Louvre.*

were often derived from sources which could only be known to accomplished hellenists. They display careful research and considerable literary knowledge.

Then it is also an allegorical art. It is François I who is glorified in the gallery which bears his name. It is Henri II's favorite who is depicted in the ball-room under the guise of the goddess of the chase.

In the realm of form, the essential novelty is the appearance of the nude. Gothic art had virtually ignored the naked human form. But at Fontainebleau, we see the Danaë, Venus unveiled beneath a fountain, Diana and a whole multitude of nymphs and fauns revealing the harmonious rhythms of the body liberated at last from its fetters. There are also nudes portrayed through the studied subtlety of transparent veils or clinging damp draperies.

Taking for points of comparison and analysis the decorations and engravings of Fontainebleau, it has been possible to classify a group of paintings and sculptures—most of them anonymous, but with more or less accentuated common characteristics—as belonging to the School. At the Louvre we can see the slender Diana starting for the hunt, known as the *Fontainebleau Diana*, then the *Continence of Scipio, Moses Rescued From the Nile*, and in Rennes, *The Young Woman, The Young Man and the Old Man*. At Potsdam there is an Allegory in honor of the birth of a son to Henri II and at Dijon a *Lady Making Her Toilet*. The National Gallery possesses a *Leda* by Rosso, long attributed to Michael-Angelo. Further examples are to be found in private collections; there are the *Scenes From the Life of Ulysses* in the Comte de Germiny's collection, which probably constitute Primaticcio's plans for the Gallery of Ulysses in the Château, the *Young Woman with A Red Lily* from the Marquis de Biencourt's collection and *Ulysses and Penelope* from the Wildenstein collection. The Fontainebleau Museum exhibits a painting with an unusual subject, *Threshing The Corn*, which is believed to be by Niccolò dell'Abbate.

But if we want to separate the work of the Italians from the work of the French, we are very much at sea. The Italians very soon began to think and feel like their French hosts. Certáin of these creations give a very strange impression. They are not completely Italian, nor are they French. It can only be said that they belong to the " School ". However it seems that we can attribute, with considerable likelihood of being right, several paintings to French masters. And then, an indigenous style makes its appearance.

It is a style not dependent on copying, but primarily on interpretation and transposition; intentional interpretation —inverted subjects, for example, probably suggested by engravings—and transposition arising from the imagination of the artists, as in the *Young Woman With A Red Lily* for which the model was Raphael's *Fornarina*. Thus it is that, compared to the works of the masters from Florence and from Parma (Bronzino and Parmigiano come to mind), those by French masters have a very particular flavor of ingenuousness. These painters know the principles and the rules, but they apply them with considerable naïveté. They are primitives. Into the painting of their great mythological figures, they put the application to detail of an illuminator. But reality is missing. The *Diana Bathing* from the Rouen Museum is attributed to François Clouet, son of Jean Clouet, who painted the portrait of François I to be seen in the Louvre. There is nothing real in the painting except the horseman, and the stag at bay. The *Eva Prima Pandora* by Jean Cousin, which is in the Louvre, displays the same characteristics of studied ingenuousness and application.

Why was it that the Fontainebleau School failed to make a profound impression on the sculptors employed by

Lady at her Toilet (detail). This is said to be the portrait of Diane de Poitiers. The subject with her tightly coiled hair and her nudity accentuated by transparent veiling represents the feminine ideal of the Fontainebleau School. Kunstmuseum, Basle.

Paris, and also for fêtes and masquerades. We come across them at Saint-Germain, at Vincennes, in Paris at the Hôtel de Montmorency and at Ancy-le-Franc. Finally, both they and their pupils did easel paintings.

From what remains of all these works, is it possible to attempt to define, in what is probably its most important aspect—that of painting—the characteristics of the royal taste in art ?

It is primarily a humanist and scholarly art. The myths and legends that it employed, borrowed from Greek antiquity,

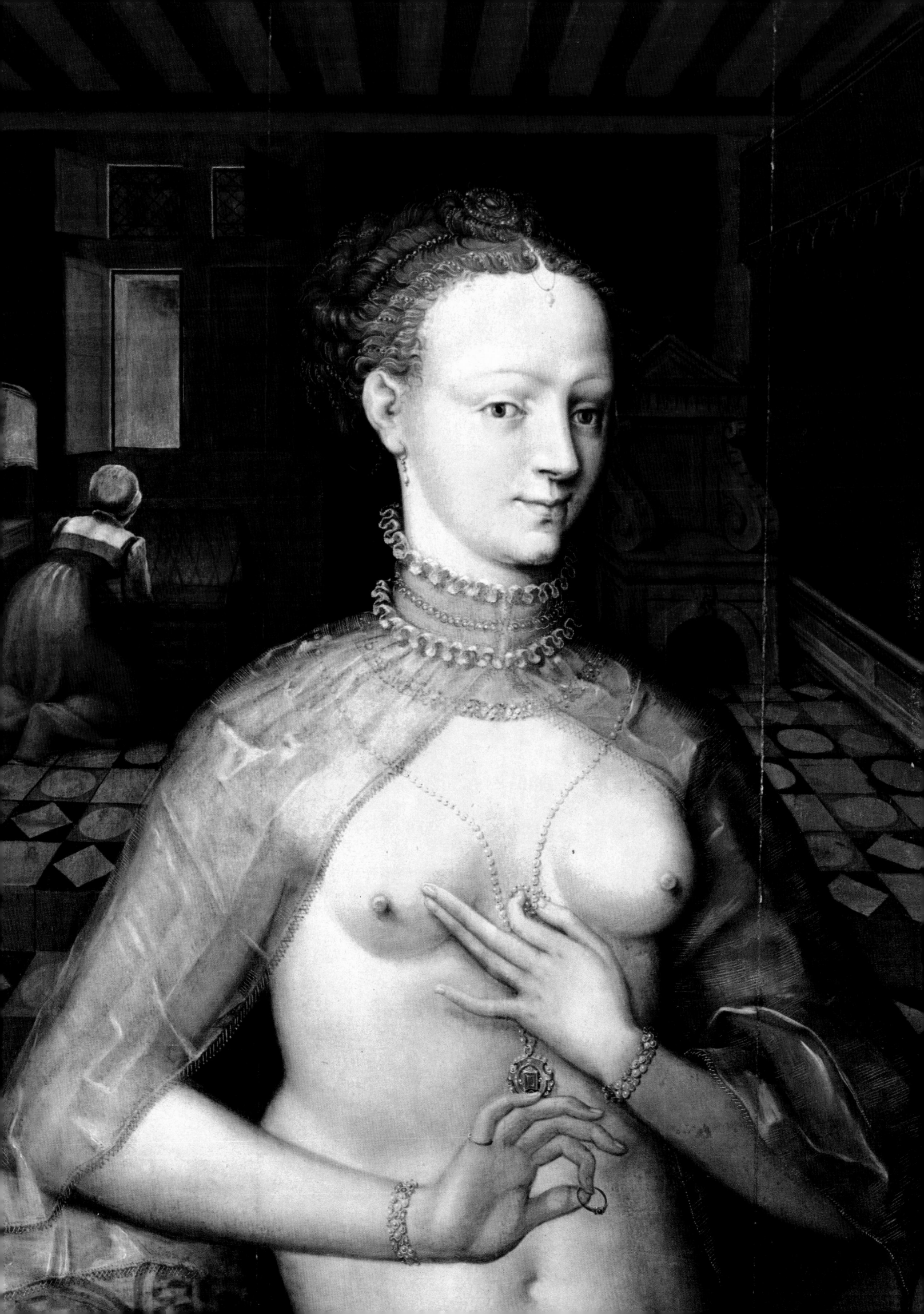

The Banquet, *oil on wood. (41¾ × 52½″) The costumes indicate this might be a late work of about 1590.*

the King? Pierre Bontemps, Jean Goujon, and Germain Pilon were part of the School. Without even mentioning the tombs in Saint Denis, of which one, the tomb of François I and of Claude of France, is partially the work of Primaticcio, and of which another, that of Henri II and Catherine of Medici, was constructed according to his designs, it was Primaticcio who produced the model for the monument for the heart of François I, carved by Pierre Bontemps. Jean Goujon, in sculpting the *Fame Marching* on the mantlepiece at Ecouen, transposed into marble a design by Rosso of which we know from the engraving, and, for his *Nymphs* for the *Fountains of the Innocents,* he refers to the sinuous grace of the nymphs in the room of the Duchesse d'Etampes.

In the field of architecture, Fontainebleau introduced hardly any novelty except the grotto in the Jardin des Pins. Its vault was ornamented with a mosaic of colored stones and shells which has now disappeared ; but it is prefigured on the exterior of the grotto by a design which still exists. It is possible that this grotto was the work of Serlio, an architect who was in the service of the King from 1540 on. Fantasies of this kind already existed at the Palazzo del Té in Mantua and at the Palazzo Capracola in Rome. The grotto at Fontainebleau can be related to that of the Bâtie d'Urfé which still exists today.

Then silence falls over the Château, lost in the surrounding forest, and from about 1570 until the last years of the century the kingdom is rent with discord. However a few disciples of the School continue to apply the scientific and allegorical tradition. Such is Antoine Caron of Beauvais, who delighted

in multiplying, in strange compositions, scenes, figures and monuments of the ancient world.

It was in Flanders that the art of Fontainebleau again appeared. It sprang into new life there in the studios of painters such as Hieronymus Franken, Bartolomeo Spranger —two faithful pupils of Primaticcio and Niccolò dell'Abbate— and Abraham Bloemaert. And it is from Flanders that it returned to Fontainebleau, at the end of the century, with Toussaint Dubreuil, and Ambroise Dubois, artists who were summoned by Henri IV. This was the beginning of the second School of Fontainebleau. For fifteen years these two artists worked in the Château which Henri IV, who dreamed of equalling the splendors of François I, enlarged without end. The work accomplished under Henri IV was, in fact, considerable. Hardly anything remains but the King's study, where Ambroise Dubois tells, in sixteen panels, the history of Theagene and Chariclee, and the chapel of the Trinity, the vault of which was decorated by Fréminet. Everything that the King commissioned, as far as we can judge from what remains at Fontainebleau and by what we know elsewhere, is balanced, robust, and has a tendency towards the grandiose. In the King's study it is not nymphs with sinuous bodies who separate the paintings on the walls but heavy cascades of leaves and fruit. The period is already addicted to the serious and the pompous. And Henri, the King, who used to climb the scaffolding and insisted that ambassadors climb with him, would sometimes sigh, in the presence of his intimates, because he was unable to recreate, in the Fontainebleau of his period, the fantasy of Rosso, or the grace of Primaticcio.

and Venus. *Oil on wood. (38½ × 31½″) Petit Palais, Paris.*

The Big

PARADE

BY DOUGLAS COOPER

This analysis of Fernand Léger's last great canvas was written by a close friend
a short while before the artist's death

During the last hundred years the circus has provided many great French artists with subject-matter for pictures. For example Daumier, whose sympathetic eye saw that, underneath their trappings and their clamor, *saltimbanques* are really commonplace mortals plying a wearisome and sordid trade. After him, Renoir, who lingered on the sparkling costumes of circus performers and on their physical charms, and Degas, whose analytical eye fastened on the expressive movements of an acrobat like Miss La-La. Seurat, on the other hand, took in the spectacle as a whole and made both a gay picture out of the athletic feats of clowns and equestriennes in the ring as well as a melancholy one out of the ritual of parading the troupe at the entrance to the tent before the performance begins. By contrast, Toulouse-Lautrec seized on the gaiety, elegance, daring and absurdity which go to make up the spectacle in the ring. Not so Rouault, who has always tended to give his clowns an exaggerated expression of physical and moral suffering because he likes to see them as tragic symbols of "man's inhumanity to man." Lastly there has been Picasso, whose vision—I am referring to the period around 1904-05—of emaciated circus-folk permanently on the move, living a communal existence in which they are obliged to share the bare necessities of life but are none the less victims of passionate private emotions, has an essentially pathetic, human significance.

In his turn, Fernand Léger has recently completed a great painting inspired by a troupe of circus performers, and once again it is different in character. There is no symbolism in Léger's image, no sadness, no pathos, no sensuous charm, no posing of human problems and no acrobatic feats. This is a composite image of the circus and all it stands for in the popular imagination. The subject is the '*Big Parade*' which takes place on a raised platform outside the fair-ground tent, and since the artist himself has written about this spectacle in his book *Cirque* (Tériade, 1950) I cannot perhaps do better than to quote his own words. "The box-office", Léger says, "depends on this parade and it is this that makes it powerful and dynamic." No comment on his picture could be more apposite. But let me quote a little more of Léger's description because it helps to explain why he has chosen to present his subject in an unusual way. "It hits you right in the face, right in the chest, and it's like a magic spell. From behind, from in front, from all sides, figures appear and disappear, dancers, clowns, arms and legs, scarlet faces, pink limbs, a negro who eats fire and an acrobat who walks on his hands." It is this enthralling scene that Léger determined to translate into a pictorial image capable of expressing the essence of a circus performance. "Nothing is as round as a circus" says Léger. "It's an enormous basin in which circular forms develop... The ring dominates, commands, absorbs... Go to the circus. You leave your rectangles, your geometric windows and you go to the land of the circle in action." But by taking the *Parade* as his subject Léger was able to present the performers as a frieze of figures against a flat background. All that is missing is the inevitable accompaniment of blaring music, for which on this occasion the artist has substituted the *tintamarre* of vigorously contrasted pure colors.

Such then is the subject and the inspiration of *The Big Parade*. Now let us see how the artist arrived at his ultimate pictorial image. I should begin by emphasizing that nothing in this picture is accidental, that every part of it has been carefully thought out and that it is based on direct observation. Léger has always been fascinated by the spectacle of the circus and as long ago as 1919 he painted a picture of

One of many preparatory ink sketches, 1953. In the final state,
horse looks to right instead of left. Opposite: Léger in front
of finished Parade, *leaning on* Country Outing with a Car, *1953.*

Preparatory sketch, 1953, seven figures and a landscape. The final picture has nine figures, no landscape. Douglas Cooper coll.

two acrobats. But it is only during the last ten years that he has really concentrated on exploring its pictorial possibilities. Léger's first idea for an important picture with a circus subject seems to have taken form in a large gouache *The Clowns (1st state)* executed in Paris in 1939-40. This was followed by a large canvas *Musicians and Acrobats* painted in New York in 1945. These must have been the first stages in the evolution of *The Big Parade*, for many elements of the composition are the same. Thus the conception of *The Big Parade* has been evolving over a long period. However, the painting itself—completed during the summer of 1954 and exhibited in Paris in November of that year—is essentially the culmination of all the work that Léger has done in France since his return in 1946. Indeed one might say that its immediate starting-point must be looked for in the immense amount of circus material which Léger accumulated between 1947 and 1950 while he was working on the great series of lithographs for his book *Cirque*. All the components of the final composition can be identified in one or other of its pages.

As soon as Léger began to work seriously on the theme of the circus, the idea of a monumental composition started to evolve in his mind. And as a matter of fact he made so many preparatory drawings, gouaches and oil studies with this end in view that it is possible to follow its evolution step by step over the last six years. Each group, each object to be included was studied and worked out in detail while the whole was put together bit by bit, so that when it came to executing the final painting Léger was able to carry out his task virtually without *pentimenti*. Thus this picture has an air of freshness unusual in a work of its size. The musicians disappeared at an early

stage ; then Léger tried setting the *Parade* against a landscape background ; he varied the arrangement as well as the composition of the different groups of figures constantly ; letters such as 'CIR' were inserted, abandoned, then re-inserted in an abbreviated form, and today only the letter 'C' remains ; the entire composition was reversed at one stage ; a horse was introduced, looking first to the left, but then ultimately to the right ; even the headgear of the performers was frequently modified or changed. But perhaps Léger's most notable experiment in this picture—and it is triumphantly justified by the result—has been his handling of color.

In *The Big Parade (1st stage)* Léger began by using color literally and descriptively : the negress has a black skin, the acrobat next to her has a red bodice and a blue skirt, the clown a white coat with blue trimmings and so on. However he quickly realized that this was not appropriate to his conception of a monumental frieze of figures and, drawing on the experience he had gained recently while working on polychrome ceramic decorations, he decided to attempt an effect of low relief in paint. The result was the version known as *The Big Parade against a Red Background* in which the composition of figures and objects, executed entirely in black and white, is projected forward from a flat background of dullish red. The result is both fascinating and impressive, but nevertheless Léger saw that this was not really a solution of his pictorial problem, for his picture—or, more accurately, his drawing—amounted to little more than an illusion of a ceramic wall-panel. Then it was that he resorted to the experiment of enlivening his black and white figure composition by projecting into it a complex interplay of free colors. So he made a new series of gouaches in which he

116

The Big Parade Against a Red Background *1953* (44½×61″). *Below : another preparatory sketch, of acrobats, 1953.*

experimented with various combinations of colors in order to find both the forms, the rhythm and the tonal balance most appropriate to his figure composition. Léger has often made use of this procedure during the last few years, though never on such an ambitious scale. He takes as a basis for his picture an abstract design of colored shapes over which he then imposes a pre-determined linear composition. In short, he builds up his picture out of two basically unrelated and separable elements. This makes it possible for him to respect the flatness of his canvas and limit perspective lines to a minimum because, by the juxtaposition of colors, some of which recede while others advance, he can set up a sufficient feeling of space which in turn enhances the sense of movement in his linear composition.

Such then are the principles which have determined the final form of *The Big Parade*. Perhaps it all sounds rather simple. Nothing could be further from the truth. Every detail of this picture has been studied and re-studied until the artist was absolutely satisfied that he had found the correct forms, that despite simplification he had preserved a sufficient degree of resemblance to natural models and that everything in the picture was harmonious. The spirit of this picture is romantic, its imagery popular. Its mood is gay and dynamic, its character forceful, and its composition classical in the strictest sense. Compare it with *The Parade* of Seurat and one sees at once that it is a continuation of the same artistic tradition. But we can, I think, look for ancestors among an earlier generation of French artists, for *The Big Parade* is also in the tradition of the brothers Le Nain and Poussin. Unquestionably this painting is Léger's outstanding achievement of the last twenty-five years, and

I cannot help feeling that it is also the most important produced by any artist of the *Ecole de Paris* since *Guernica*. What is more, though it is a consummation of all that Léger has discovered about painting during the last fifty years, it also represents a considerable stylistic innovation. When one considers the impoverished state of painting in France today, it is exciting to discover that, at the age of seventy three, Léger has just painted not merely one of the masterpieces of his lifetime but one of the great paintings of the twentieth century.

Following pages : The Big Parade, *final version with bands of color, 1954* (118½×158″).   117

When The Cubists Were Young

A RECORDED INTERVIEW BETWEEN DANIEL-HENRY KAHNWEILER AND GEORGES BERNIER

Kahnweiler sold Cubist painting before there was any real market for it, and is still selling it today.
He is one of the world's best-informed people about the inside and over-all history of contemporary art.

Bernier./ *Between 1902, when you arrived in Paris from Frankfurt, and 1907, when you opened your gallery, did you know many painters?*

Kahnweiler./ No, none at all, it's a much more peculiar story than that. I came to Paris because my parents, who were bankers, sent me there to work in a broker's office. They couldn't imagine any other future for an offspring of the family except a career in finance. I went to the *Bourse* for a few minutes every day so as to be seen by my employer and then I took off to the Louvre. I continued this stratagem for two and a half years; then in 1905 my parents sent me to London where my two uncles had settled down — one of them, Sigmund Neuman, later became a Baronet; he was one of the men responsible for developing gold mining in South Africa. There, as in Paris, I did my best to do as little work as possible.

In December 1906 the family decided that I should go to Johannesburg. It was then that I said : " As you must have noticed already, I have absolutely no inclination for banking or for the stock exchange."—" Then what do you want to do ?"—" I'd much prefer to be a picture dealer. " I had not seen any painters in Paris, where I knew no one, but I had spent a great deal of time at exhibitions and I had begun to make a small collection of engravings, in particular some etchings by Manet and some lithographs by Lautrec and Cézanne. My uncles did not utter loud cries of protest, as my parents would certainly have done. They decided to have me pass a kind of examination. For this, they sent me to Wertheimer, one of the biggest dealers in the town, who dealt primarily in XVIIIth century paintings—Gainsboroughs and so on. He was a very honest man and certainly, in his way, an excellent dealer. He asked me, for example : "What do you particularly like in the National Gallery ?" I purposely took the opposite point of view to his. If I had told him that I liked Velasquez—whom I actually did like very much—he would have been delighted. I declared : "I like El Greco."

Now at that time, El Greco was still highly suspect. I also said that I admired Vermeer who was not very much appreciated in those days and I cited two or three names of that sort. Then he said to me : "But after all you're thinking of opening a gallery ; what would you buy ?" I already knew of the existence of Derain, Matisse—in other words of the *Fauves*. I said to myself : If I mention those names to him, he'll answer : "Don't know them." I decided to name Bonnard and Vuillard of whom I thought he might have heard. He answered : "Don't know them."

Nevertheless my uncles, who were very understanding men, made me the following offer : "We're going to give you twenty five thousand francs and one year. If at the end of the year you've achieved any results you can continue ; if not you'll go to South Africa." When the bargain had been struck, I left immediately. My wife and I arrived in Paris on the twenty second of February 1907. I soon found a gallery in the Rue Vignon. The *Salon des Indépendants* opened in March and it was there that I made my first purchases, works by Derain, Vlaminck, Braque, by the *Fauves* in fact.

B./ *What could a young man passionately interested in the arts, like you, see of contemporary painting at the time?*

K./ The Luxembourg, as you know, was still the dumping ground for all the glories of official painting. There was only the tiny Salle Caillebotte where one could see living painting. On the walls of the *Salons* could be found works by the painters who had joined together, in 1903, to found the *Salon d'Automne*: Matisse (Picasso never exhibited), Braque, Vlaminck, Dufy, Friesz and Rouault.

B./ *Cézanne was still alive. Was his work well-known?*

K./ There had been—at the *Salon d'Automne* of 1904, to be exact —a big retrospective exhibition of Cézanne. The Independants had also held retrospective exhibitions of Seurat and Van Gogh

about that time. These painters thus had a group of admirers who formed a small but enthusiastic minority. Personally I admired them too, but it seemed to me that from the point of view of business it was already too late.

B./ *But apart from Cézanne, Seurat or Van Gogh, did Impressionist paintings, which were already more widely appreciated, seem "comprehensible" to the general public?*

K./ Ah, not at all. Even the Impressionists were still very far from being under-

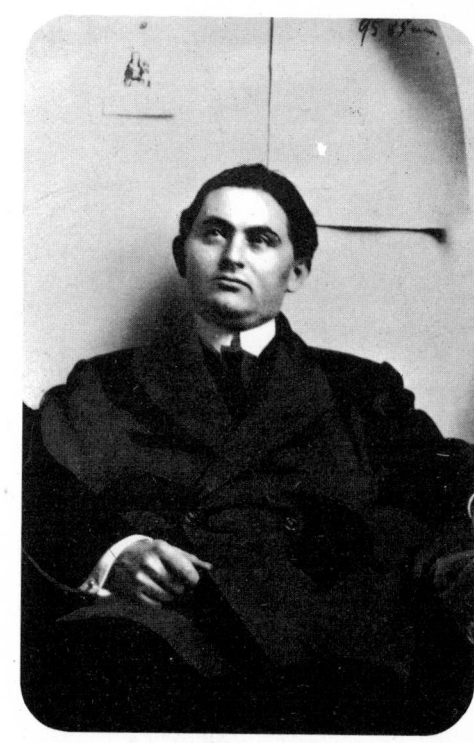

Picasso took this photograph of his friend and dealer Daniel-Henry Kahnweiler in 1912.

stood. In 1904, during a Monet exhibition at Durand-Ruel's, I remember seeing two cab drivers, convulsed with hatred shaking their fists. They obviously would have liked to demolish the gallery-window because they were so enraged by these paintings.

ue : The Table (45½ x 31½") 1911; Museum of Modern Art, Paris.

121

Monsieur, je viens de voir vos Oeuvres aux Indépendants et j'ai offert au secrétariat cent vingt francs pour acquérir N° 722 (L'olivier). Je serais reconnaissant pour une réponse vite ; car en cas de refus de votre part je pourrais disposer autrement de mes moyens assez limités. Agréez, monsieur, l'assurance de mes sentiments les plus distingués.

Facsimile of the first letter sent to Georges Braque by the collector-dealer Wilhelm Uhde.

B. / *In fact the public, even the initiates, who still hardly knew how to look at Impressionist painting and still less at works such as those by Seurat, Cézanne and Van Gogh, found itself suddenly telescoped into the presence of the Cubist revolution.*

K. / Quite so, but to be more precise, the public did not exactly find itself confronted with Cubism because the great painters of this movement did not care to exhibit at the Paris *Salons*. Picasso never participated in any of them ; he showed his painting once at Vollard's in 1901. Braque showed some *fauve* canvases at the *Salons*. In 1908 he sent some Cubist paintings to the *Salon d'Automne*. They were rejected but two of them were retrieved thanks to the intervention of Marquet and of Charles Guérin. Braque, nevertheless, withdrew all his entries, and in November 1908 I organized the exhibition that was to give birth to the word "Cubism" which was coined, as you know, by the critic Louis Vauxcelles who used it in a derogatory sense. Léger, whose Cubism only began in 1910, exhibited that year and the following year and then he too stopped exhibiting. Gris, who only began to paint in 1911, only made a very brief appearance in the *Salons* because in 1912 I began to handle his work and after that he no longer exhibited anywhere else.

B. / *We've mentioned Cézanne, Van Gogh and Seurat. Did Gauguin make much of an impression among young painters at the time ?*

K. / Among some of them, yes, and Gauguin's influence was certainly considerable. Personally I think it was disastrous and I have often said and written so. Even Picasso was influenced by Gauguin ; obviously so during the Blue Period, but not after, while a man like Derain, up to 1908, was still completely under the influence of Gauguin. I consider that Gauguin is at the root of the whole school of decorative and ornamental painting which we are seeing at the moment. A man like Cézanne obviously gave considerable thought to the construction of his composition but he never distorted a single line in order to obtain a pleasing or ornamental effect. Gauguin did and so did many painters after him. I think that he is even responsible for abstract painting.

B. / *Just before Cubism began, were there any contacts between the painters who were about to found this school and their elders : Gauguin's old friends and the Nabis ?*

K. / No, all the groups were very much separated and everybody did not know everybody else as they do today. Just think, I myself never knew Vuillard or Bonnard, or even Lautrec. I met no one of that generation, except Odilon Redon.

F. Léger (right) during the first World War. A series of Cubist drawings date from this period.

B. / *Who were the first painters that you took on at your gallery in the Rue Vignon ?*

K. / They were Derain, Vlaminck and Braque. Then Van Dongen. I had Van Dongen for quite a while and I still think today that his *fauve* work was very good.

B. / *Were you interested, at the same time when the Cubist painters made their debut, in the* Fauves *?*

K. / Cubism only appeared during 1907 and when I arrived in Paris at the beginning of that year I found myself surrounded by *Fauvism*. *Fauvism* was then really in full bloom. I admired Matisse—and I still admire him very much—but from the commercial point of view it was too late for me. Matisse was being sold by Bernheim and even then I had made up my mind positively to have the exclusive rights to the works of any painter whom I would handle.

B. / *When did you get to know Picasso ?*

K. / I went up to see him for the first time in his studio in the Rue Ravignan in the spring of 1907. There I saw the *Demoiselles d'Avignon*, which he had finished during the previous weeks and which, as you know, marked the beginning of Cubism.

B. / *What made you go to see him ?*

K. / He was being talked about among young painters. I can even tell you in exactly what circumstances I heard about the *Demoiselles d'Avignon*. Shortly after the opening of my gallery, I got to know Wilhelm Uhde, who knew Picasso already. He told me that Picasso had just painted a very strange painting "something Assyrian". I thought to myself : "I must see this" and I went up to the Rue Ravignan in Montmartre. Picasso, who had just got out of bed, came and opened the door bare-foot and wearing only a shirt. He knew me by sight, having already been to the Rue Vignon.

B. / *Had Braque and Picasso met at that time ?*

K. / They got to know each other through Apollinaire in 1907. Braque said at the time about the *Demoiselles d'Avignon* that it was as if one drank gasoline so as to be able to spit fire. But it must have started him thinking because between the autumn of 1907 and the spring of 1908 he evolved from *Fauvism* to Cubism and became one of the two creators of the Cubist movement.

B. / *So this moment marked a kind of aesthetic revolution ? By 1910-1911 the Cubist phenomenon was something which could no longer be ignored ?*

K. / Definitely.

B. / *And how did the movement continue to develop up to the time of the first World War ?*

K. / First there was what is called analytical Cubism which, as Gris said himself, was more a means of exploring the

Picasso photographed in Barcelona in 1905, between Fernande Olivier and the Catalan writer, Ramon Raventos.

world than of representing it. Obviously this was a profound break with the accepted habits of painting, in that what was being represented was not only one view of an object—of a bottle for example —but a view from the side, from above and from the inside as well. In other words, an object was described in terms of what was known about it and not only in terms of what could be seen of it.

B. / *In fact, the artist represented several aspects of the same object simultaneously according to different angles of vision, and projected onto this his own personal experience.*

K. / Yes, but he was also trying to represent his memory of the many different aspects that the object had assumed for him.

B. / *Do you consider that this attempt had had, in one form or another, any precedents in the history of painting?*

K. / I don't know of any. In the "Lives of the Saints" as depicted by the primitives, which some people have mentioned in this context, it is different events taking place at different times which are represented. There is a progression in time. In Cubism we are dealing with the same object at the same moment

but it is portrayed simultaneously in a variety of ways.

But analytical Cubism became increasingly difficult to interpret. Moreover it limited the use of color in paintings. It is this that undoubtedly led painters to what was afterwards called synthetic Cubism. This was an attempt to create symbols or, if you prefer, colored forms which represent an object, but still giving multiple aspects of it. Look how Picasso continues to use simultaneous representation even today. I'm thinking of those women in profile and full-face which he was still doing quite recently.

B. / *Yes, there is no doubt that the broadening of vision has been one of Picasso's constant preoccupations and also of great importance to every valid painter in the last fifty years.*

K. / The Cubist contribution is essentially this : to have broken with the tradition of direct imitation of the exterior world and to have created a form of representation that was not direct imitation. One may say there is not a single French painter of merit who was not Cubist in manner at the time. It is a phenomenon which, in retrospect, is rather fascinating. Segonzac, for instance, who today cannot find words insulting enough to describe Cubism, was one of the Cubists, as Cubist

as could be, using facets and all the rest of it.

B. / *And Derain?*

K. / Yes, but he was completely aware of what he was doing. At that time he was in the same state of mind as Braque and Picasso with whom he was on very close terms. He knew what it was all about and he wanted to do the same thing that his friends were doing, only in another form. It was less artificial, less exterior than with Luc-Albert Moreau, Chagall, Boussingault and many others who, at that time, called themselves Cubists.

B. / *What were Matisse's relations with the Cubists?*

K. / They were never bad. Matisse was a man of remarkable intelligence who was always on very good terms with Picasso and Braque and who always followed the activities of the Cubists with great interest.

B. / *Did this go any further?*

K. / Matisse and Juan Gris found themselves together at Céret in 1914. There are distinct traces of his conversations with Gris in Matisse's work of the period... in particular in a very large painting

of an interior with a piano painted in flat tones, but this remains an isolated example amongst the rest of his work.

B. / *And a minor master like La Fresnaye, would you say that he is a Cubist?*

K. / I don't think so at all. Every time that the organizers of Cubist exhibitions asked me for advice, I said that La Fresnaye should not be included. I consider that he too is very close to Gauguin. Like everybody at that period, he more or less took on a Cubist appearance but he was never a Cubist at heart.

B. / *And if you were to organize a Cubist exhibition whom would you include?*

K. / I did organize one, several years ago, at the Venice Biennale with Douglas Cooper. There were Picasso, Braque, Gris and Léger. Not the others who were only imitators.

B. / *In the early period of struggle, did you find any collectors who understood Cubist painting?*

K. / A few. Don't forget that at that time a gallery, its proprietor and its painters could live with the help of just a very few collectors, three or four, but it's true that in those days there were some faithful friends. First of all, in France, there was Roger Dutilleuil, who from the very beginning was a real enthusiast, and then there was one of my personal friends, called Hermann Rupf, with whom I had worked in a bank in Frankfurt, in 1901. I sold him my first picture, and today he owns a magnificent collection in Switzerland.

B. / *Did you know Tchoukine the Russian who bought so many Fauves and Cubists?*

K. / Tchoukine came to my gallery about 1908. He did not stop buying until the war and he bought in vast quantities. Some of his paintings were on view in Paris in the spring of 1954. There was also another Russian, Morosov. But he collected very few Cubists and preferred Blue Period and Rose Period Picassos. As for Gertrude Stein, she met Picasso two years before

I did. She already owned some of his paintings and continued to buy them from me.

B. / *She collected Blue and Rose Period Picassos and did not stop buying in the Cubist period. Were there some people, among those who bought Picasso, who did stop at that time?*

K. / I could name Vollard among the dealers and also several collectors. However, Vollard began buying again later. On the other hand someone who was never frightened by Cubism and whose behavior was always courageous was Wilhelm Uhde. I also had a Czech art historian, Vincenc Kramar, among my clients.

B. / *So, on the eve of the first World War, Cubism was already known all over the world?*

K. / All over the world if you like, but only among a few hundred people, and these people tended to indentify Cubism

B. / *Do you consider that, in the militant period of Cubism, there was any focal point outside Paris ?*

K. / No, absolutely none. There wasn't even a question of such a thing. I organized many exhibitions abroad ; other people did the same and promoted the Cubist painters. But there was no other creative nucleus but Paris.

B. / *What about Klee whom you knew and who worked in a style that one can safely say owed nothing to anyone—was he familiar with Cubism at a very early date ?*

K. / Yes, Klee never lived in Paris but he came there. And then there were exhibitions in Munich, in particular an important Picasso exhibition at the Tannhauser Gallery in 1912. So he knew Cubist painting very well at an early date. The German painters of the period, who called themselves Expressionists, believed, what is more, that their work and Cubism were one and the same thing. In this they were wrong. This confusion persisted : for a very long time in Germany Cubism was considered a kind of sub-division of Expressionism.

B. / *To return to France, isn't it true that there was another stronghold of Cubism near Paris : Jacques Villon's studio ?*

K. / Villon tried to do something which, in my opinion, is quite impossible : to fuse Impressionism and Cubism. But the real problems which agitated the Cubists never engaged Jacques Villon.

B./ *But don't you think, all the same, that Villon is a very gifted painter ?*

K. / Yes, and a thoroughly admirable man, full of talent, taste and intelligence.

▶ **When the Fauves were first struggling for recognition, opening day at the official Salons was a very elegant affair.**

Braque in his studio playing the accordion.

But his painting is not the sort to open up new paths.

B. / *To your mind, what use are contemporary painters making of the great discoveries of Cubism ?*

K. / I think the best use to be made of them is to do the opposite of what the Cubists did. I believe that, in the final analysis, Cubism was not a school of discipline, as we thought at the beginning, but a school of freedom. It demonstrated the possibilities of a plastic method of communication completely independent of straight-forward observation. I think however that the use to be made of this method of communication ought to be in tune with the spirit of a completely different generation.

with Picasso. Braque was very wrongly considered to be a plagiarist by almost everybody. Picasso always defended him with great generosity, and said : "Not at all, he's an absolutely authentic creator who paints in his own style."

B. / *What happened during the 1914 war and immediately afterwards ?*

K. / During the war, Leonce Rosenberg started his gallery and protected the painters whom I couldn't look after at that moment because of my German nationality. He failed completely from the business point of view, since he was not commercially minded. At the same time, it is quite likely that the alliance between Picasso and the *Ballets Russes* played a useful publicity role. That also coincided, as you know, with Picasso's Classicist period. Many collectors who had not bought Picasso during his Cubist period now returned to a painter whom they could easily understand.

Matisse with his sons Jean and Pierre, 1912.

"Il faut de l'enfance répandue partout."
Louis XIV to Mansart, 1699.

Discovery and Praise of Rococo

BY CYRIL CONNOLLY

To Sacheverell Sitwell.

One can describe a passion only in terms of passion. Many years ago I noticed that certain works of art brought tears to my eyes. Lines of Horace, Dryden, Rochester, Pope, the last paintings of Watteau, Mozart's *Voi che sapete*, while in the summer of 1938 two small buildings—Palladio's Roman theatre at Vicenza and the Amalienberg pavilion outside Munich—were added to my list. What had they in common? Perfection or the ideal of perfection—a lyrical conception of humanity, a response to all that is transitory and fugacious, a calligraphy of farewell. I have, of course, been more deeply moved by that art which springs from the tragic sense of life, I have been fissured by romanticism, spell-bound by Baudelaire or Wagner, yet I have come to believe that there exist also an unselfconscious gaiety, an acceptance of human limitation quite as significant as the romantic protest and no less congenial an incubator of works of art. The Amalienberg, a royal huntman's bagatelle which Mr. Sacheverell Sitwell calls "a supreme monument of the period", was the first rococo I had seen, for of my youthful visits to Potsdam and Dresden I have no clear recollection. Here in that round room of blue and silver with its long mirrors and hanging chandelier was a poetry of living, a revelation of intimacy and delight that I had not thought possible.

> "Ci-gît, dans une paix profonde,
> Cette dame de volupté
> Qui pour plus grande sûreté
> Fit son paradis en ce monde."

So familiar are we to-day with the rococo that it comes as a surprise to learn that the cult is very recent. To love and understand the first half of the XVIIIth century would seem a prerogative of the present. Here are two early definitions :

"Rococo is a term applied specifically to a type of ornament, style or design belonging to the reign of Louis XV and the beginning of the reign of Louis XVI. In general, it applies to everything that is old and out of fashion in the arts, literature, costume, manners, etc. 'To like the rococo,' 'to fall into the rococo,' 'that is very rococo'."—Dictionary of the Académie Française, 1842.

"Rococo. A debased variety of the Louis XIV style of ornament, proceeding from it through the degeneracy of the Louis XV. It is generally a meaningless assemblage of scrolls and crimped conventional shell-work wrought into all sorts of irregular and indescribable forms, without individuality and without expression. The term is also sometimes applied in contempt to anything bad or tasteless in decorative art."—Chambers, 1882.

The first allusions to the new style referred to it as '*goût moderne*' or '*goût du siècle*' (Blondel 1738). The expressions 'Pompadour,' 'Rococo,' came from the studios and were first used by Maurice Quai in 1796-97. In 1828 Stendhal writes: "Bernini was the father of that bad taste called in the studios by the somewhat vulgar term Rococo." Victor Hugo is the first to admire it: "The belfries of the Cathedral (in Nancy) are Pompadour pepper-mills... the square of the Town Hall is one of the gayest, prettiest and most complete of any rococo square I have ever seen... It is a marquise of a square." (1839)

In 1836, the word appeared in English, in 1843 Burckhardt uses the term in Germany whose art historians have slowly succeeded in stripping it of its pejorative meaning. Since it is now international I am in favor of keeping it, not of bringing forward the French *rocaille* which is apt to create a false distinction, being used by French apologists in order to disassociate their country from the extreme consequences of its own invention. *Le style Louis XV* is more familiar but imposes an artificial chronology.

We must now face the problem of what rococo is and where it came from. Mr. Fiske Kimball of Philadelphia has settled this question in his monumental *Creation of Rococo* (1943). He proves, I think, conclusively, that the movement begins as a breaking up of the massive baroque of Louis XIV into contrasting asymmetrical curvilinear forms, an invasion of architecture by decoration until (as in some German churches) decoration creates its own architecture. He is thus at variance with the German theory that rococo is but another name for late baroque, which came as an organic development from Italy to Vienna and Vienna to Germany. Nor does he believe that it was evolved by the Nordic 'will-to-form' nor by direct observation from nature nor from the properties of new materials such as stucco and porcelain. Its genesis is in the arabesques of Bérain which Lepautre translated into decoration and which were carved in hard oak panelling around Versailles about 1699, the artists being stimulated by demands for the new Palaces of Marly and Meudon, for the King's

œil-de-bœuf room and chapel and for the night nursery of the young Duke of Burgundy. By close study of the original drawings and builders' accounts Mr. Kimball has sorted out the possessors of inventive genius from the hierarchy of official craftsmen: the great precursors, Bérain and Lepautre who soften up the heavy baroque, Oppenordt and Vassé who lead the first attack under the Regent, Audran and Watteau with their arabesques, Pineau, Meissonier and Lajoue, the brilliant general staff of *le style pittoresque* in the victorious years 1730-1735, and finally Babel and Cuvilliès. We watch the somewhat finicky *Régence* line struggling with the heavy shapes of doors and windows, furniture and paneling and gradually controlling the shape of the object itself until by the late 1730's every article in use, view and vista, palace or summerhouse, temple or tomb, begins to be subjugated to the line of ebb and flow, the convolu-tions which govern both water and the shells and rocks which are formed by it and the sprays and tendrils which drink it in.

The reaction begins after 1750 when the younger Cochin, the antiquarian Caylus and the Abbé Leblanc take up the cudgels in the name of French good taste, when the youthful Marigny sets out on his Italian journey and returns with all Pompeii, when Servandoni's St. Sulpice and Soufflot's Pantheon arise, when Gabriel replaces Boffrand and, above all, when England is victorious in the Seven Years War (1759). Pedantic England which, led by Burlington and William Kent, had side-stepped the rococo and gone straight from classical Palladio to neo-classical Adam (who returned from his Dalmatian trip in 1759)—with Horace Walpole's neo-gothic as the only deviation! The rococo was not a movement to outstay its welcome, there was no decadence, its latest achievements are among its best; rather was it displaced by the overwhelming reality of the new vision of the classical world which had materialized in all its simplicity and strength in Herculaneum, Spalato, Greece and Asia Minor before the eyes of XVIIIth century travellers. The magic of the rococo is in that it is a European movement of spontaneous originality, a true *style moderne* arising between two backward-looking periods, the grandiose baroque and the academic neo-classical.

Mr. Kimball builds his case on correct dating and the personality of artists; for him it is the last years of Louis XIV (Bérain, Lepautre) and the *Régence* (Oppenordt) together with the decorative wood-carving of Pineau after his return from Russia (1727) and the genius of the architect and goldsmith Meissonier that are truly important. The hotels de Roquelaure, de Rouilly, de Soubise and some rooms at Rambouillet (all before 1740) are what he considers the peak.

The soft paste of Vincennes and Sèvres, St. Cloud and Mennecy, the faïences of Strasburg and Marseille, the tapestries of Boucher, the lacquers of Martin, the engravings of Gravelot and Eisen, the bindings of Pasdeloup, the silver of Thomas Germain, the snuff boxes, the *petits riens* and even the whole gamut of Louis XV furniture he sees as secondary artefacts of the architect's creation.

He also minimizes political and economic influences, although it is clear that the rococo was an explosive affirmation of the private life, an escape from Versailles ; its great phase opens with the stage of the reign of Louis XV referred to as *les premières infidélités*. In fact the whole of Europe needed liberation from heroics, and the rococo is an art sponsored by leading personalities ; the Regent Orléans, Louis XV, Stanislas of Lorraine, Frederick the Great, Maria Teresa, Madame de Pompadour ('*Reine et Marraine du rococo*', Goncourt), Count Brühl, the Schönborns, the Wittelsbachs and Spanish Bourbons, The Margraves of Bayreuth and Ansbach, which caught on immediately with the humblest of their subjects and united all in a masquerade of gaiety and pleasure terminated (as is every European aesthetic movement) by an internecine war.

Let us suppose that the imagination of some studious American is kindled by the Bouchers in the Frick collection (formerly in Madame de Pompadour's collection at Crécy) or his tapestries in Philadelphia, from the oval room of the

Far left and left : figures by the master of Bavarian rococo sculpture, F. I. Günther. Right : rococo library, St. Gall, Switzerland

hotel de Soubise, and that he decides on a journey to learn more about the civilization that produced them. Where should he go?

He might stop off at London's Wallace collection where he can study the basic rhythms among some of the finest furniture, china and paintings of the period. England was to the fore in three minor examples of the rococo : the so-called Chippendale furniture, Lamerie's silver and the china of Chelsea and Bow, so luxurious, fresh and countrified. London's masterpiece was the interior of Ware's Chesterfield house decorated by the best French workmen (1749) and demolished in 1934. There is, however, a surprising amount of stucco, often by Italian workmen.

In France he would visit the *petits appartements* at Versailles, now in course of restoration, the hotels already mentioned (especially Soubise) and various rooms, doorways and staircases of the Faubourg St. Germain and the Place Vendôme. But Paris, despite the Place de la Concorde, is not the capital of rococo ; the opposition to the style there was strong and constant. Mr. Kimball quotes from Cochin's secret memoirs : "At that time there were any number of makers of bad ornaments who enjoyed the most brilliant reputation ; like Pineau who ruined all the architecture of the period with his sculpture, like La Joue, who was a rather mediocre painter of architecture and who designed some miserable ornaments which sold with the greatest rapidity. It was M. Openor, the architect, who began the

flight from the good taste of Louis XIV's reign... and things went from excess to excess reaching the height of absurdity which we know only too well."

This attitude persists two hundred years later when in his *Architecture Française* (1951), M. Hautecœur writes of the creators of the *style pittoresque* in words which might easily be applied to cubists or surrealists : "When we find some form of exaggeration in France, we must discover its perpetrators and these perpetrators are Oppenordt, son of a Dutchman, Meissonier, born in Turin, Pineau, who returned after a long stay in Russia, Cuvilliès, born in Hainault or Lajoue, who was not an architect, but a painter."

If, then, there is so little left, it is not entirely due to the *guerre aux châteaux*' of the Revolution but because the style was itself revolutionary, abandoned later by the fashionable and the conservatives through a mistaken worship of straight lines and moderation. Only in Nancy, fief of Louis XV's Polish father-in-law Stanislas, is there a rococo architectural ensemble, one of the loveliest agglomerations north of the Alps, where Heré's planning is enriched by Lamour's exquisite ironwork. The situation there and in Germany was quite different from France ; the country was proud of its rococo and the princelings were seldom in a position to re-decorate, while their descendants regarded the splendid rooms which they inherited as a symbol of a golden age. Here the devastation is entirely due to the last war and irreparable damage has

been done in the three capitals of the rococo, Würtzburg, Munich and Berlin. Those who find Cuvilliès' surviving work in Munich cloying or overcrowded should study the vanished decoration of the golden hall of Charlottenburg and Voltaire's rooms in Sans-Souci, the work of the more sober yet no less gifted the court architects returned from Paris with new books of ornament and design.

In central Germany the position is clearer. Here the great family of Schönborn, Prince Bishops who traded and mediated between Vienna and the West, controlled Würtzburg, Bamberg, ceiling in which Jupiter's envoys carry the good news of the establishment of Apollo's reign to the four continents almost makes one forget the war damage in their airy serenity. For Tiepolo (as can be seen from his 'rooms' in the 'Ca' Rezzonico') is the quintessence of the spirit of the rococo in painting. (It is misleading to talk about 'a rococo painter' but there are clearly some artists such as Boucher, Huet, Pillement, Longhi, Devis and Laroon who abandon themselves to the movement as wholeheartedly as the great porcelain modellers Kändler and Bustelli.)

Besides work on seventy churches, Neumann was also in charge of artillery fortifications, waterworks, roads, bridges, factories in all the Schönborn dominions; he even held a scientific chair at the university and left behind an unfinished theoretical textbook. He also built Schloss Werneck outside Würtzburg and the lovely staircase hall at Bruchsal near Karlsruhe, an apricot palace once full of exquisite rococo work by Feichtmayer, now badly damaged. Two chapels for the Schönborns in the Würtzburg Residence, and attached to the cathedral, lead on to his other masterpiece, the pilgrimage church of Vierzehnheiligen (1743 onwards) between Bamberg and Bayreuth. Every aspect of this church is grand, warm, welcoming and lovely. Twin towers of golden stone rise above the fields and woods while all within is light and harmony. Like Wies (though much larger), it is a church in which every square foot is exquisitely decorated.

Feichtmayer's confessionals suggest sedan chairs or boxes at the opera and (as at Wies) the main feature is an oval shrine with a colonnade of colored

![Rococo library of the Schussenreid monastery]

Rococo library of the Schussenreid monastery, 1752, by D. Zimmermann. Eddies of white and gold stucco foam around the oval ceiling painted in clear-toned frescos. Book cases and gallery follow undulating lines. Allegorical statuary below, gesticulating cherubs above.

Johann August Nahl. Of Hoppenhaupt's silver room in the Potsdam Neue Schloss (removed in its entirety by the Russians), Mr. Sitwell writes, "the boiseried rooms decorated in silver are quite inconceivable in their loveliness; many of the doors have a wavelike waterfall treatment which is again echoed in some of the wall panels in two shades of gold, or with a greenish silver that gives variety to that more conventional shade of moonlight. Pictures by Watteau can surely have never found a more congenial environment."

I do not think that the ecclesiastical rococo of southern Germany can be attributed entirely to French sources. There would seem to have been some instantaneous fusion around the lake of Constance of French, Italian and Austrian influences among the deeply religious yet pageant-loving master-craftsmen and wood-carvers of Wurtemberg and Bavaria. The impulse to build or renovate large monasteries spread westward from baroque Vienna along the Danube and the Inn while the stucco workers came up from the Ticino and Mainz, Speyer and Trèves. In 1719 Johann Philip Franz, succeeding to his estates, announced to the alarm of his Chapter that the building bug *(Bau-Wurm)* had got him. He chose as his architect a young captain of engineers who had just returned from the Turkish wars where he had visited Vienna and Belgrade. This specialist in fortifications and canon founderies became one of the great architects of the XVIIIth century, a large, generous, serene and triumphant personality. Johann Baltazar Neumann's first plans for the Residence of Würtzburg were made in 1719, and in 1723 he was in Paris consulting Boffrand and Robert de Cotte. The Palace took from 1720 to 1744 and included much exquisite decoration by Bossi, a card room in green lacquer, a mirror room with Chinese ceiling in gold, gray-blue and white with a black marble chimney piece, all destroyed by incendiaries in the raid of March 16th, 1945. The great staircase hall and three other sumptuous rooms remain. The Tiepolo

A summit of rococo religious art: the little pilgrimage church of Die Wies built and decorated by the Zimmermann brot

marbles built in the oval centre of the church and removing emphasis from the altar at the end of the nave. This feature distinguishes those churches which are built in the XVIIIth century from those which are merely renovated, for the oval form satisfies an aesthetic need of the age. Neumann is thus a link between French rococo and south German church interiors, though in Tiepolo's fresco (1753) it is neither as a pilgrim nor as a court architect that he chooses to be represented but as a full colonel of artillery meditating beside his cannon.

The Goethean genius of Neumann sub-divides into two, in the brothers Zimmermann who came from a family of craftsmen in Wessobrunn. Johann Baptist (1680-1758) went forward in court circles as a painter and decorator and drove back from Paris to Munich in a golden coach while Domenico (1685-1766) became an architect for the humbler monasteries, living all the time in the country at Landsberg or Wies where he died quietly at the age of eighty one. He was uninstructed and could hardly get his drawings correct, using wood and stucco to solve problems in stone while his more wordly brother was working with Cuvilliès on the 'rich rooms' of the Munich Residence.

Yet at Gunzbourg, Steinhausen and Wies he produced works abounding in natural genius. Steinhausen is a small pilgrimage church near Biberach in Wurtemberg with a ceiling fresco by J. B. The church is elliptic in shape and decorated in white, pink, beige and pale blue; even the lettering of 'Jesus'

Carved façade with figures and playfull cherubs of the "Asam House", built by the Asam brothers Cosmo Damian (frescos) and Egid Quirin (sculpture), 1733-1746. Between the two of them they built and decorated important churches, including the hand some though damaged St. Johann Nepomuk next to this house in mid-town Munich.

is rococo while the circular fresco of Mary as Queen of Heaven, full of green paradisal scenery, is bounded by a Versailles vision of a fountain in a glade. These upward leaping fountains (there is another in the Asam fresco of St. Maria Victoria in Ingolstadt) suggest the rococo title page of Meissonier or the imaginary ornaments of Cuvilliès and Lajoue. Yet Steinhausen is but a preparation for Wies (near Füssen), the supreme achievement of the two brothers. The outside is plain: fields, dark woods and distant mountains (often under snow), frame the lonely scene so that the contrast within is all the more striking, a pilgrim's dream of pastel perfection. The painter to the Munich court and the rural master builder have here fused all their separate capacities. Such interiors are impossible to describe, they must be illustrated by color and diagram and then a prolonged visit must be undertaken. Wies, Vierzehnheiligen, Zwei-

falten, Birnau, Ottobeuren, Weltenburg —these have to be studied, then seen, then relearnt over again, for no words can evoke both light and space and color. J. B.'s ceiling at Wies is a Day of Judgement where all is charity and forgiveness and Christ descends on a rainbow; the whole small edifice breathes delight and serenity. After the two old brothers' work at Wies was done Domenico retired to a nearby cottage where he could contemplate his handiwork and remained there until his death.

The brothers Asam (Cosmo Damian 1686-1739 and Egid Quirin 1692-1750) are more famous, for they too were capable of building and decorating a whole church between them, but their work is not so well known as their name, for the best of it is somewhat inaccessible. Their genius is more agited than that of the Zimmermanns, they too worked best away from cities in the remote monastic lands that bordered

ail of the pulpit, Die Wies. Around its shining garlands, fresco scenes of the Last Judgment.

on the Danube. Their youthful master-piece is Weltemburg with its magical statue of St.George slaying the dragon and its enchanting bust of Cosmo by his brother, a Cherubino arising from the stucco, while at Rohr the younger brother Egid Quirin went on to create his sensational altar-piece—a theatrical tableau of the Assumption. Osterhofen and Straubing are considered their finest late work while at Munich their carved rococo house front can still be seen next to the dark, damaged, some-what occluded church they built toge-ther for St. Johann Nepomuk. The brothers are the earliest of the rococo church architects of southern Germany, they studied in Rome which must have developed their sense of theatre and began to work at home in the 1720's. They combine a brillant invention, grace and wit with the fresco-gift of Cosmo Damian and the outstanding sculptural talent of Egid Quirin.

One more church architect must be mentioned, Johann Maria Fischer (1691-1766), who sprang from a line of upper palatinante masons and began to work in Munich with the Asam's and Cuvilliès, then became the architect for the greater monastic orders, especially the Benedictines. In richness of conception he was the equal of Neumann and, like him, finished off his work with superb decoration. He too was extremely pro-lific and was connected with thirty-two churches and twenty-three convents but he never became a builder of palaces and of his life we know next to nothing. Although his designs go back to Austria and Italy and he was well versed in French art, he never travelled. His finest churches are Diessen (on the Ammersee), Ottobeuren (near Memmingen south of Bavaria) and Zweifalten in Wurtem-berg. This is indeed a marvellous creation where his lofty spiritual qua-lity combines with the dazzling stucco of J. M. Feichtmayer and the moving sculpture of Christian. The church is surrounded by hills and woods, its precinct encircled by a quiet little stream. The exterior is billowing and gracious, the inside extraordinarily rich ; the pulpit drips with golden waterfalls and is ornamented with skeletons rising from the dead, while greenery cascades to the serpent on its base, and it is faced by another full scale model by Christian of the vision of Ezekiel in the valley of dry bones. The art of rococo here brings the whole of the great church under its genial domination. There is a throne with rococo chair and two confessionals by the entrance which must be unique, one is a stucco box carved with a swaying palm grove, the columns encrusted with vegetation, while in the other the stucco is carved into a catas-trophe of falling columns. Ottobeuren is on an even grander scale.

One other exquisite church remains of the mid century, Neu Birnau, a pilgrimage church at the west end of the Lake of Constance, on a hillside among meadows and orchards. Peter Thumb was the architect and Joseph Anton Feuchtmayer in charge of the stucco. The entrance doors are grey with pink facing. Inside is a blaze of color, a ceiling fresco containing a real mirror with gold busts below to catch the sun reflected from it and every-where patches of green—in interstices in the scroll work or at the top of the pink altar columns where it is echoed by green plants and the green in the cracks of the honeycomb pergola above the altar and again in St. John the Baptist's outspreading tree. There are several fine statues of an elongated El Greco character and on a wall-memorial Death has been reduced to the dimen-sions of a dried sea-horse while from the pulpit nearby a girl's head as fresh and secular as Mozart's German dances looks out while from below another head peers.

The strangest figure of the German rococo is certainly Cuvilliès (1695-1768); this Walloon from Soignies was a dwarf of under four feet high. Although of French origin, he worked entirely abroad and before 1711 had become the page of the exiled Elector Max Emmanuel of Bavaria with whom he returned to Munich from Brussels in 1715. After an apprenticeship as a military engineer, he was sent to Paris where he studied under Blondel from 1720 to 1724. In 1725 he became court architect to the Elector and succeeded Effner, the creator of Nymphenburg and Schliessheim. His books of orna-ments are fertile and original variations on the themes of Lajoue but his oppor-tunities for realizing them on the grand scale were much greater. Apart from work (now badly damaged) at Brühl outside Cologne, he produced three triumphant interiors, the five rich rooms in the Residence (1730-1737), the Amalienberg (1734-1739) both deco-rated by J. B. Zimmermann, and the Residence theatre (1753). Both the theatre and these rooms in the Palace have now vanished utterly. Jacob Burckhardt considered these rich rooms "the most beautiful rococo which exists on earth, excelling in inventiveness and subtle elegance anything I have seen." There were particularly fine *chinoiseries*, a bedroom in white and gold and wine-red, a long picture gallery hung with silk and a blending of all the sea-borne themes of French *rocaille* with German hunting scenes and northern woods. Here the Elector Karl Albrecht dreamt his luckless dream of Empire which was to end so tragically. The theatre ('rococo art at its absolute culmination.' S. Sitwell) was a vision of white, gold and crimson, the key note of which was

the Royal Box and four circular tiers of boxes each with rococo ornamentation ; it held only six hundred and thirty-seven people, and here Mozart conducted the first performance of his opera *Idomeneo* (1781).

A link between church and state is formed by the monastic libraries whose frescoed oval ceilings, undulating book cases and allegorical statuary proclaim an opulent calm where the atmosphere is deeply religious yet no detail can offend the delicate susceptibilities of an unbeliever. St. Gall in Switzerland, Für-stenzell, Wiblingen near Ulm, Dillingen and Schussenried in Wurtemburg are among the loveliest. There are also rococo gardens, like the Jardin de la Fontaine at Nîmes and above all at Veitshöcheim outside .Würtzburg. Driven out of the shrubs which are confined to nigh enormous formal hedges forming a series of '*cabinets particuliers*', Nature seems to flower in Tietz' statuary, exquisitely exuberant and robust, yet like rococo china, touching, even pathe-tic. Trains, trams, gasworks and factory chimneys, waiting greedily for the end, cluster and hoot round the alleys and the delicate grottos.

"Unwater'd see the drooping sea-horse mourn, and swallows roost in Nilus' dusty urn"

One last word to those who want to study the rococo, Hurry ! A style which ignored frontiers, which convoluted all it touched from a cathedral to a chamber pot, which included all classes, whose message was movement, spon-taneity, intimacy, formal extravagance and spiritual delight, which brought love and warmth for a half a life-time into gloomy interiors, which in its day was daring and contemporary and universal as no other has been since— unless we elevate art nouveau, cubism and surrealism to a status they do not merit,—such a creative fire as swept through every capital from Lisbon to Leningrad, Cork to Constantinople, is nothing if not perishable and attracts to itself an undeviating hatred. Even as I write some façade is crumbling, a ceiling flakes, pannelling is being stript, plaster-work crushed, chimney pieces torn out, a Chippendale looking glass cracks and innumerable pieces of china are thumbed and shattered—("the period of rococo may well be called the age of porcelain and without a sympathetic understanding of rococo no apprecia-tion of the art is possible." Honey.) So hurry, before the last cartouche, the fading arabesque, the final *cul-de-lampe* goes the way of Sans-Souci and Schönbornslust, Belle-Vue and Bruch-sal.

"Another age shall see the golden ear im-brown the slope and nod on the parterre, Deep harvests bury all his pride has plann'd And laughing Ceres re-assume the land."

BY JEROME MELLQUIST

*The mathematician of color waited fifty years for fame
in the same suburban villa*

Jacques Villon might well be compared to a Renaissance figure. His character might even be said to make him an exact counterpart of those early Humanists. Though living in almost total obscurity while elaborating his "screen" technique, he still managed to participate in many of the most essential group shows of the last fifty years and never closed his mind to the work of other experimenters.

His life presents no snarls of ambiguity. Born in Normandy (at Damville, Eure) in 1875, he apparently underwent no major frustrations when growing up in nearby Blainville-Crevon, the very country of Emma Bovary. His family was neither dry nor crusty, and its noncon-

formity encouraged whatever was talented in its members. The mother painted and etched with ability, and her father, Emile Nicolle, a commission-merchant from Rouen, also practiced the craft of etching, and to such effect that certain of his architectural views are today reposing in the Print Department at the Louvre. Villon himself has recalled that "At an early age I was accustomed to handling copper plates, to the smell of etching acid and the sound of melting varnish." Among his six brothers and sisters, one (who later took the name of Duchamp-Villon) eventually became a sculptor-architect; another (Marcel Duchamp) devoted himself to painting, and so did a sister, Suzanne. When

they sat about the family lamp, it was not apparently to play cards but rather to compare their respective drawings, etchings and modelings. Villon has said that he attempted his first etching at sixteen. "We were in the country and I had neither ground nor mordant for biting the copper. I prepared my plate with melted candle wax and bought acid at the pharmacist's. I used the acid undiluted and the result was catastrophic. I was obliged to begin all over again. After some reflection I diluted the turbulent · solution with water. The result, a portrait of my father was my first etching — signed and dated *G. Duchamp* 1891. My second print done in that same year was a portrait

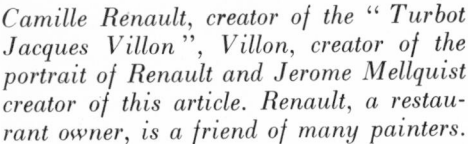

Camille Renault, creator of the " Turbot Jacques Villon", Villon, creator of the portrait of Renault and Jerome Mellquist creator of this article. Renault, a restaurant owner, is a friend of many painters.

This first stage of a poster for the cabaret Le Grillon was one of Villon's early works. 1897. A poet named Levet posed for the large figure. Forty years later Villon added a portrait of Renault, who owns the poster.

of my grandfather. After that I did no more etching until 1899."

The Normandy landscape further imprinted itself on his mind, as his primary schooling was conducted under the shade of its apple-trees, and later, when he entered the *lycée* at Rouen, his etcher-grandfather was delegated to look after him, and also of course to guide him, when he bit out the first of his plates. Before finishing the university and starting his studies in law, he submitted waggish drawings to a local newspaper and they so amused the public that henceforth they were published rather regularly. Nevertheless, obeying his father, he finished his preliminary legal studies and installed himself amidst the foolscap and high stools of a lawyer's office. He would often visit his father on Sundays and they would walk among woodlots where timber was being sold. Once, on such a stroll, a friend had drawn the father aside and urged him not merely to withdraw his son from the law office, but to lend

Villon has worked in this studio at Puteaux, near Paris, for over fifty years. Around him, souvenirs of his sculptor-brother Duchamp-Villon; the latter's bust of Baudelaire (behind the easel) became the subject of a famous Villon etching. The Section d'Or discussion group used to meet here on Sunday afternoons in 1912.

unqualified encouragement to him as an artist. This the enlightened father did, so that when Gaston (who now named himself Jacques Villon both to distinguish himself from other artists in the family and to signify his admiration for the poet-litanist of medieval Paris) reached the capital in 1895, he was given an allowance of one hundred and fifty

francs a month, a comfortable sum for the day. The newly-christened Villon started his professional career without the drawbacks of poverty.

After a brief period in Cormon's atelier Villon became a draughtsman-collaborator of various humorous magazines : *Le Courrier Français, L'Assiette au Beurre, Le Rire, Gil Blas, Le Chat Noir.* He visited the Moulin Rouge, as did Toulouse-Lautrec (who drew, incidentally, for some of the same papers), and led a boisterous life with such friends as Juan Gris, Pascin, who had worked on *Simplicissimus,* and Kupka who once celebrated the New Year for three solid days.

He soon settled himself in the Rue Caulaincourt, and he drank many a glass with his artist friends in the neighboring *bistrots.* Yet he was no idler; his brother Marcel Duchamp has said that almost invariably Villon carried a sketch-pad in his pocket and that sometimes, pencil in hand, he would actually draw figures in the air. This quickened his faculties of observation, while his proximity to such draughtsmen as Forain, Toulouse-Lautrec and Steinlen taught him very much about linear precision. Even today this is reflected in a recent portrait by Villon of the *St Louis Post-Dispatch* publisher, Joseph Pulitzer, Jr. The line of the jaw, the blue glint to the eyes, the strength of the torso—these he noted accurately and well in his preliminary

Jacques Villon meticulously prepares his mixtures of color on small pieces of paper, before starting his canvas.

sketch, and one finds a similar record in much of his work from the late nineties and the first years of the present century. But what sets the drawings of Villon apart from those of his more caustic colleagues attached to the humorous magazines is that his line never stung. It eliminated, twinkled, or insinuated—never did it lacerate. His was too kindly a nature for such a mode of attack.

Marcel Duchamp has also revealed that, in those years, his brother painted very few oils. He sometimes did portraits of his family on his Normandy vacations, and perhaps he undertook an occasional landscape. Otherwise his daily tasks occupied him too fully. Between 1895 and 1907 he produced over thirty lithographs, mostly in color, as well as a few posters resembling those by Chéret—then to be seen all over the city. One of the best however, *Le Grillon*, is more reminiscent of Toulouse-Lautrec than of Chéret. As for his etchings, he once again started using this medium in 1899 and produced by 1910 a total of one hundred and seventy-five prints—repentant ladies, spinning hurdy-gurdies, beach scenes, family views and sometimes a portrait. His portraits of the period are somewhat similar to the cameo-like productions of Helleu, then a favorite with the general public. A lively plate showed Bibi la Purée, a Montmartre figure of those days who insisted that his only shirt had been given to him by Verlaine.

This stay in Montmartre, at least in its first phase, took place during what was to be a last pause before the upheavals of the *Fauves* and Cubists. The Villon of the time painted rather little, but he did come under

" I start from studies made from nature. From them I derive a construction, and a play of arabesques and rythms." Villon.

The plane, *1954* (25½×36″). *Collection Joseph Pulitzer Jr, St. Louis, Missouri.*

The Normandy field, *1953* (15 × 21″). *City Art Museum, Saint Louis, Missouri.*

The mechanical workshop, *1946* (32 × 46″). *Phillips Memorial coll., Washington.*

the influence of Degas' biting line, of Bonnard's melting color, and Forain's satiric pen. He participated as a member in the *Salon d'Automne*'s famous show of 1903 (in his *Portrait* color was broken up in Impressionistic patches), and since then he has always continued to exhibit at this *Salon*. But he did not concentrate upon oils until his principal source of support, *Le Courrier Français*, had ceased publication in 1910. (It could hardly be said that his practice of tinting certain etchings with watercolor developed his capacities as a painter).

However Villon, the observer, was struck one day by the stresses in a group of men pulling at a cable along the Seine and he put the forward pitch of their bodies into an aquatint dated 1907. The next year he expanded this work into a painting, entitled *The Haulers*, and thus emphasized still further his early preoccupation with movement, anticipating the Italian Futurists by two years, despite their subsequent trumpeting about pioneering. Gradually, as Villon stopped drawing for humorous publications, he increased his output of paintings. He studied the

composition of Cézanne, and once, when painting his father, used the receding planes of the Aix master. Associating himself with the Cubists (his brother Marcel, after all, being one of the more advanced among these pioneers), he soon strove for a similar discipline, both in etching and oils.

His next step was to join a group of painters known as the *Section d'Or*. This comprised a faction of Cubists who would meet at the studio of Gleizes, at Courbevoie near Paris, a short walk from Villon's own quarters at Puteaux. Soon these men began to meet weekly at

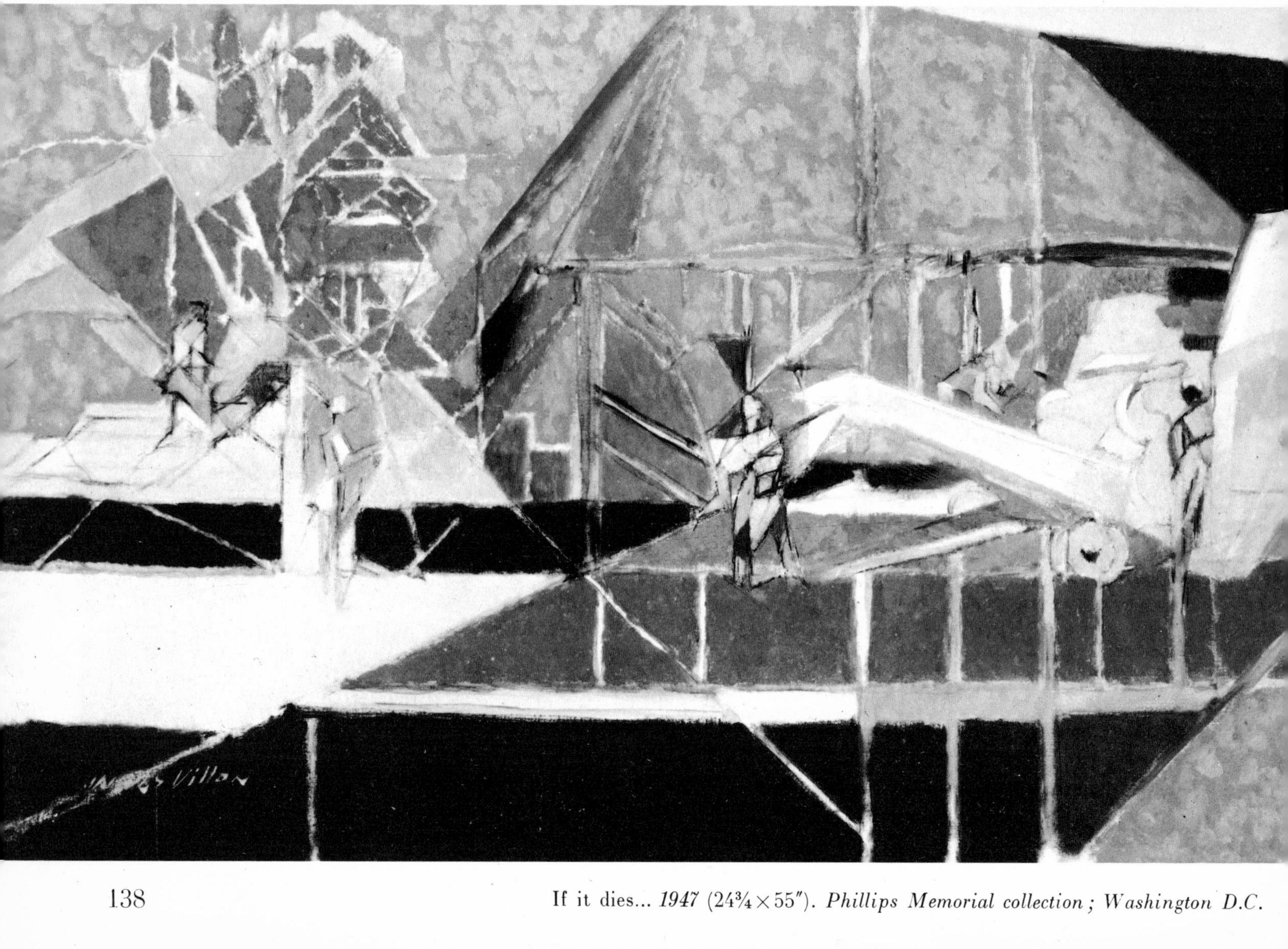

If it dies... *1947* (24¾×55″). *Phillips Memorial collection; Washington D.C.*

his studio, for it was capacious and could hold them all. Here there were battles over the new basic principles of art, participated in by Gleizes and Metzinger, who published the first systematic study on Cubism, Fernand Léger, who would journey over from his trap-like atelier in The Hive, as it was called, Marie Laurencin, Kupka the Czech abstractionist and former illustrator, Delaunay, Le Fauconnier, Picabia and Villon's two brothers, the sculptor-architect Duchamp-Villon, and the resilient-minded Marcel Duchamp ; and finally such bold intellects as Roger Allard, Valensi, André Mare, and the poet-critic Apollinaire. They wondered if a new and ideal canon of form could not be invented. Convinced that it could, they recalled how the Egyptians, with their pyramids, the Greeks, with their hermetic thinkers like Prothagoras, and, still later, Leonardo, Dürer and even Seurat had searched for reality in the light of such conceptions. They even organized a show, calling it the *Section d'Or*, and exhibited as a group in 1912. Perhaps Villon, who sometimes is cre-

Villon made his first etching when he was sixteen, copying his grandfather, Emile Nicolle, an engraver. Unlike most painters who only engrave occasionally between canvases, Villon has always pursued a parallel path, treating the same subject both in paint and in prints. His graphic work includes over nine hundred engravings and lithographs.

dited with being responsible for these sessions, profited most. He became increasingly interested in planning his canvases in terms of pyramidal divisions, recalling, no doubt, how Leonardo had recommended the same approach. He would dissect a canvas by lines from given points, cutting it into smaller areas always subject to the ideal proportion, as was discussed by the group. This procedure did not degenerate into a formula, for each subject required a fresh approach. And then, having found his method, having produced with some regularity as a painter, he was called to the colors in the First World War.

Five years elapsed before he again returned to painting — two years while he served as an infantry corporal in the front lines in Champagne and Artois— and three years more in a camouflage unit. On his return to civilian life he tried to resume his earlier technique, attempting, for instance, to render galloping horses through a series of super-imposed planes, or making etchings in similar style of the bust of Baudelaire by his brother, Duchamp-Villon (a casualty at the very end of the War), or once again experimenting in the abstract manner. Economic need prevented him from devoting

himself entirely to such experiments, and he was obliged, until 1930, to spend most of his energies on various etching commissions. One, undertaken for a platonic dialogue of Paul Valéry, *Eupalinos or the Architect,* involved the preparation of thirty engravings to illustrate

Chess is a favorite game of the whole family. Villon has made several etchings of his sister Suzanne and his brother Marcel playing as children. Marcel Duchamp eventually spent more time at chess than at painting. Here : Villon's Chess board.

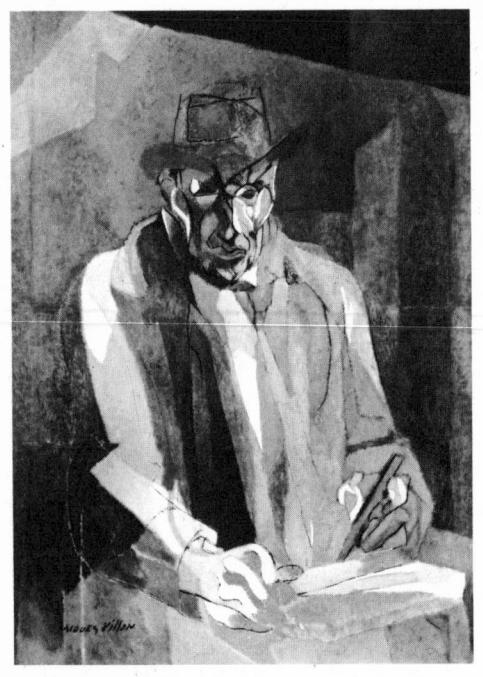

a de luxe edition published by the *Nouvelle Revue Française*. Then, in 1922, he agreed to furnish Bernheim-Jeune with some forty colored intaglio plates : reproductions of paintings by Renoir, Cézanne, Manet, Monet, Picasso and Derain, among others. These plates turned out to be unequalled of their kind. Villon, giving sometimes ten weeks to a single plate, spent himself on the project, and it allowed too little margin for other work. Sometimes he painted semi-abstract oils, recalling his old predilection for horses and movement ; or he composed still-lives, often using the objects on his etching table as subject matter. These same compositions also reappeared in the form of etchings. He exhibited as always at the *Salon d'Automne*. He took part in the vast New York Armory Show of 1913 (where Marcel Duchamp's *Nude Descending A Staircase* provoked both derision and applause), and was shown successfully by the New York dealer, Joseph Brummer. But recognition in the form of support was slow to come and Villon had not yet attracted a regular dealer.

At last, his reproductions were completed and, after 1930, he could devote himself more intensively to painting. Again he applied himself to still-life subjects, depicting spirals or other non-figurative elements within a series of receding planes. He analyzed himself in a painting called *Man Drawing*, and did steady portraits of such friends as the American novelist Francis Steegmuller and his wife Beatrice, who studied with Villon, though officially he never has taken pupils. He seldom

painted a landscape, the first of consequence appearing in 1935. But, nevertheless, this decade was particularly fruitful for Villon, who belongs to that rare species, the late-flowering artist.

The war struck, Paris fell, and Villon fled to the Tarn, near Toulouse. In the summer of 1940, the reticent, patient recluse was driven from his studio by the pressure of events and compelled to stand his easel outdoors. Strange lights shimmered in his work, unforeseen color combinations of citron, rose and airy blue dominated his canvases. A diamond-cutter might have chiselled out the forms in his *Vegetable Gardens at Brunier*. Later, at Beaugency, he painted its still-standing bridge and synthesized in *The Three Orders* the hierarchy of ancient France—the nobles, the clergy and the third estate. After this, he began to use the colors which are now so particularly his, in landscapes at Mougins, in the south, and, much later on, in his panoramic harvest-fields. His palette altered again, black and sultry orange now augmenting his earlier colors. Even the portraits were on a larger scale. Then, as always, he continued etching the same subjects he painted.

His light had penetrated the very shadows. Younger painters, men like Bazaine, Estève, Pignon and Manessier, rallied around him. They came not only for some moral conviction inseparable from the man and his work, but because he had devised a communicable method —his screenlike analysis of color—by which he situated a subject far back within the canvas, settling it there as if to satisfy some philosophic preoccupation with space and balance.

Finally came Villon's official "consecration" : in 1950 an entire room was devoted to him at the Venice Biennale, and he won the first prize at the Carnegie International Exhibition at Pittsburgh. Recognition came late, when he was already seventy-five. His reaction was typical : "This should help me to five more years of good painting". This proved to be an understatement —at eighty the modest master of Puteaux is producing some of his finest work.

Top : Portrait of the artist (39 ½ × 29″). *Carnegie Institute, Pittsburgh. This canvas of 1949 is one of the numerous Villon self-portraits. Like all his portraits, it interprets the human face by geometrical planes and flat surfaces of color, and bears a striking resemblance to the sitter.*

Center : The black stamp, *1926* (36 × 28½″), *Louis Carré collection. Here the artist depicts his work table with his engraving implements. Villon has used this theme on several occasions, both for prints and for paintings. This canvas dates from a figurative manner that occured between two abstract periods.*

Left : Space, *1932* (15½ × 35″), *Louis Carré collection. Villon has worked in the abstract style during two periods : first immediately after the first World War, and then for three years starting in 1931.*

Right : The Three Orders, *1944* (39 ½ × 28¾″), *Louis Carré collection. Painted after the war, at Beaugency, this canvas, by its cathedral, castle and fields, symbolizes the three orders of ancient France.*

Sixteenth Century Cinemascope

BY HANS THOMA

*Trompe-l'œil paintings in a Bavarian castle
evoke the Commedia dell'Arte*

Landshut, an hour by car from Munich, is a typical small Bavarian town which has preserved its medieval atmosphere almost intact. The name means "Defender of the Land" and it still recalls its original function. Landshut was, from 1204, the residence of the Dukes of the house of Wittelsbach—whose descendants were first Electors and, later, Kings of Bavaria until 1918.

At that time, these Princes lived at the castle of Trausnitz, a stronghold whose monumental walls and fortified towers still dominate the town.

Landshut—where the world of the Middle Ages and that of the Renaissance coexist without any visible transition—has a brick church in flamboyant Gothic style and a Renaissance palace built in 1536 by architects from Mantua. The new forms of Italian art reached Bavaria much sooner than they did any of the other German States, partly because of the close commercial relations between the two countries through the neighboring alpine passes, but mainly, because of the dynastic bonds which united the House of Bavaria and the princely Courts of Italy.

Duke Albrecht V, the founder of the celebrated art collections of Munich, was the first great Renaissance Bavarian prince. His eldest son who was to succeed him under the name of Wilhelm V married a daugher of the Duke of Lorraine, in 1536, and, for six years, the Castle of Trausnitz was the principal scene for the amusements of this lively young couple.

Prince Wilhelm, like his father, was a friend and generous patron of the arts. His first preoccupation was to transform the medieval fortress into a castle in tune with the new spirit of the times. He imported gardeners from France and,

with their assistance, laid out some attractive gardens, unfortunately no longer in existence, for the pleasure of his wife. The Castle chapel was famous and for it he engaged Orlando di Lasso, one of the greatest masters of music of the times. There is little trace of all this lavishness. All that remains is the architectural work which transformed the original warrior's keep into a magnificent Renaissance castle. The lively frescos which he had painted to decorate the royal apartments still tell, today, of the gaieties of that brilliant court.

It was the painter Frederick Sustris who presided over the transformation of the castle. This Hollander, born in Italy, had worked in Vasari's studio in Florence. In 1560 he went to Augsburg and a short while afterwards settled in Landshut. Among his collaborators was his brother-in-law Alessandro Scalzi, known as the Paduan, to whom we owe the *trompe-l'œil* frescos reproduced here for the first time, which illustrate so vividly the theatrical taste of the time.

From the second half of the XVth century, the comedies of Plautus and Terence had been acted at the courts of Italy; but along with this intellectual and sometimes boring art there was developing, particularly in Northern Italy, an impromptu form of comedy played by troupes of strolling players, usually in the open air, at first, only patronized by the bourgeoisie and the lower classes. It was an art of pure entertainment, composed of satiric allusions, witty sarcasms, quick repartee and puns often not in the best of taste. The plot and the order of the scenes were the only established factors in this form of theatre which included of endless misunderstandings, intrigues and amorous adventures of the most fantastic kind.

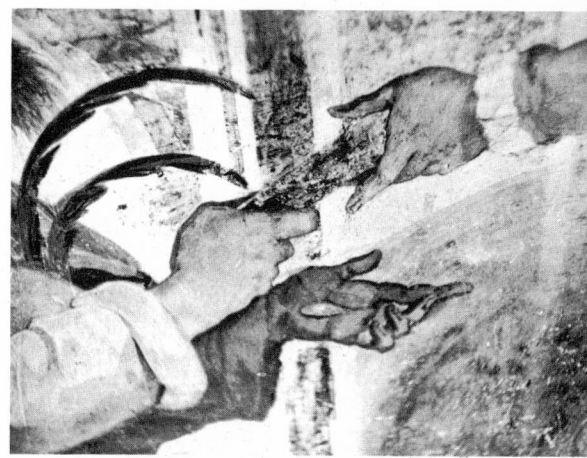

On these pages, details of the frescos that wind up the staircase at Trausnitz Castle, Landshut. Rowdy incidents succeed each other, painted in life-like trompe-l'œil *by Alessandro Scalzi. It is not known if the scenes refer to a specific play.*

Here are various members of the Commedia dell'Arte cast as they appear on the castle walls. From top to bottom: a disapproving onlooker; Zanno with his feathered hat; Pantaloon the elderly gallant. Opposite: a noble lady and her companion apparently melting into the steps.

The actors soon acquired a great public following. In imitation of the Italian courts, the nobles who surrounded the Crown Prince of Bavaria, at Landshut, were highly appreciative of the *Commedia dell'Arte* performances. Audiences easily became familiar with the varied aspects of the characteristic male types featured in what was called, from then on, the *Commedia dell'Arte*: "Pantaloon", the wealthy, miserly bourgeois who is always being tricked and deceived, his carefree servant and companion "Zanno", the "Doctor" from Bologna, so delighted with himself, the "Captain" a blustering soldier who is a coward at heart, "Harlequin", the clown, in a gaudy, close-fitting tunic and many other members of the motley crew. For all these comic and often very vulgar roles, less attention was paid to the text than to miming and to acrobatic skill (how really very clever it is to give someone a slap in the face with one's feet!) The actors had to be musicians, dancers, and acrobats at one and the same time. In intentional contrast to these mountebanks, the actresses were often remarkable for their elegance and charm: they represented true love, under many guises, and also "Cortigiana" (Columbine), the capricious flirt; the only exception to this was an elderly, repellent lady in search of romance.

Several documents of the period mention these quarrelsome, wandering Italian players who disturbed the peaceful life of the city. It is therefore not surprising that their compatriot Alessandro Scalzi chose to depict them when he was called upon to decorate the walls of one of the new staircases at Trausnitz, where thanks to him they live again. The spiral staircase known as the "Clowns' Steps" was constructed to connect every floor of the castle from the cellars to the attic. It was built around a square central frame decorated with slender Tuscan columns and equipped for installing a dumbwaiter. The steps were separated by four landings; the narrowness of the stair-well perhaps explaining the deterioration of the murals which had to be restored in 1597 and again in 1679.

To choose characters from the *Commedia dell'Arte* as a theme for a large-scale fresco was, at that time, a completely revolutionary idea; unfortunately, we possess no contemporary description of these paintings. Are they a simple juxtaposition of the best-known figures from the *Commedia dell'Arte* or are we being shown a succession of scenes from a performance which, per-

haps, took place at the Castle? We can only surmise.

But although we cannot interpret the meaning of the frescos with complete accuracy, they continue to enchant us not only by the wit of their motifs but also by the originality of the treatment. We can imagine the sensation they must have caused almost four hundred years ago.

As it does today, the cinemascopic technique seems to confer on the flat, two-dimensional surface a third dimension, vividly evocative of XVIth century life. The *trompe-l'œil* of Landshut must have fascinated the ladies and gentlemen of the Court by its powers of illusion. No one had ever yet seen the steps of a staircase melt imperceptibly into the frescos surrounding them. No one had ever yet seen characters as large as life, and almost alive, spring from the walls with terrifying reality.

Descending the staircase from the main living quarters, each scene unfolds like a short sequence on the screen. But the staircase is so narrow that it is almost impossible to take in everything with the eye and, even more difficult, with a camera.

The scenes begin with a small negro, framed in a half-open door, holding a dog on a leash. Then, in front of a painting representing Vanity, we see a young girl crowned with flowers: this is Cortigiana. On a balustrade, beneath a pointed arch, stands Harlequin in his motley tunic, while a masked and bearded valet leads a pretty woman away from the steps. Then Pantaloon appears accompanied by his servant; he is singing to someone off stage and nostalgically raises his eyes towards a window where only a cat condescends to appear. Zanno and Pantaloon advance towards each other, and while Zanno pathetically waves his cap, Pantaloon raises a finger. The theme of the half-open door is repeated: a bearded old man follows a gentleman who is signalling to his valet: the latter holds a note in his left hand, a cock in his right and is looking towards a window out of which a young girl is leaning. Servants enter the scene while, further down a man with a plate in his hand (might he have stolen it?) is trying to disappear into the shadow of a door-way. Next we see a dwarf and an old woman with the aspect of a witch and then a man wearing enormous spectacles looking out of a window.

The following scene contains five characters: two servants hold the (stolen?) plate, Pantaloon is threatening two others with a cudgel. An idyllic scene—an elegant young man holding a glass of wine towards a young girl—precedes a more violent one : one valet throws another to the bottom of the stairs. Pantaloon, with a dagger in each hand, runs towards him, while in the background a night-watchman appears with a pike and a lantern. Meanwhile the young girl at the window does not remain inactive ; she empties the contents of her chamber-pot onto the people beneath. And so the game continues, always grotesque and sometimes scurrilous. Here is Pantaloon climbing the staircase astride a donkey, into whose behind Zanno is vainly trying to introduce an enema ; he is greeted by an old man leaning on a crutch and holding a crown of roses and by his servant who is wearing a chamber-pot on his head. Another old man is drinking from a gourd. Then come two figures, with raised daggers, mounting guard over a door. Pantaloon appears, once more, being sprinkled with water by an old woman while he threatens Zanno who is descending the staircase playing the violin. With his right hand Pantaloon seizes the carnation that the beautiful Cortigiana offers him from her window. Cortigiana accompanied by a procuress appears at her door and tries to put a red cap on the head of a young man kneeling at her feet, while Pantaloon hides his face. Another young girl, her valet and a nobleman contemplate the scene. Next it seems that a solution has been found to all the misunderstandings : in the last sequence the old dotard accompanies a lady dressed with great distinction and her elegant cavalier. The servant holding his plate, Pantaloon crouched over a basin vomiting and Zanno carrying his master on his back appear once more. The game is over and it seems almost possible to hear the applause of the delighted audience whose minds had been distracted from the severities of court etiquette by these provocative scenes.

The frescos at Trausnitz are a valuable documentary record of a form of dramatic art which, at that period, was beginning to win public favor. Besides their purely amusement value these paintings constitute one of the first pictorial representations of the *Commedia dell'Arte* and for this reason they are the forerunners of a whole series of masterpieces including the engravings of Jacques Callot, in the XVIIth century, and in the rococo period, the paintings of Watteau and the porcelain figures of Bustelli.

GAUDI

From Nature

to Geometry

BY JOSÉ-LUIS SERT

Those outside Spain who have heard of Antoni Gaudi usually associate his name only with the vast, unorthodox Cathedral of the Sagrada Familia in Barcelona. That enormous, unfinished and extraordinary structure, the epitome of *art nouveau* and a real shock to the unprepared observer, with its decorative sculptures of human and animal forms molded from nature, earned for this Catalan architect-sculptor-builder a reputation as a flamboyant eccentric. Nevertheless his remarkable structural innovations, imaginative and far in advance of his time, have made a contribution of lasting value.

He was born in June 1852, at Reus, near Tarragona, where the man-made landscape of cultivated terraces and the clear light of the region that accentuates the sculptural quality of every natural object, must undoubtedly have influenced him. At sixteen he left Reus and went to study at the Barcelona School of Architecture. Settling in Barcelona, he remained and worked there the rest of his life, seldom leaving it even to travel. His career, especially toward its latter end, was that of an explorer in his craft, devoted single-mindedly to the building arts.

When Gaudi arrived in Barcelona the town had demolished its medieval walls only a few decades before and was rapidly extending its limits. It was a period of extraordinary industrial flowering. Factories—in particular textile works—were springing up everywhere and attracting an increasing number of workers. Building went on at enormous speed. In the field of the Arts, there was a veritable Catalan Renaissance during the last years of the century. Poets, writers, sculptors, painters and architects gathered nightly in cafés and clubs for passionate discussions. A few artists like Picasso left Barcelona for Paris, but Gaudi, bound to his country by the nature of his work, stayed resolutely at home.

Barcelona is near the French border, this kept it in close contact with currents from outside that reached the city in successive waves. The Gothic revival, the writings of Ruskin, the works of the Pre-Raphaelite painters, Wagner's music, the florid *art nouveau* style, and Impressionism all left a permanent mark on many young artists. Gaudi himself was of course influenced, but not deeply changed, by these trends. His work, when studied with care, shows a continuous development, and he undoubtedly owes his liberation from con-

ventional historic styles, and his passionate interest in the forms of nature, to *art nouveau*. Though *art nouveau*, in general, had only a superficial influence and was almost exclusively applied to decoration, it was nevertheless an incentive in leading Gaudi toward a greater freedom in structure and toward experimenting with new materials and forms.

Through his friends in the " Circol de Sant Lluc " and the " Ateneu Club " and through his patron, Count Güell, Gaudi got to know the writings of Ruskin. Güell, who was a great patron of the Arts, travelled constantly to England, France, Italy and Central Europe. But little by little Gaudi ceased to see his friends. During his last few years when he had discovered and defined the definitive form of his highly personal style, he lived the life of a recluse in his studio near the huge Sagrada Familia church and devoted himself entirely to his work. He considered the other buildings he constructed as only experiments for his " Cathedral of the Poor," as the population of Barcelona called it, for it was financed, at the beginning, by public charity. Gaudi, hat in hand, helped to collect the funds. A fervent Catholic, it was in the street in front of

unfinished Sagrada Familia cathedral, Barcelona.

the cathedral that he was killed by a bus one day in June 1926.

It is only in recent years that Gaudi's name has begun reappearing in international art magazines and in books. He had long been forgotten. And yet, if we examine his work closely there is no doubt that he was one of the most remarkable architects of his time. He was a creative researcher, experimenting all his life with new forms and methods of building, and he made a series of very interesting discoveries. Why, then, was recognition so late in coming?

Possibly because Gaudi worked in isolation, did not travel, or write or publicize his work in any way. Perhaps also because his most popular works are those that were most influenced by the bad taste of his time and are correspondingly outmoded today. This is particularly true of the portal of the Sagrada Familia over-decorated with mouldings in the exhuberant manner of *art nouveau*. Salvador Dali and the surrealists seem only to have appreciated the " delirious " aspect of his work which is entirely superficial and they were not interested at all in the more serious side of his experiments.

Most of Gaudi's works remained unfinished, for a very sound reason—finances. Gaudi's buildings, because of their sculptural character and the mate-

These giant stone snails lie abandoned outside the atelier, at the foot of the Sagrada Familia cathedral, where Gaudi worked until his death. He had intended them to be placed on the exterior walls. In a desire to renew decorative style, the architect turned to forms of nature. He often made castings directly from shells, animals and even humans.

Opposite : a massive decorative motif high up on the cathedral façade. Representing a cluster of stars and a bird, it rises from a balcony outside one of the four labyranthine interior staircases. These link the spires. Of the twelve spires planned, only four were finished. Beyond the balcony, a view of mid-town Barcelona.

Gaudi liked to design even the fixtures and interiors of his buildings. He conceived the chair, below, looking like a recent functional model, in 1905. Its concave seat and the angle of the back make it remarkably comfortable. Below, right, a font at the Güell chapel near Barcelona, made from a giant shell and wrought iron.

rials he used, cost fabulous sums. By the square yard, Gaudi was without doubt the most " expensive " architect of his period. There always came a moment when the money gave out.

It was during the last quarter of the

XIXth century, one of the most confused periods of architecture in world history, that Gaudi began his researches into new structural forms. His position is unique and can only be compared to that of Viollet-le-Duc, whose ideas, as expressed in his book " Conversations on Architecture ", greatly influenced Gaudi in his student years. Gaudi's attitude toward the architecture of the past and to the revival of former styles was identical to Viollet-le-Duc's, but the latter was not a creator. Gaudi carried out what Viollet could only write about.

In examining Gaudi's early work, and to appreciate it as it deserves, we must take into consideration the fact that these buildings were designed at a time when other architects were only inspired by styles from the past—styles that no longer had any real validity. Architects had ceased to be builders and had become decorators. Structural problems had come to be only the concern of engineers. The Gothic revival was followed by Romanesque, Byzantine and Moorish styles—all applied superficially to any type of building : apartment houses, private homes, concert halls or railroad stations. The Moorish manner became a favorite for public baths—perhaps because there was no such tradition among the Christians.

Gaudi's early buildings, such as the Vicens house (1878-1888) show some of these revivalist trends ; for example

151

The snail-like form, right, is a chimney stack on the Milá apartment house roof. It is covered in white ceramic fragments.

Moorish decoration in plaster and ceramic tile. He soon abandoned these tendencies and developed more individuality, as in the house in the village of Comillas in the north of Spain known as " El Capricho " and, particularly in the Güell house (1885-1889) built for his patron in Barcelona. Some of it recalls Eastern architecture and the Venitian palaces. Gaudi never saw Venice or the Near East, but he must have been influenced by the books of Ruskin.

Even at this period, the parabolic arches in the entrance, the light structure of the dome in the main living room, and the imaginative chimneys on the roof forecast the best of Gaudi's later work. The dome is three stories high, built so airily that it seems to rest on nothing, a piece of architectural virtuosity. Another interesting feature of this house is the glazed openings between rooms which give a continuity of space and show the contrasted shapes of the various rooms flowing into one another. Many years were to pass before other architects became aware of the possibilities of this innovation.

In wanting to liberate himself from the styles of the past and by rejecting the backward trends of his time, Gaudi searched, even in his early years, for new elements of decoration in the forms of nature. He reproduced flora and fauna

A newspaper stand installed outside the Milá house. The curved lines of this window are repeated throughout the building.

directly from life : large ceramic sunflowers in " El Capricho ", floral designs in wrought iron for the Güell house, a dragon on the gateway of the Güell villa, shells and lizards on a colossal scale for the Sagrada Familia, some of which can still be seen on the grass outside his studio. His interest in natural forms led him to make plaster casts of men and animals to be used as elements of sculpture.

His careful observation of nature and of the structure and appearance of natural elements led Gaudi to a deeper study of the laws that govern them. What started as a search for new decorative subjects became of increasing importance when applied to buildings as a whole. And so this study of natural forms developed into the search for static laws and geometric principles governing these forms and their behavior (resistance to loads, to changes of temperature and to rain, etc.). His profound and sincere approach to religion which increased as he grew older, coincided with his growing admiration for nature that initiated him to his greatest discoveries.

In the Calvet house (1894-1904) columns are decorated to look like trees, but this has no structural significance. In later years, especially in his last studies for the Güell Chapel and the Sagrada Familia, the " tree column " developed its full significance. These columns do not only resemble trees, they also behave like them, with a definite purpose, transmitting separ-

Towering chimney stacks and stair outlets on the roof of the Milá apartment house, Barcelona. Here, although they are invisible from below, the exuberant Catalan architect created plastic shapes entirely for his own pleasure. These constructions resemble medieval knights or abstract sculpture ; they were designed in various materials between 1905 and 1910.

ate roof loads, spreading different branches in order to fulfill their structural function better. Something similar happens with his roofs and vaultings as they tend to become light, shell-like structures, with a strength derived from their warped shapes. Gaudi had observed corrugations and curvatures in nature and had noticed their rigidity and resistance despite their apparent lightness.

The Batlló house (1905-1907) marked a great step forward in the direction of functionalism. There superimposed decoration is greatly reduced and the overall forms are emphasized. The furniture that he designed at the time goes through the same evolution. Its form becomes purer and discards ornament in favor of comfort : it is definitely conceived in terms of its function as furniture and even today is astonishingly modern in appearance.

The trend is carried even further in the Milá house (1905-1910)—his last apartment building. For it, he conceived a flexible interior where columns

would replace bearing walls, and where only screen partitions would be needed. This system which later became standard in office buildings, would permit each tenant to subdivide interior space to suit his needs best. The heavy stone façade, magnificent in its sculptural quality, contrasts with the lightness of other parts of the building, such as the attic under the roof, where parabolic arches, in thin brick partitions, act as ribs and their height, varying with the changing widths, determines the undulating lines of the roof. Iron and glass are used for the entrances and balconies. The general design suggests the forms of nature, but it is no longer a direct transcription of these forms.

Gaudi experimented as much and as often as he could with the sculptural possibilities of architecture; this he did for his own pleasure, for example on the roofs of the Güell, Batlló and Milá houses, in places that cannot be seen from below, only visited by maids coming up to hang laundry. Although some of his earlier work was more colorful because of his use of tile mosaic, the sculptural elements of the Milá roof—chimney stacks and stair outlets—show Gaudi's real plastic gifts. They have the fullness, the monumental quality of traditional Mediterranean sculpture, not unrelated to the work of Picasso and Maillol.

Soon after Gaudi undertook the building of the Sagrada Familia in 1883, he realized that he would never be satisfied by applying the Gothic revivalist principles that were then the accepted formula. He wanted to modernize Gothic—in his own words to "continue the work where the great builders of the Middle Ages left off." He soon decided to do away with buttresses, "crutches" as he liked to call them. This brought him to one of his greatest discoveries, the tilted column, designed to take the diagonal thrust. He carried this idea further until he gave it full-scale application in the Güell park (1900-1914) and the Güell chapel (1898-1914).

The Güell park rises in terraces on the side of a hill. Gaudi wanted to preserve and even accentuate the natural characteristics of the site. With this in mind, he used stone quarried from

Serpentine bench at the Güell park, on a hill near Barcelona, winds its brightly-colored path above the retaining wall. It is encrusted with odd pieces of broken ceramics. The mosaic face in the foreground recalls Miro, who played here as a child.

the hillside, so that the structures seem to spring from the soil itself. The plan he formed was as follows: to build retaining walls, viaducts and terraces. which would follow exactly and prolong the undulations of the hillside. The curved lines of the walls were determined with mathematical preciseness. The tree-columns supporting the viaducts and the terraces were designed by the same process—their form and angle were those most suited to their function. But Gaudi was aware that these forms could be more than merely functional. He gave them an exciting sculptural quality and the most varied textures. These range from rough stone found on the site, to different shapes of bricks forming patterns of light and shade, to mosaics made with ceramic tiles and glass of the most contrasting designs and colors.

From the vast terrace of the Güell park there is a magnificent panorama of the city and of the distant Mediterranean. Benches, also serving as balustrades, follow a continuous undulating line that recalls the pattern left upon the sand by the receding tide. These benches are entirely covered in mosaics made of broken ceramic tiles whose contrasting and unexpected colors and shapes speak of most varied origins. Gaudi had two problems to solve when covering these benches : one technical, the other financial. Winding along for several miles, their curved surfaces could not be covered with ordinary flat tiles. Gaudi's solution consisted in using the valueless broken tiles, left-overs from

The porter's lodge at the entrance of the Güell park, glistening with polychrome mosaics.

the tile-ovens. The Güell Park is consequently an enchanting playground for children, exciting their imagination with the free fantasy of its colors and forms.

Gaudi also planned a small housing center for the workers of the Güell textile mills in Santa Coloma de Cervelló, near Barcelona. This included a chapel, that was to become a laboratory in which he tested his new theories. Only the crypt was ever finished, as Count Güell died before Gaudi had completed his most ambitious project. Nevertheless, the part that does exist is the best and most interesting example of Gaudi's late work.

The chapel is situated in the midst of a pine grove. The tilted columns of the entrance porch—of different diameters, shapes and materials—twist and branch out like real trees. Their branches support the vaulting which, like the columns, is in varied shapes and textures. The outside walls follow undulating lines and are inclined like the columns. All the elements of the building, columns, walls and ceiling have warped forms—in this precise case hyperbolic paraboloids. The sections of the columns vary in relation to the loads they carry and the resistance of the materials used. The branches of the columns fan out in different directions like ribs or the veins of leaves, creating varied effects of light and shadow on the ceilings. Parts of these are decorated with broken tiles, mosaics forming

crosses, or other religious symbols. The windows of different sizes are also defined by their interesting warped forms. The great variety of elements of different shapes and sizes in this building hold together because they all belong to the same family of forms— and what otherwise might have been totally devoid of harmony, achieves a miraculous unity. Gaudi, who was very well aware of the law of nature which groups forms, in plants or animals, by families, applied the same basic principles to his architecture.

He used some of the discoveries he made in the Güell chapel when working on the models for the Sagrada Familia. But he constantly corrected and improved these models which began as diagrammatic skeletons of string and wire in which loads were represented by small proportionate weights. In all his later models, hyperboloids replaced hyperbolic paraboloids. His forms were so rigorously governed by geometric principles that, by following the principles he used, it was possible to reconstruct, with the utmost precision, the models which were destroyed during the Spanish Civil War. These final models represent some of his very best work.

It was only when Gaudi, in his study of natural forms and their behavior, discovered the structural and geometric laws that govern these forms, that he was able to give real unity and sculptural quality to his buildings. The contrast between his earlier works and the more

Windows of the Güell chapel like open mouths, framed in multicolored mosaic.

sharply defined shapes of his later work is clearly evident if we compare the portal of the Nativity and the lower part of what is finished of the Sagrada Familia with the magnificent contours of its four spires. The difference is also evident between the existing portals and those planned for the west entrance of the church.

Gaudi's Cathedral remains unfinished. Though it has no roof, with but one portal and only four spires out of the twelve planned, it stands as a symbol of faith and courage. One can like it or not like it, but it is impossible to remain indifferent to its grandeur. Certain modern artists and engineers are making more and more specific use of light structures which resemble, in form, shells and other elements of nature. These forms, some of which are warped, are obviously going to play an increasingly important role in the future. We cannot continue to construct our cities limiting ourselves to edifices exactly like boxes, exclusively inspired by the system of the slab and the pillar. In the continuous evolution of modern architecture, it is more than likely that Gaudi's last experiments will acquire increasing value and will be more fully appreciated. Then his importance as a pioneer and a prophet will be acknowledged.

Gaudi tested his most daring theories at the Güell chapel, near Barcelona. He used inclined columns for the porch, their varying tilts and textures suggest the tree trunks outside.

The retaining walls, viaducts and terraces of the Güell park follow the curving lines of the hillside. These supporting tree-columns are built out of stone from the site; they are inclined to take the diagonal thrust, in application of Gaudi's curious principle of the tilted column. As usual, Gaudi's use of texture is striking.

Le Comte de Guitaut

Pomp and Propaganda

BY HENRI HELL

A book made for Louis XIV brings back to life a magnificent fête
staged to extol the glory of the young King

The Library of Versailles, now housed in the former Ministry of Foreign Affairs, still in the same condition in which it was at the time of the Revolution, contains many precious volumes from the royal collections and from the libraries of Madame de Pompadour and Madame du Barry. One of the most remarkable of these books is the copy of The Carrousel of 1662 *that belonged to Louis XIV. We shall see presently what this "Carrousel" was. But first let us look at the book from which some of the best plates are reproduced on the following pages.*

It appeared in 1670—eight years after the event it commemorated. Its publication marked the inauguration of the Bureau of Engravings, founded by Colbert. The plates, of which there were thirty-seven, were commissioned from the engraver, Sylvestre, who received eight thousand livres for the work. It is worth noting that Mignard only received three hundred livres for a portrait of Louis XIV. The text was entrusted to Charles Perrault, the author of the celebrated fairy-tales. Some copies, intended for foreign courts, were issued with a text in Latin. Books of this sort, published with very definite purposes in view, would, today, be called propaganda. The Livres de fête, *elaborate illustrated descriptions of "the entries of sovereigns into their loyal towns," printed in various countries of Europe from the XVIth century on, were aimed at promoting policy by prestige, much as do the publications put out by official information services today.*

The copy from which the plates we reproduce are taken, was painted in gouache for Louis XIV by Jacques Bailly (1629-1679), an artist of astonishing versatility, who devoted his talent to the glorification of the King. He painted mostly flowers and miniatures, and designed the tapestries of the Elements and the Seasons preserved in the Paris Bibliothèque Nationale.

The "Carrousel" of 1662 was one of the most sumptuous fêtes of the Roi Soleil's reign. It was the only one witnessed by the populace. It took three months of preparation. The Court architect, Ludovic Vigarini, constructed a wooden amphitheatre with fifteen thousand seats, which was set up in the garden of the Grande Mademoiselle, the King's cousin, opposite the

Le Duc d'Anguin　　　*Le Marquis de Canaple*

ESCVYER ET PAGE TVRCS

L A Coiffure étoit moitié Bonnet & moitié Turban. Le Bonnet étoit de fatin bleu brodé d'argent, & le Turban étoit de toille d'argent rayé de bleu: Outre les plumes ordinaires, il y en avoit encore en forme d'ailles, tant fur le Bonnet qu'aux deux épaules, de couleur de la Quadrille.

La vefte étoit de fatin bleu, doublée de toille d'argent, & bordée de fatin brodé d'or & d'argent.

Le caparaçon du cheval de l'Ecuyer étoit une peau de Lyon, dont la crinière étoit d'or.

Et le caparaçon du cheval du Page étoit de fatin bleu brodé d'argent, & bandé de fatin noir brodé d'or, avec des Croiffans d'argent.

TIMBALIER ET TROMPETTE INDIENS

LA Coiffure du Timbalier étoit un grand Perroquet, accompagné de deux petits ſur ſes épaules avec leurs plumes de couleur naturelle.

Le fonds de l'habit étoit couleur de chair brune chamaré de jaune & de noir: le jaune étoit brodé d'argent, & le noir étoit brodé d'or. Le caparaçon & banderolle étoit des bandes de ſatin jaune & de ſatin noir brodé d'or & d'argent.

Tuileries. Henri de Gissey, the designer for the "Royal Pleasures and Ballets", was entrusted with creating the costumes.

"Carrousels" are not a French form of fête; they were unknown in France before the reign of Henri IV. They were a kind of equestrian spectacle on the most lavish scale, with magnificent amphitheatres, floats, musicians, songs, recitations of verse and equestrian ballets. In this sense, the "Carrousel" of 1662 was a real carrousel in name only. In actual fact, it was a kind of elaborate sporting event which gave the nobles an occasion to cavort and parade before the King. It was very exclusive;

Le Cheualier du Plessys   *Le Marquis de Genlis*

PAGES ROMAINS

LE bonnet étoit de ſatin couleur de feu brodé en bandes d'or & d'argent. Les Pages étoient vétus des mêmes étoffes, & des mêmes couleurs que les précédans Officiers de la Quadrille, à la reſerve que le corps étoit de brocart d'or brodé par écailles d'argent, & que les lambrequins tant des hauts des manches que de la ceinture, étoient taillées en écailles de ſatin couleur de feu, brodé d'or & doublé de toile d'argent.

the participants were hand-picked by the King himself. The five brigades or troops of horse which took part in the carrousel were led by the greatest names in the kingdom and arrived in the exact order of rank that each of them occupied in the State. First came the King's troop, dressed as Romans. Then, successively, the troop of Monsieur, the King's brother, as Persians; a Turkish and an Indian troop led respectively by the Prince de Condé and the Duc d'Enghien, both of whom were Princes of the blood; finally, a troop of "Americans", led by the Duc de Guise.

The parade started from the Hôtel de Vendôme and marched down the Rue de Richelieu, the Rue Saint-Honoré and the Rue Saint-Nicaise. Each troop was composed as follows: the trumpets in the front rank, followed by the drums, then slaves on foot leading horses, and finally pages on horse-back. The leader of the troop rode either in front or behind. The people of Paris— a huge crowd massed even on the roof-tops—were thus able to admire a dazzling and colorful cavalcade in which good taste was rivalled by splendor. The Romans were dressed in flame and gold, the Persians in silver and pink, the Turks in blue and black, the Indians in every color of the rainbow, while the "Americans" wore green and violet. The costumes, which were all of the same style, displayed an astonishing variety. There was an extraordinary profusion of plumes, ribbons, embroideries and precious stones. Each costume deserves a separate and detailed description.

160

LE DVC DE GVYSE, ROY AMERIQVAIN

LA cuiraſſe étoit de peau de Dragons, dont les deux teſtes ſe rencontrant ſur les épaules, vomiſſoient les manches, dont celle de deſſus étoit de brocart vert, rebrodé de même que l'habit, & celle de deſſous de toile d'argent qui deſcendoit juſque ſur le poignet, étoit liée d'un bracelet de groſſes Emeraudes, & les quëües de Dragons faiſoient des lambrequins; le tout chargé d'une broderie de perles & de rubis, ainſi que les brodequins.

A mere Indian drummer had a huge parrot as a headdress and two smaller ones perched on his shoulders. A Turkish equerry wore plumes in the shape of wings (on his cap and on both shoulders) and the mane of his horse, caparisoned in lion-skin, was threaded with gold. The Duc de Guise as an American king was perhaps the most extraordinary of all: his breast-plate was decorated with dragon scales (with two dragons' heads on the shoulders): his head-dress was of green and white feathers, surmounted by three enormous plumes; a horn transformed his horse into a unicorn. It's mane and tail were covered with writhing serpents. Louis XIV, as a Roman Emperor, sparkled with jewels. It is amusing to note that most of these jewels were nothing but ordinary glass and that the few real diamonds the King wore did not belong to him but had been rented from jewellers.

The emblem on the King's shield was the sun with, as a motto, the phrase Ut vidi vici, inspired by Julius Caesar's phrase: Veni, vidi, vici. In imitation, the nobles also had emblems and mottos which were variations on the theme of the sun. The emblem of the Comte de Vivonne represented a burning-glass, that of the Comte de Navailles an eagle looking at the sun, that of the Comte de Saint-Aignan a laurel exposed to the sun, that of the Comte de Lude a sun-dial exposed to the sun, that of the Comte de Feuillade a sun-flower turning towards the sun, etc.

Several of the mottos proclaimed much personal pride, such as the Prince de Condé's: "He grows while you watch" or that of the Marquis d'Illiers: "It matters not how long I endure providing I rise".

After parading through the streets, and after enjoying the admiration of the crowds, the procession emerged into the amphitheatre, the entrance to which was covered by French and Swiss guards. The boxes, hung with violet velvet embroidered with fleur-de-lys, were occupied by the most distinguished members of the public—none but the greatest names in France— Queen Maria-Theresa, the Queen of England, Henrietta of France, Madame, Mademoiselle, etc. The cavalcade paraded three times round the amphitheatre beneath the eyes of the great ladies. When the parade was over, the jousting began. It lasted two days (the third and fourth of June). They tilted at the ring, hurled lances and wielded their swords. These exercices, with no element of violence, would seem very monotonous today. They were games of skill, very like those played by children, riding the roundabouts in public gardens, which consist of trying to thrust a stick through a ring while the wooden horses revolve.

The king gave

> *"... so many fair signs*
> *of his great dexterity,*
> *one would think in verity,*
> *(so determined was he on victory)*
> *that only he would have the glory."*

This clumsy verse is meant to convey that he did not achieve the particular glory of victory but was content to be admired in all his solar brilliance. The winners were the Marquis de Bellefonds (who was in Monsieur's troop) and the Comte de Sault (who was in Monsieur le Prince's troop) whose motto was "He always rises in the esteem of his forebears." The former received as a prize, at the hands of Queen Maria-Theresa, a diamond worth nine thousand livres, and the latte a box embellished with a portrait of the King, valued at eight th usand six hundred livres.

After the Carrousel of 1662 the remainder of the "chaotic garden" where it had taken place was levelled and transformed into an "orderly tilt-yard" which ever since has been called, in honor of the event, the Place du Carrousel.

What was the pretext for this Carrousel? What was the occasion for the display of such magnificence? The official reason seems to have been the birth of the Dauphin, to whom the principal nations of the world came to pay homage. But nothing is less certain. It was long claimed, repeating what Voltaire had said in "The Century of Louis XIV", that it was organized so as to seduce Mademoiselle de la Vallière: the King was said to have wanted to display himself to her in all his glory. But, romantic and appealing as this hypothesis is, it too must be abandoned. The King, always fickle, was courting the favors of Mademoiselle de la Motte-Houdancourt at the time.

Probably the Carrousel was organized without any particular motive, except that of allowing the young King, then in his prime and at the height of his power, to give his subjects and foreign courts visible proof of the magnificence of his reign. Or perhaps it was intended to leave to posterity a perfect picture of the pomp in which he lived.

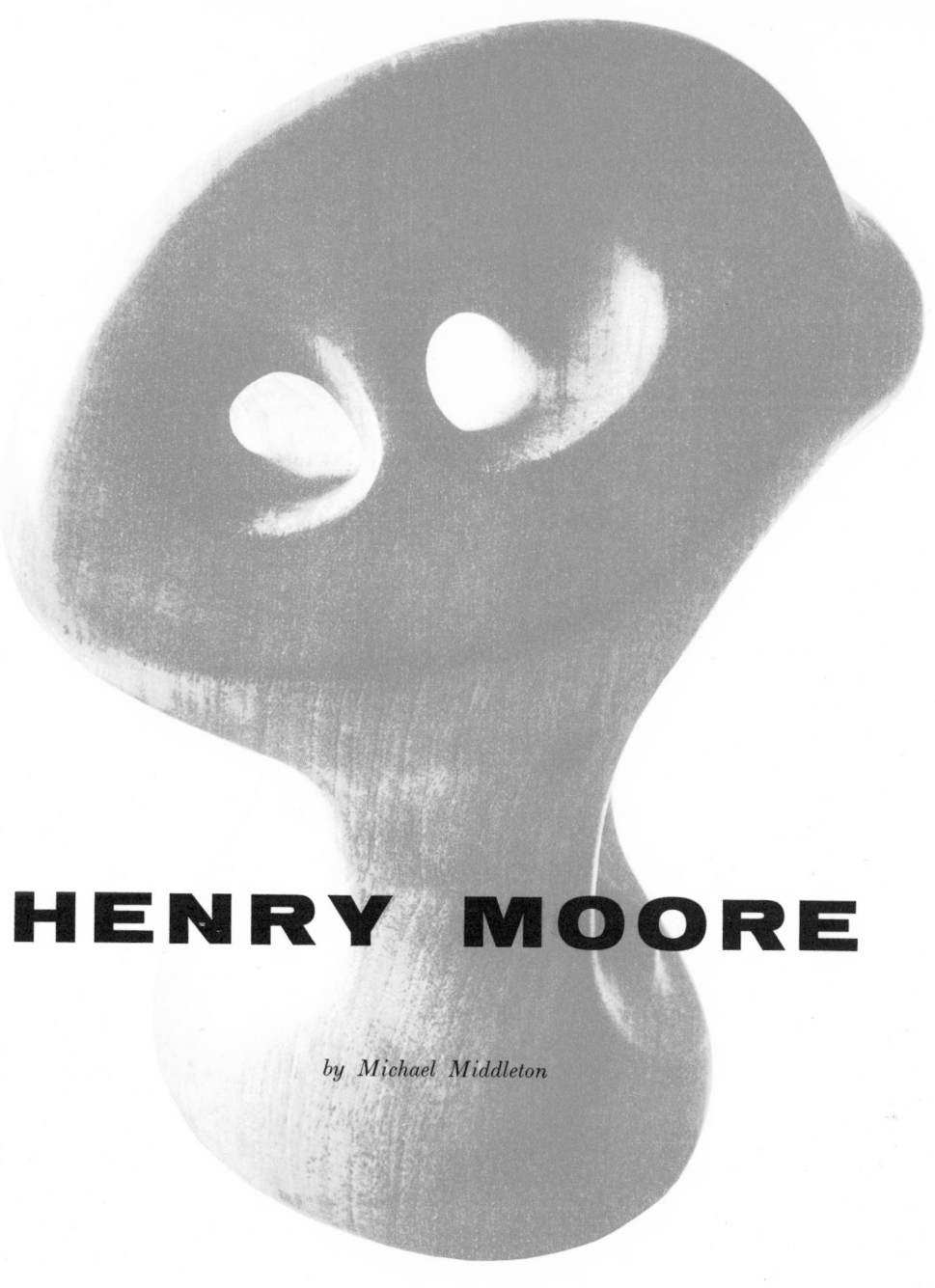

HENRY MOORE

by Michael Middleton

Perry Green is about thirty miles north of London, a mere cluster of cottages. Set back from the road by a great fore-court, the house is low, whitewashed, with a steeply-pitched roof. There are two studios to the side, amongst a little clutter of shacks ; the larger was a stable, the smaller, until very recently, was the village shop. But sculpture can be very big, and if it is destined to be placed in the open it is best carved in the open, under the sun and the sky. So often, across the hedge, the sculptor can be seen at work in this forecourt ; sometimes, when there is a rush on, he is there with his assistants working into the night by the glare of floodlights.

This is the home of Henry Moore. Here, tramping through the lanes of the gently rolling Hertfordshire landscape, come the unannounced strangers from across the world ; and in their cars, the publishers, the critics, the museum directors, the collectors. There is a tea-urn in the kitchen now, for on a Saturday afternoon there may be twenty or thirty visitors at a time.

Moore at fifty-seven is generally recognized as the foremost sculptor of his generation. Since the war, important collections of his work have been shown in forty-five cities in sixteen foreign countries ; sculptures and drawings by him may be found in the permanent collections of at least twenty-five museums throughout the world ; to him have come the two most important international sculpture awards, at the Venice Biennale in 1948 and the São Paolo Biennale in 1953.

Great pressures are brought to bear upon the artist who becomes a world figure. As well as artist he must become ambassador and businessman. He is expected to sit on committees, lead delegations, be filmed and photographed ; his wastepaper-basket will be scavenged, his smallest doodle framed. Commissions will flood in upon him from all over the world, but he must rigorously exclude those to which his art is not properly attuned, must always leave himself time for his own work and study. These things have not changed Henry Moore. In England, the northcountryman has a reputation for shrewd commonsense and Moore has little use for the outward trappings of success (he is reputed to have declined the honor of a Knighthood).

re in front of a wood sculpture Internal and External Forms, *1953.*

In build be is shortish and stocky—not heavy, but with a certain sturdiness that suggests the workman and the craftsman. His father was a miner, and you feel that his own two feet are set firmly on the ground in a way that recalls Picasso and Braque and Léger. He is a friendly man, quite without pretensions, at once quick and gentle and firm, unaggressive but sure of himself. It is noticeable that the wider public in Britain, even when it has failed to understand his work, seems always to have sensed its dignity and integrity. Moore has never been subjected to attacks as virulent as those upon, say, Epstein or Reg Butler in an earlier, and a later generation.

He was born on July 30th 1898, at Castleford in Yorkshire. Barbara Hepworth, who lived only a few miles away, has described the noise, dirt and smell of that industrial background of "stunted grass, collieries, slag heaps, pit ponies, foundries by the railway lines, distant hills wreathed with indigo smoke which the very earth seemed to be exhaling." Moore won a scholarship to the local Grammar School, trained as a teacher, joined the army in 1917, was gassed at Cambrai and invalided back to England. On his demobilization in 1919 he obtained a grant to attend the Leeds School of Art, moved to the Royal College of Art in London two years later, and there won a travelling scholarship in 1925 which took him to Paris and Italy. On his return, in order to supplement his income, he taught, as is the English way, in art schools until 1939. In 1928 he held his first one-man exhibition. The following year he married.

The sculpture tradition in England, unlike that of painting, is so tenuous as to be almost non-existent. The only foundations upon which a young man in the early 'twenties could build were the exuberant early promise of the young Gaudier-Brzeska, killed in the First World War, and the early carvings of Jacob Epstein, and perhaps Frank Dobson. From them sprang the most potent doctrine of the period : truth to material and the necessity for direct carving. Upon Moore the effect of this concept was powerfully reinforced by his repeated visits to the British Museum—first to the Egyptian galleries ; later to the archaic Grecian "with its lifesize female figures seated in easy, still naturalness, grand and full like Handel's music" ; and then to the Etruscan, Palaeolithic and Ethnographical rooms. Pre-Columbian Mexican sculpture in particular he found "true and right, perhaps because I immediately hit upon similarities in it with some XIth century carvings I had seen as a boy on Yorkshire churches." In its richness of form-invention it still seems to him unsurpassed by any other period of stone sculpture. Echoes of the recumbent rain-god Chacmool (into whose belly the Paris, Stockholm and London crowds attending the Mexican exhibition were throwing their votive coins a couple of years ago) may be found throughout the long series of reclining figures for which Moore is best known. Today, the only sculptures to be found in his own home, apart from one or two of his own pieces, are Mexican fragments in two wall-cabinets, one of them a chunky head given to him by Diego Rivera.

He was affected too by Masaccio and Michel-Angelo ; by Brancusi and Archipenko and above all Picasso ; by the belated impact upon Great Britain of Surrealism, and perhaps by the arrival there of Moholy-Nagy, Gabo and Mondrian. Yet, looking back upon Moore's œuvre over thirty years, what strikes one most is its consistency and its steady development. By the early, thirties the reclining-figure theme and the mother-and-child theme had both become predominant in his figurative work ; the smooth, organic forms which grew into the stringed figures or baskets of 1937-9, and the encounters between detached monolithic forms of a more square and heavy monumentality—these contained the germ of all his subsequent non-figurative work.

From 1930 onwards there was a growing sense in nearly everything he did of the mass being pushed from within by its own inner energy. "For me," says Moore, "a work must

Moore took this photograph of his Standing Figure *in the Hertfordshire plains (7 feet 3 ins. high).*

"I know nothing about photography technically, but I have been taking photographs of my own sculpture for twenty years." Here, photographed by Moore: (above) Draped Reclining Figure, bronze, 1952-1953 (5 feet 2 ins. long), Time Life Building London; (below) Reclining Figure, bronze, 1951 (7 feet 6 ins.) Arts Council coll. England. "The human figure is what interests me most."

first have a vitality of its own. . I do not mean a reflection of the vitality of life, of movement, physical action, frisking, dancing figures and so on, but that a work can have in it a pent-up energy, an intense life of its own, independant of the object it represents." This was perhaps only another aspect of the artist's growing preoccupation with opening-up the sculptural mass. "The first hole made through a piece of stone," he was to write, "is a revelation. A hole can itself have as much shape-meaning as solid mass. Sculpture in air is possible, where the stone contains only the hole, which is the intended and considered form." Moore was not the first to invest sculpture with spatial attributes which were at one time considered to be the prerogative of architecture, but he has done more to exploit those attributes in an organic sense, as opposed to a constructive sense, than any other sculptor.

From a formal point of view this penetration of the solid serves to increase our awareness of its three-dimensionality, and to make explicit the thrusts and tensions within. From a poetic point of view it touches deep chords in the human psyche. Over the surfaces of Henry Moore's figures, over breasts and thighs and head and hands, round mountain, through arch and cave and mysterious tunnel, the eye and mind of the spectator may roam as freely as in a dream-landscape, voyaging in time and space. It would be an over-

Chalk, pen and watercolor sketch, Reclining Figures, belonging to the sculptor's wife; 1947 (11×9½"). Moore has written: "Every few months I stop carving and do life drawing. My drawings are done mainly as a help towards making sculpture."

simplification to say that Graham Sutherland has turned landscape into a metaphor for the human figure, and that Moore has turned the human figure into landscape. Nevertheless there are profound affinities between the biomorphic forms that both artists have created, and here we touch upon a conception that has proved peculiarly fruitful in British art.

In the XVIIIth century Gainsborough used to construct model landscapes of cork and coal and broken stones, mosses and lichens. Paul Nash, Graham Sutherland and Henry Moore

Some years ago the sculptor executed a series using strings and wires threaded through wood or metal. This example, of lead and wire, from the Museum of Modern Art, New York; 1940.

have all likewise had about them curious objects found on their walks—strangely shaped stones, fragments of bone and bark which have served to stimulate their imagination. This same double image, this ambiguous presence, informs much of the work by Sutherland and Moore. Let me quote from Sutherland, writing of the Welsh landscape: "Sometimes, lying through sheer laziness on the warm shore, my eye became rivetted to what it would—some sea-eroded rocks, for instance, which I would notice were reproducing, precisely in miniature, the forms of the inland hills."

It was just this apprehension of what Baudelaire called "the universal analogy", this ability, like William Blake, "to see the world in a grain of sand", which led Moore for a time to associate himself with the Surrealists. Moore's substitutions and equivalences, however, unlike those of orthodox Surrealism, have always been implicit rather than explicit.

"The human figure", he has written, "is what interests me most deeply, but I have found principles of form and rhythm from the study of natural objects, such as pebbles, rocks, bones, trees, plants. Pebbles and rocks show nature's way of working stone and principles of asymmetry. Rocks show the hacked, hewn treatment of stone and have a jagged, nervous rhythm. Bones have a marvellous structural strength and hard tenseness of form, subtle transition of one shape into the next and great variety in section... Shells show nature's hard but hollow form (metal sculpture)."... Moore's most typical figures are neither human beings turned to stone, nor yet exercises in abstract form, but new realities—"object-personages", to use Paul Nash's phrase, "outside the plan of natural phenomena".

It was in 1940, with his air-raid shelter drawings, that Henry Moore really caught for the first time the imagination of the wider British public. As records of the terrifying anonymity of total war in the XXth century, these simple yet tragic drawings seem to restate Masaccio in modern terms. Since the end of the war, when sculpture became possible once more, Moore has increased the range and the richness of his output. It has included the elegiac sweetness of the *Madonna and Child* commissioned for St. Matthew's Church, Northampton, and completely non-figurative exercises in spatial relationships like the sculptural screen he has executed to shut off one end of the roof-garden on the Time/Life building in London, in addition to groups like the *Three Standing Figures* in London's Battersea Park which represent that "encounter" between object-personages in a natural setting which has been one of his long-standing obsessions. ("I would rather have a piece of my sculpture put in a landscape, almost any landscape, than in, or on, the most beautiful building I know.")

He has worked in all mediums. To the stone and wood which were his interest before the war, he has added metal—sometimes casting traditionally as in a draped reclining figure which recalls the classical world, sometimes using its structural strength to create free-standing bone-like figures in which void and solid are so intermingled that neither could exist without the other, or hollow sculptures like those called *Helmets*, in which an imprisoned inner spirit seems to look out at the world from within a smooth sheath or cage. In his studio at the beginning of this year was an immense non-figurative double sculpture of just this type, only carved out of a single elm trunk some five feet in diameter, and a new cast of a *Warrior* carrying a shield on his right arm and with a great wound-cleft frontally splitting his head. Even here, in the first single male figure he has created since his student days, Moore's preoccupation with natural forms persists. Its origin lay in a pebble, the formation of which suggested to the artist a certain configuration of the thigh and hip-bone.

The concurrent development of different idioms has sometimes confused critical judgment of Moore's work. Opposing tastes have rated the Northampton *Madonna*, for example, his best and his worst piece. The artist is untroubled by such divisions of opinion. "I don't change from week to week" he says; "if I am as bad as they say in one kind of work, then I can't be as good as they say in another. They are different sides of my nature." Indeed, throughout his life, Moore has returned to certain basic conceptions, whatever the medium, whatever the idiom, in which he may have expressed them. This central position, this constant consolidation of thought, is perhaps his greatest source of strength. He mistrusts the etiolation of art by its purification into mutually exclusive extremes. Not for Moore the whittling away, the isolation of essences; rather the enrichment of the work by the apprehension of truth at many levels simultaneously. He would like to feel that art can take account of Michel-Angelo as well as Pre-Columbian sculpture, the forces of nature as well as the aspirations of the human mind. "But of course that", he says wryly, "is the hard way."

Henry Moore at work in his Perry Green st

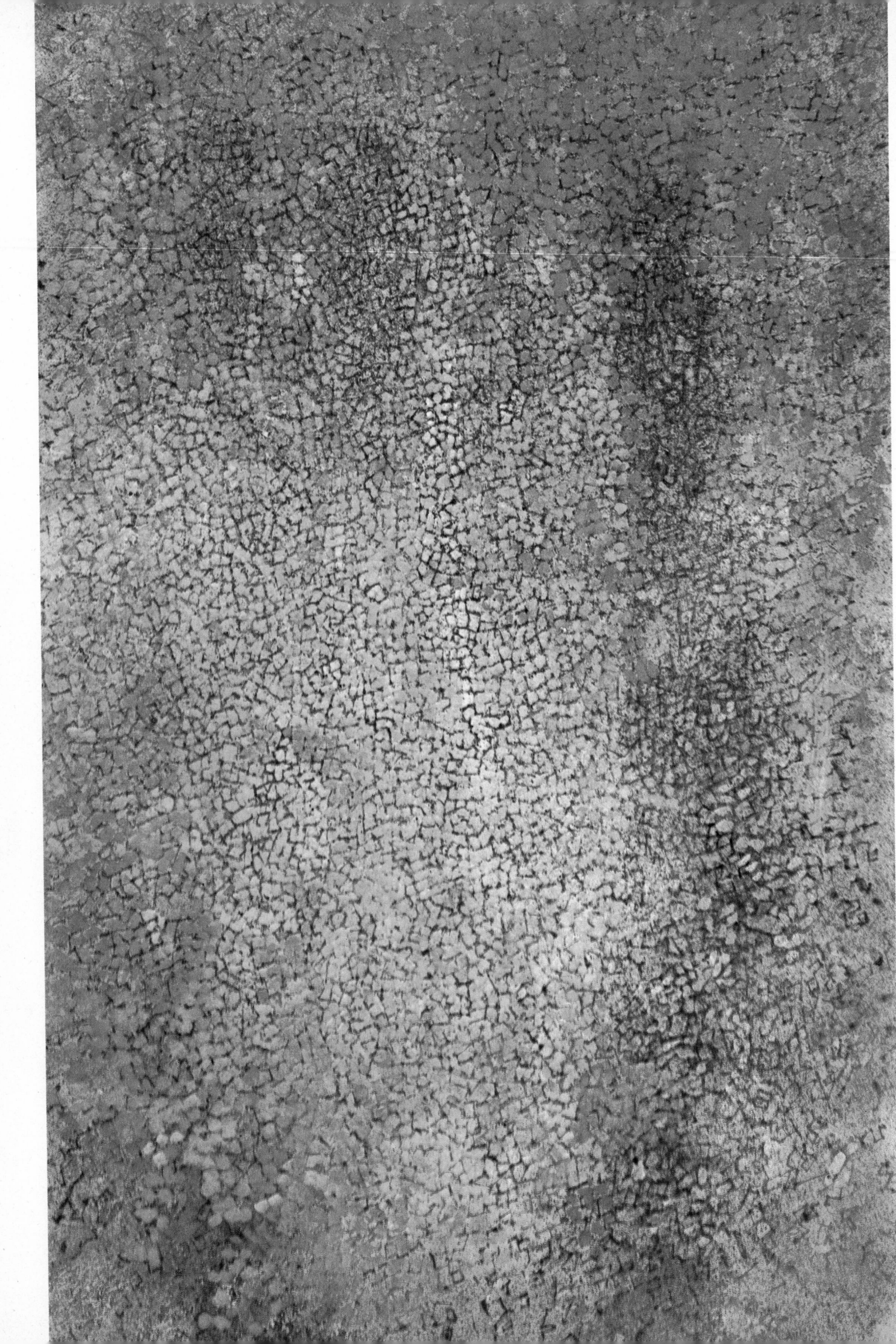

Sage from Wisconsin

BY JANET FLANNER

Opposite : Meditative series Nº 9, tempera, 1954 (17×11½"). On this page, three calligraphic gouache drawings, 1955.

The American artist, Mark Tobey, is now internationally known for his style of "white writing", almost as if he were an author rather than a painter. In truth, his calligraphy is part of his artistic biography, recording his desire to penetrate perspective, whose long view for him lies in the microcosm of colors and plastic forms that make the mystic background of his pictures and indeed the background of his lengthy, curious, rather un-American life. We Americans, having gone West from Europe to make an exported nation of ourselves, later had to import the aesthetics and cultures we had left behind in that immediate East across the Atlantic Ocean, like pictures and books we had failed in our haste to take with us on our initial voyage : specifically in aesthetic matters we have been borrowing from Europe ever since. Thus our contemporary art is mostly borrowed from France. That is to say, like most good Europeans of today, our contemporary art practise largely stems from the German *Blaue Reiter* school founded in Munich by the Russian Kandinsky or from the *Ecole de Paris* dominated by the Spaniard Picasso.

To these specific Continental influences Tobey has remained a strange American exception. The maturing influences of his life have been so Eastern that they are Oriental,—Persian philosophy and Chinese brush strokes. At the end of the first World war, aged twenty eight he was still necessitously earning his living as a commercial artist in New York, robust, handsome and already with a beard like a Titian portrait. This was the war which to the whole civilized world seemed to have achieved the horrible climax of mankind's inventive genius for destruction. In a profound individual revulsion against these aspects of Western Christian civilization, Tobey turned toward a modern Persian philosophy, Bahai, then in the process of establishing itself in the New World—a world long weakened by the multiple factionalisms of the Protestant faith. Bahai is a religion whose mystic generosity acclaims the peaceful oneness of all mankind, a mysticism taken from antique Eastern faiths stressing the sacred unity of men and of all nature in earthly harmony. To the young and uncertain artist this mystique offered the illuminating ancient dual aspect of the soul and the senses. As he turned toward his life career of serious art, Tobey carried with him this alien contemplative spirit which was to supply his work with its secret inner definition.

Then in 1922 he went West from New York to teach in the new Cornish Art School in Seattle, where influences from China and Japan were faintly deposited in exile. Through the small Chinese and Japanese colonies operating their various businesses on their special streets, aspects of their civilization, even if debased, were visible in badly colored cheap Japanese paper prints or, in nobler and more costly form in the XVIIth-XVIIIth century Chinese Ancestor Portraits, then still available ; a refined ancient art, in which, by long practise, line dominates mass and even seemingly eliminates its presence. Tobey became intensely interested in the Eastern bamboo brush stroke which produced this delicacy of speculative line. He began the study of the handling of the bamboo brush with a local Chinese artist friend, Teng Kwei. Ten years later, when Tobey was teaching at the famous Dartington Hall School in England, he was sent out on a voyage of study to Japan and China where this same Chinese artist was his guide. It was on Tobey's return from China to Dartington Hall, a noble old Devonshire castle, in the heart of a rich landscape as English as Shakespeare, that this mystic American, with a Chinese brush in his hand and an Eastern philosophy as his guiding spirit began his "white writing" paintings.

Upon a meditative background of sweeping colors, revealed and connected in small intense harmonies and enriched by their plastic relations, he has added what is called by others "white writing"—the term is not his— which as the last element of the composition is his final communication, in each picture, with form and perspective. This white writing is composed of what look like small graphic signs in patterns and contours, mysterious and personal affirmations of his inner meditative existence which for him finds its only means of communication through the medium of painting. What he seeks to paint is an equilibrium of space and matter, obtained by colors, rythmic as constellations on his canvas combined with small microcosmic elements, all dealing with form as part of motion, and with space as part of the outer balance of man's life. The mystique of his work rationally presented in his own version of today's Western art forms, remains Eastern. This harmonizing of Eastern and Western civilizations may be the result of the co-incidences of his life. He defines co-incidence as an example of growth caused by disparate elements touching each other unexpectedly.

He paints intensely and often belatedly, since the painting first composes itself to the point of completion in his mind and the act of painting is performed later. The titles of his paintings are another version of their meaning. His largest canvas

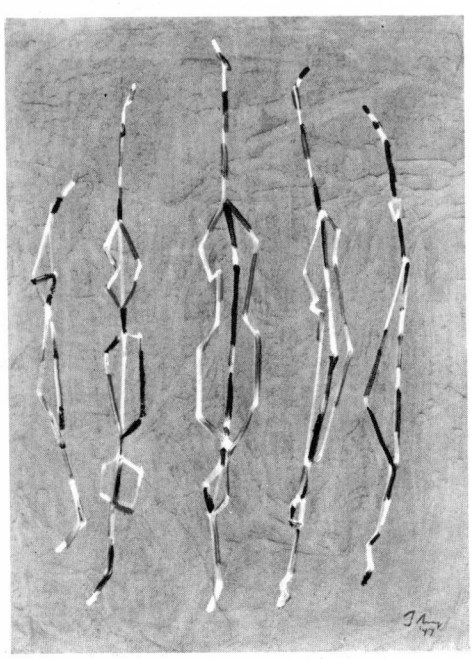

to date, *The Edge of the Month of August,* (1953), was conceived, through the poetry of the phrase itself, as a composition of a changing season, of the motion of the passage of time, with time ascertained and recorded in radiant ripe color—touching, in his imagination, the opening line of one specific harvest month. It took ten years before he painted it as he had seen it at first, complete within his inner eye.

Recognition and the elements of a certain fame in America came to him only in the middle years. Today he has paintings in the Metropolitan Museum and in the Museum of Modern Art of New York, in the museums of Brooklyn, Seattle, San Francisco and in the Chicago Art Institute. The first one man exhibition of his paintings in Paris was held in the spring of 1955 in a Montparnasse gallery. During that winter several of his paintings were shown in Paris with works by the *tachiste* group whose declaration that he had been an American influence on their work surprised him as he does not consider himself an abstract painter. In his third Paris appearance of the year, four of his canvases were included in the "Salute to France" exhibition at the *Musée d'Art Moderne* of Paris. They came from the collection of the New York Museum of Modern Art. Tobey is the American painter who has roused the most interest in France since the war and has been treated as a master of his métier. American art critics early ceded that he was the only American who had brought something so new to the native art scene that it could not be classified, which was exasperating to some of them.

His Dartington Hall experience in England unexpectedly furnished one more long foreign influence. He had gone there supposedly for six months in 1930, at

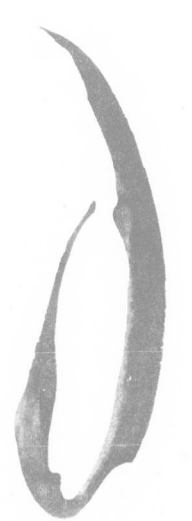

the beginning of the American depression which not only left millionaires without money but often left artists and painters without bread. He remained for seven years, completing another stage in his diverse development as an American. Dartington Hall, a progressive school, was one of the most notable educational and social experiments of that period. It aimed at uniting laborers on the land with the intellectuals of the school, in an ideal community and was indeed a venture into the modern philosophy of living. Its classes ran from kindergarten to preparation for Oxford or Cambridge. Arthur Waley, the Chinese scholar, lived in residence at the Hall while doing some of his translations into English of *Princess Gengi* The Shankar Indian dancers and the Joos Ballet often worked and resided there. This was the longest period Tobey had ever lived outside his own country. He had once spent a winter in France, in 1925, painting outside Chartres, after journeying to the Near East, Greece and Constantinople. Those seven English years were pastoral and poetic influences after the *Sturm und Drang* of American city life.

Tobey was born in Wisconsin in 1890, "the year van Gogh died, of whom I never even heard till perhaps a quarter century later," he recently said, in Paris. He says he had a beautiful childhood with nature, no culture, few books and that the word art was never spoken. As a boy he lived in the village of Trempleau, founded by early French explorers of the Mississippi River on whose headwaters it was built. It contained six hundred inhabitants and one saloon which the adults considered wicked but necessary. In winter when the river froze in the bitter cold of forty degrees below zero, he skated and in summer he fished and swam. Beginning with spring, small sidewheel steamers visited Trempleau bay which was mysteriously fringed with yellow Egyptian lotus lilies, blooming exotically in that septentrional region. His boyhood contained elements of youthful American life left over from Mark Twain's "Tom Sawyer" and Fenimore Cooper's "Last of the Mohicans". Indians had inhabited the region and had used a local red stone for making their peace-pipes which they ceremoniously smoked in pow-pows. Tobey's father who was a housebuilder with intelligent hands, used to carve red stone animals for his son, squirrels, chipmunks, beavers. In the forested hills above Trempleau and its steamboats were caves to which the boy would climb and from where he could see lying below a watery pleiad of seven lakes, shining together on the distant primitive landscape. When he was sixteen his family moved to a steel mill town near Chicago. Tobey began earning his living in a variety of unpleasant ways such as working in the steel mill and later working in Chicago for one dollar a week drawing pretty girl faces for a mail order catalog of womans wear, with Saturday afternoon off for a water-color class at the Art Institute where at first he learned nothing. He says he learns slowly and by osmosis. Suddenly roused by an exposition of paintings by the lush Spanish painter Zuloaga to whom he is still grateful, the whole world began opening up on all sides. In that disorderly digestive appetite of youth he flung himself hungrily on Rembrandt, Raphael, Dostoievski, Artchibascheff, Gorki, Tintoretto and Greco, first educators of his artist's eye and young thinking mind. He went to New York, doing highly paid fashion drawings, moved to the painters quarter in Washington Square and began a series of remarkable sanguine, charcoal and pencil portraits, the latter with a line as fine as a silver point. Most of this young work is lost today though the Knoedler Gallery gave him a show that included a portrait of Mary Garden who had become his patron, of Jacques Copeau and of a governor of New York whose name now is also lost to mind. His artist's life had begun.

He has spent much of his life teaching which he found informative. In teaching he was forced to definitions. He says that he arrived at the conviction that the laws of space and sight in painting correlate the laws of space and time in living; that the journey of the eye in looking at a painting correlates the journey of an individual aware that he is covering a certain distance and who when he looks at a painting is, with equal awareness, following the journey in space which the artist has recorded on his canvas. For Tobey line, not mass, is his preoccupation, which is what led to his so-called white writing as a form of mobile of moving line. What first interested him in the Chinese brush stroke was that it gave a springing line to creation as against the architectonic arrangement of mass known as "building a painting" which he then believed to predominate in Western contemporary art. He thinks a painting is constructed upon the edge of given lines, that the pictorial drama of two walls, for instance, is the point where they meet, which becomes the threshold of new shared life. To him painting is not a profession or a career but a profound emotional part of life, like love in the minds of men who do not paint.

Of friends of his own generation among serious American painters, the closest was the late Marsden Hartley, whose talent was so deeply appreciated too late. Today the only survivor of them all is Lyonnel Feininger, the oldest, most masterly, European-trained painter left in America, Tobey thinks, and the best with whom to talk painting. For the technique of painting can be discussed only between artists just as the painter's imagination is a form of silence which is confided only to the canvas.

The Sleeping Midas of Art

BY PASCAL PIA

Ambroise Vollard, the Creole dealer and publisher, realized at the turn
of the century that academic art had run its course

Ambroise Vollard was very proud of being a Creole. He had first seen the light of day on Reunion Island and it pleased him to believe, as a sop to his conscience, that his sun-drenched birthplace provided a ready-made excuse for his indolence, his pronounced taste for siestas and for his often rather sulky air—like a baby who has been lifted out of its cradle too soon. His father had come to the colony as a very young man, to be a notary's clerk, had married, eventually acquired his employer's practice and had bravely sired ten children. Ambroise was the eldest of these ten little notaries.

Undoubtedly, his being the eldest had something to do with the decision to send Ambroise to France after he had taken his Bachelor's degree. There was nothing whatsoever to suggest that two years at the Faculty of Law in Montpellier, a graduation thesis successfully submitted in Paris and tentative preparations for a Doctorate, would finally lead Monsieur Ambroise Vollard to become a dealer in a kind of painting the mere existence of which was not even suspected by his fellow islanders.

In all probability, it was thanks to a taste for strolling that Vollard succeeded in deviating from the path his family had mapped out for him. In 1889, the quays along the Seine were no less attractive than they are today. In fact they were even more so, for the dealers in books and prints displayed a larger and more varied selection than is now to be seen on their stalls. Had he been better off, who knows if young Vollard might not have wasted more *louis d'or* on engravings in the style of Meissonier or Bouguereau than the number of francs he spent on the purchase of etchings,

lithographs and original drawings. Sketches by Constantin Guys could be found on the quays from two francs up. Two gold francs, it is true, but that is still only three hundred paper francs of today.

Wandering along the quays, browsing through gallery after gallery looking at paintings and prints, Vollard began to discover a vocation as a dealer, which soon led him to abandon the Law completely. To initiate himself into the mysteries of the dealer's trade, Vollard became, at a salary of one hundred and twenty-five francs a month, an employee of a gallery, the *Union Artistique* which dealt only in academic painting.

Outside his job, he dealt, on his own account, in engravings by Rops and drawings by Forain, Willette and Steinlen, which he would buy cheap after they had been used by the illustrated weeklies: *Chat Noir, Pierrot* or *Le Courrier Français. Le Courrier Français* led him from Willette to Louis Legrand, thus putting him on the road which led, inevitably, to his meeting with Degas. In the same way, his first dealings with Steinlen, Bruant's regular illustrator, provided him with the occasion for approaching Lautrec. To advance from Degas to John Lewis Brown, from Lautrec to Bonnard, to Vuillard, to Maurice Denis, and from these to Cézanne whom they had recognized as their master, Vollard had often only to take a step or to cross a road. Having

Above: details from portraits of Vollard by Bonnard, Picasso, Cézanne and Renoir. Right: Vollard in 1925 at the home of the painter Roussel near Paris; he spent every Sunday here for forty years. Bonnard and Vuillard were also frequent visitors.

Engraving by Picasso for Balzac's Chef-d'Œuvre Inconnu, *one of two books illustrated by Picasso for Vollard.*

found his artists, he gave up his job at the *Union Artistique* and determined to live economically so as to have sufficient funds to be a dealer himself. As a precaution, he provided himself with a cask of sea-biscuits, or army biscuits, a form of nourishment which keeps easily and which, when moistened and consumed, dispels hunger pangs by swelling up like a poultice in the stomach.

At that time, which was about 1890, Vollard still did not have a gallery. He worked "from home" as the expression was. To his drawings and engravings had been added a *Nude* by Renoir for which he was vainly asking two hundred and fifty francs and which he later sold for four hundred. Today it is to be found in the Musée Rodin, after the sculptor had finally bought it for twenty-five thousand francs. It must be added here that, for a beginner like Vollard, owning a Renoir was already something of an achievement. Although no one was clamoring to buy Renoirs, his paintings, like those by most of the good Impressionists, had already begun to find an outlet in the Rue Laffitte, particularly at Durand-Ruel's.

The Rue Laffitte, in the 'nineties' already had the same significance for painting as the Rue La Boétie and the Rue de Seine were to assume later. The popularity of the Boulevards and the proximity of the auction rooms of the Hôtel Drouot had determined all the dealers to set themselves up

between the Carrefour Drouot and Notre-Dame de Lorette. Monsieur Vollard was determined, as soon as he could, to have a gallery in the street down which walked all the Paris collectors and all the most serious connoisseurs from the provinces and from abroad. In 1893 he rented, at 39, Rue Laffite, between the Rue Lafayette and the Rue de la Victoire, a modest gallery now occupied by a shoe-maker. It was there that he had his first private exhibition, consisting of a group of sketches by Manet bought from his widow.

The following year, Vollard "expanded". From 39 Rue Laffitte he moved to more spacious premises at number 41, now demolished. In December 1895 he presented the first important collection of canvases by Cézanne. Vollard was introduced to Cézanne by Emile Bernard and Maurice Denis, and succeeded in persuading him to show his pictures which he still was reluctant to expose to the sneers of the public and the condemnation of the critics. Did Vollard himself believe in Cézanne's future? It would be hard to say. Perhaps he said to himself that among the veterans of modern painting, Cézanne was the only one whom Durand-Ruel and the Bernheim brothers had left to his initiative. Convinced or not of the value of Cézanne's art, in any case, he did what none of the other dealers had dared to do: he devoted his whole window space and all his walls to

In his autobiography Souvenirs d'un Marchand de Tableaux *Ambroise Vollard wrote : "I was the subject of one of Picasso's most important portraits. Naturally certain connoisseurs made the obvious joke asking what it represented. The son of one of my friends, a little boy of four, put his finger on it and, without hesitating, said : "that's Voyard". To the left, the portrait. Hermetic Cubist period. Moscow Museum, (36 × 25").*

Following page : Picasso illustration for Balzac's Chef-d'Œuvre Inconnu, 1931. *Vollard wrote—"of all the works I ever published, the one that proved the most intriguing to bibliophiles." Picasso's "introduction" is comprised of abstract linear patterns but the text itself is accompanied by engravings in his classic manner. Facing following page :* Interior with pink wall-paper, *a lithograph by Vuillard, from an album published by Vollard.*

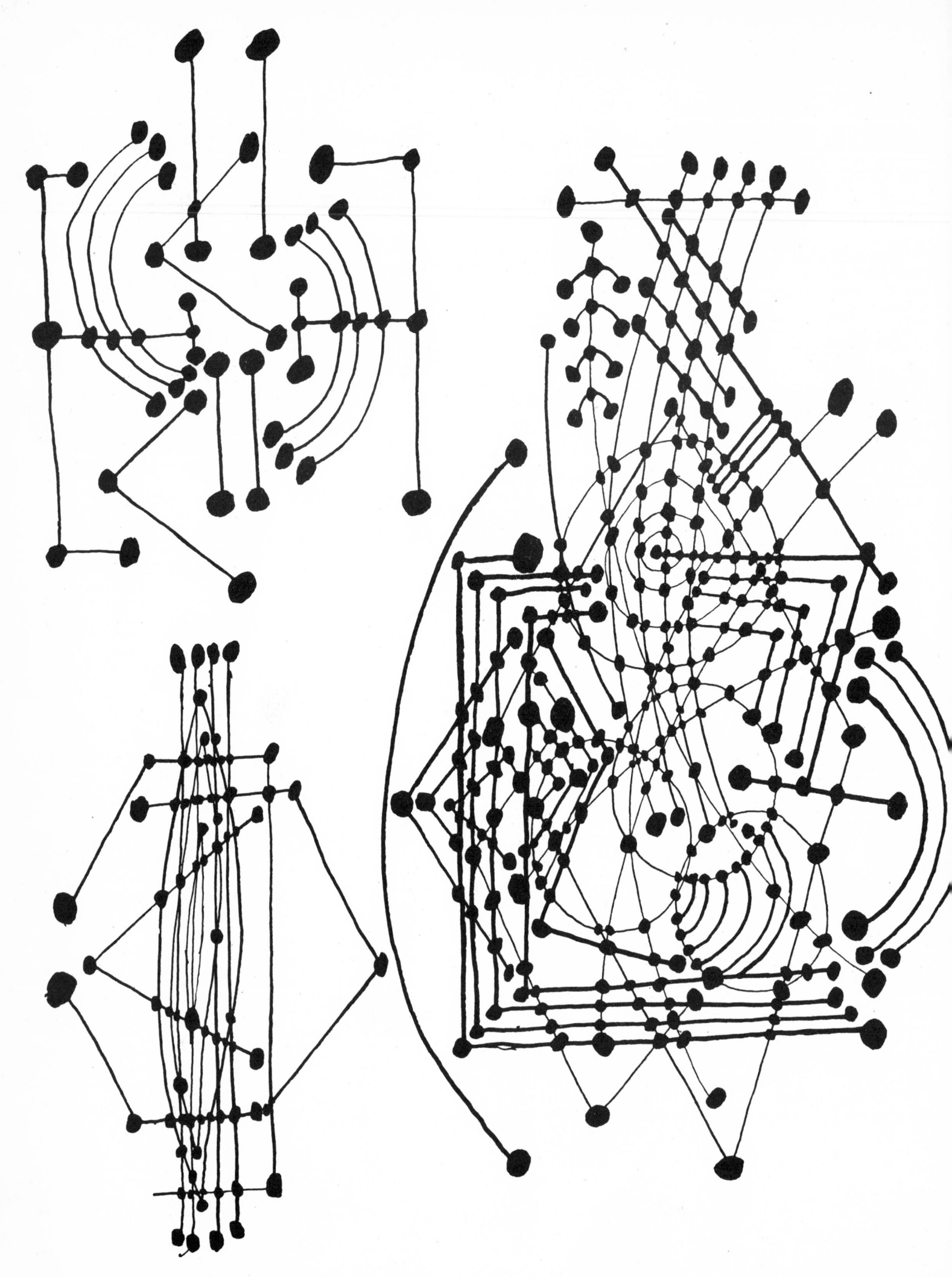

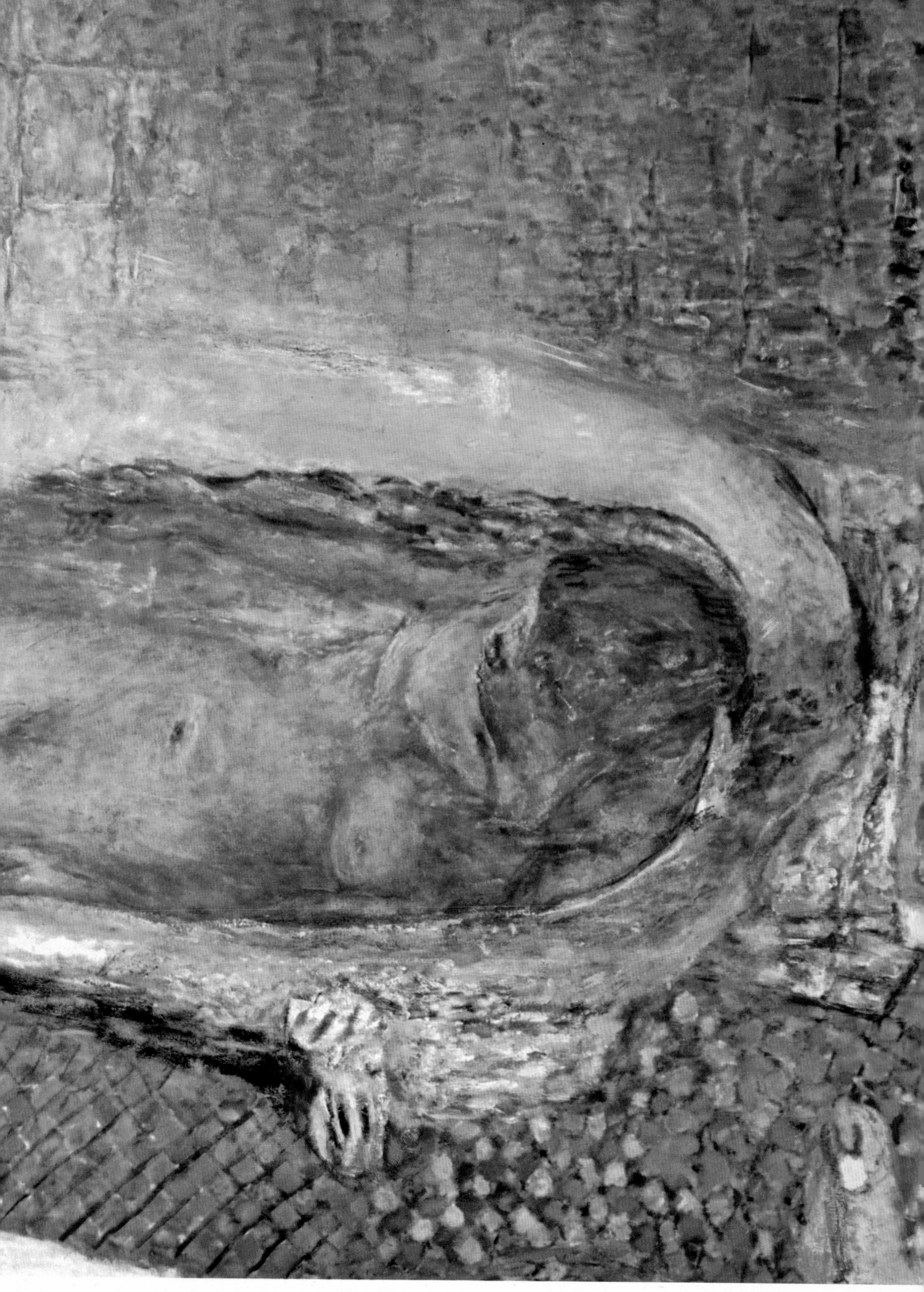

Pierre Bonnard : Nude in Bath. *1930. Petit Palais, Paris. 36½ × 57½″. Bonnard was one of Vollard's outstanding painters.*

A **Matisse reproduced for the first time**: Saint-Tropez, *oil on cardboard*, (10 × 15"). *This painting from the little museum in the town hall of Bagnols-sur-Cèze, in the south of France, has remained almost unknown. It dates back to 1904 ; in June of that year Vollard organized the first Matisse exhibition ; it was not a success. After the show young Matisse left for Saint-Tropez with his family. During his summer stay there he changed his manner, brightening his palette under the influence of Signac.*

Cézanne's work. On that particular day, Fate smiled on Vollard. There is no doubt that his success was decided by the Cézanne exhibition in December 1895. It was not that the sales were sensational, but the show attracted many connoisseurs. Until then the only person to exhibit Cézanne had been old Tanguy the proprietor of an art supply shop in the Rue Clauzel, who asked from forty to one hundred francs for the paintings without ever finding a purchaser. At the opening of the exhibition in the Rue Laffite, Claude Monet bought three Cézannes from Vollard. Auguste Pellerin, a rich margarine manufacturer, acquired the most important picture for his own collection. An unknown buyer carried off a minuscule still life of a pot of jam for ten francs.

The Cézanne exhibition was to a large degree responsible for Vollard's success as a dealer for it brought him, as of 1896, an entirely new group of painters : Denis, Bonnard, Vuillard, Roussel, Vallotton—in short all the artists of the *Revue Blanche*, all the painters in the entourage of Félix Fénéon and Alfred Jarry.

Vollard's faults, his bursts of anger, his bored or contemptuous airs, his grumbling, his systematic rudeness, have been remarked upon by too many witnesses for it to be possible to ignore them. But it is worth noting that he has never been severely criticized except by those who only met him after he had become a "success". To the later Impressionists, to the Pointillists, to Signac, to Maximilien Luce, to the

Nabis and their friends, Monsieur Vollard, despite his rudenesses, remained, more or less confusedly, the architect of Cézanne's glory.

To return to Vollard's history as a dealer, his zenith, in our sense, was reached in the fifteen years which preceded the first World War. In 1899, Vollard, continuing his ascent, had climbed from the end to the beginning of the Rue Laffitte—from number 41 to number 6 to be precise. There he had found a gallery with a mezzanine and a basement. This basement was "Vollard's cellar" described by so many people who had probably never seen it, except through the ventilator, where Vollard had installed a dining-room and kitchen. Apollinaire wrote of this tiled cellar whose dead white walls gave it the aspect of a "monk's refectory" where the dealer entertained carefully selected guests to meals of curried chicken and other elaborately prepared dishes : his painters, Alfred Jarry, Claude Terrasse the composer, some of his compatriots, Dierx and Marius-Ary Leblond—collectors like Count Kessler and even society women like Madame Missia Sert. As for his gallery, Vollard seemed to want it to have a decrepit air. Through the dusty windows of its broad façade, passers-by could see canvases piled up in a corner, boxes of biscuits, dirty collars and old bits of wrapping paper. A Van Gogh exhibition—the most complete there has ever been—marked the opening of this particular Vollard gallery. In 1904, it was the scene of the first Matisse exhibition.

From then on—and success had obviously come to him in a manner that was indisputable—Vollard gave up organizing exhibitions in the formal sense. He now only showed canvases to prospective buyers who insisted on seeing them. His own collection had been increased by a considerable number of Renoirs, Degas, Lautrecs, and to his Bonnards, Vuillards, Denis and Roussels, had gradually been added works by Picasso, Derain, Vlaminck and Rouault. However Vollard always displayed a marked reserve in regard to Cubism.

In fact, from 1908, Vollard had entered upon what can be called his period of digestion, which lasted until his death. He had become rich enough to buy a great deal and only to sell in his own time and at his own price. As he liked to sleep and as he could do so without his prosperity suffering, he dozed away freely in his gallery, hardly even lifting his heavy eyelids when a visitor entered.

Four years after the armistice he bought a house at 28 Rue de Martignac which was henceforth to be both his home and his place of business. It was from the Rue Martignac that the last of the Vollard editions were issued the first of them dating from the beginning of the century and from the dinners in the cellar. According to Vollard, he had became a publisher because of his first name and because, on the quays, he had come across a book published by the famous firm of Ambroise Firmin-Didot. The real truth, rather more banal, is that he was only looking for a new mode of expression for his painters through the medium of books. He had previously published single engravings before he began to publish books of engravings. Some of his publications are among the most beautiful in existence—in particular, *Parallèlement* with lithographs by Bonnard, printed in raspberry pink. Others are sumptuous rather than really beautiful, and their plates would gain by being separated from the text which they in no way illustrate. It is not hard to find the reason for this inconsistency. Vollard only published books on account of plates which he had already had engraved or which had been lying in a drawer for some time. The text meant very little to him, and he did not hesitate to illustrate

Above, one of the 82 wood-cuts made by Rouault to illustrate Suarès' Passion, *published by Ambroise Vollard in 1939.*

the *Mimes of Courtesans* with scenes of brothels by Degas which made no claim to depict the heroines portrayed by Lucian.

A great deal has been said about how much time and money Vollard spent on his editions. We may perhaps be permitted to think that the results would have been better still if some of these publications had been conceived with less lack of constraint or by an editor less inclined to somnolence. But we may be thought too severe: Vollard is dead having left a fortune valued at more than a billion francs. Is not this a perfect answer to every criticism? And does not his boldness of 1895 largely compensate for the indifference he displayed, during his last years, towards every neophyte?

◄ *Left: Renoir's* Portrait of Vollard as a Toreador *Walter P. Chrysler Jr. coll. New York; 1917 (40 ½ × 32 ½"). Paul Léautaud tells the following story about this portrait and the relations between Vollard and Renoir in* Théâtre de Maurice Boissard *: "In order to enjoy this story one must know that Ambroise Vollard has a face... how to describe it? a face... I can't get the word out!... a face... that's slightly simian, yes, that's it, slightly simian and at the same time very sympathetic. One day he went to see Renoir in his garden at Cagnes in the south of France. They were both in the garden. At one point Vollard, as a joke, started swinging by his two hands from the branch of a tree. Renoir looked at him. 'Vollard, my friend,' he said to him, 'that's not a cocoanut tree'... And too, you have to see Renoir's portrait of Vollard as a toreador, with its oh! so pink stockings and its oh! so green jacket! It's marvellous!"*

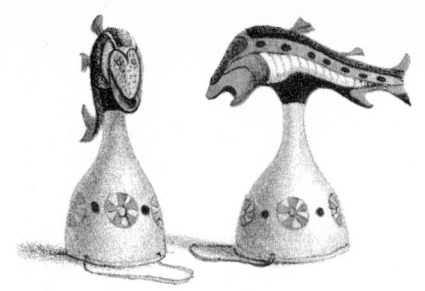

This was Brazil

BY HENRI HELL

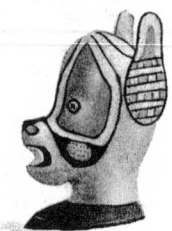

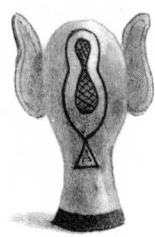

How a pupil of Jean-Louis David became a reporter
on the banks of the Amazon

On the 26th of March in the year of grace 1816, after a crossing that lasted two months, a colony of French artists landed at Rio de Janeiro where the coronation of King Juan VI of Portugal was being celebrated. There were six of them : Monsieur Le Breton, permanent secretary of the Fine Arts Department at the Institut de France and leader of the little colony, Monsieur Taunay, a sculptor, Monsieur Grandjean, an architect, Monsieur Pradier, a copperplate engraver, Monsieur Ovide, a Professor of mechanics and Monsieur Jean-Baptiste Debret, a painter.

They were not a group of hardy travel enthusiasts in search of adventure in Brazil. They were minor ambassadors, civil servants by appointment. They had come at the request of the Brazilian Government, to found the Academy of Fine Arts of Rio de Janeiro.

They had a powerful protector, the Count d'Abarca, Minister of Foreign Affairs. They were received at Court and receptions were given for them. They were full of plans and enthusiasm. Everything began under the best auspices. Alas ! it was not until ten years after the arrival of the French artists that the buildings of the Academy of Fine Arts were finished — on the 5th of November 1826. The Frenchmen had not reckoned with the jealousies they were going to arouse among the local artists, the obstacles that the latter were going to put in their way, or the intrigues and political passions they were to encounter. The very year of their arrival, the Count d'Abarca, their principal supporter died. With his disappearance their troubles began. Le Breton, the virtual director of the Academy, was replaced by a mediocre local artist, the

father of twelve children, who made the lives of the French artists almost unbearable. However they bravely held out until final victory — with Jean-Baptiste Debret at their head, Le Breton having died in the meantime.

Debret accepted all the disappointments philosophically : "Nothing will alter my conviction of my usefulness or the great enthusiasm which the development of my art inspires in me beneath so pure a sky and in a place where nature deploys, before the eyes of the painter with a philosophical bent, a profusion of riches unknown to a European. This is an inexhaustible source of delightful memories which will enchant me for the rest of my days."

Jean-Baptiste Debret wrote these lines upon his return to France in 1831, after fifteen years absence. These "delightful" memories were soon to assume a concrete form : lithographs in color, executed to illustrate a very important work in three volumes, published in Paris by Firmin-Didot under the title "Picturesque and Historical Journey to Brazil".

There was nothing that predisposed Debret to write and illustrate such a book. He did not have a very pronounced artistic personality and, before his journey

On the left : Indian carnival led by a musician. On the right : not bop in Brazil but, according to Debret, a dance by « civilized Indians ». The ornaments around the title are headpieces.

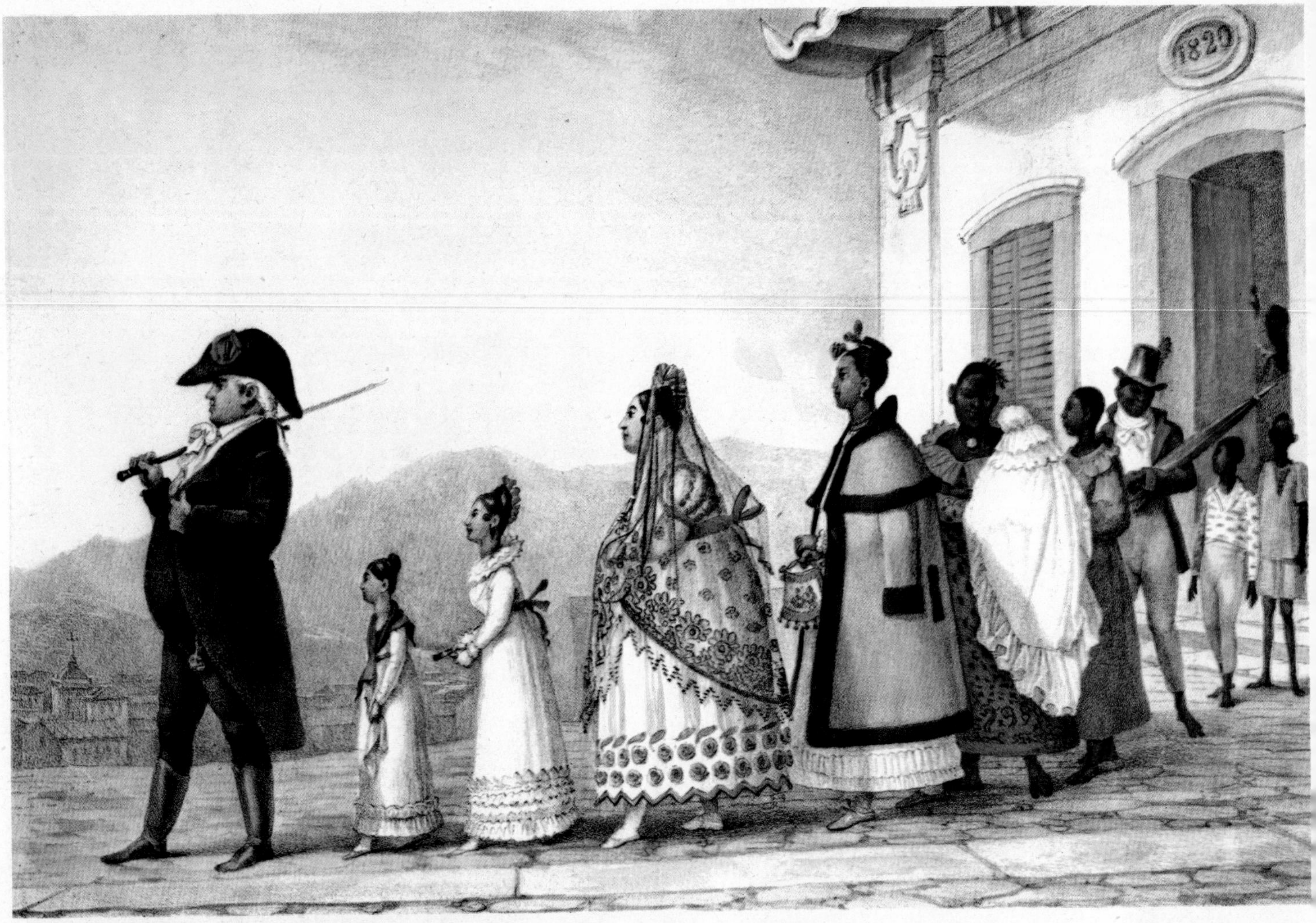
1820

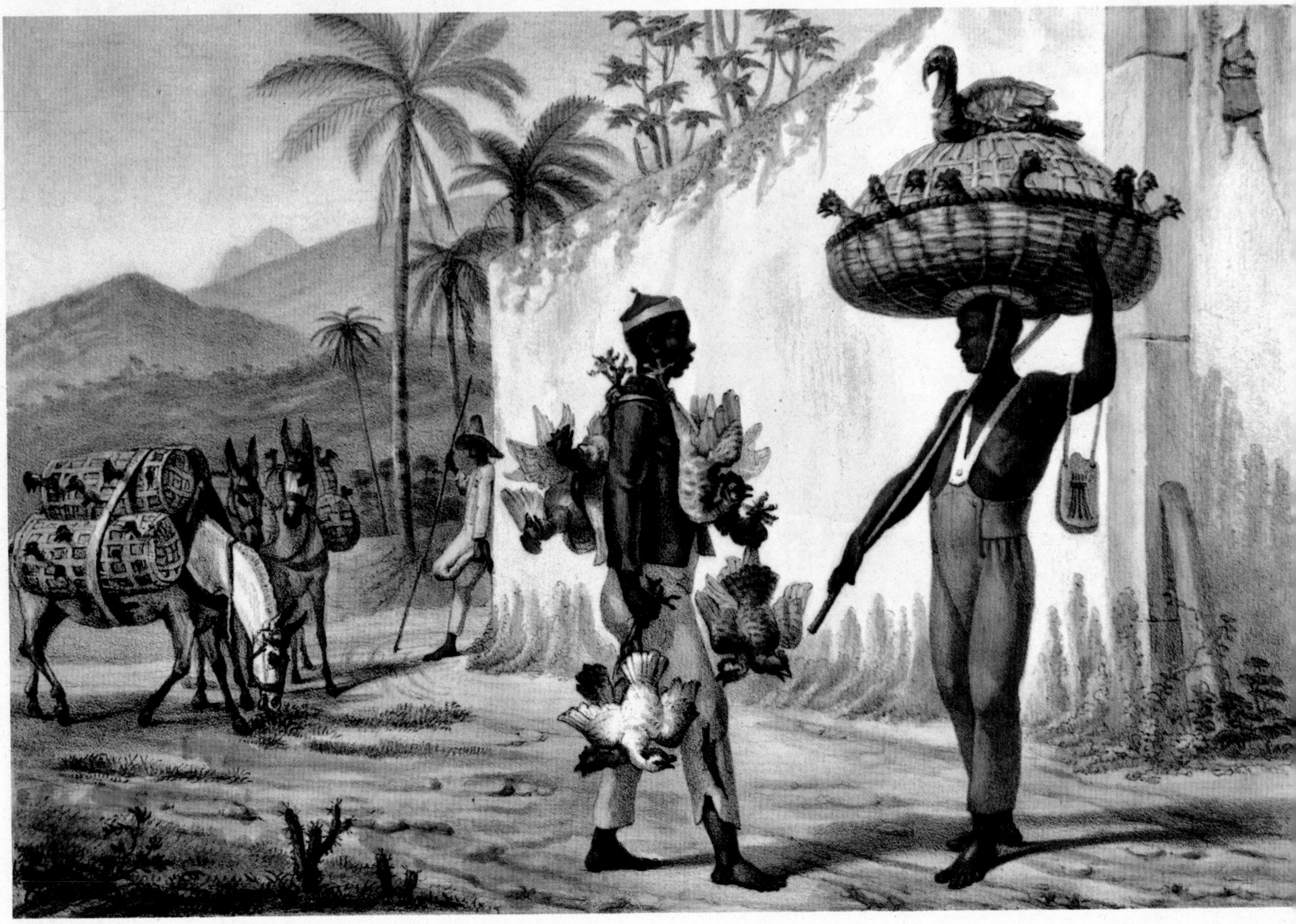

to Brazil, pursued the career of an official painter in the purest academic tradition. He imitated David whose pupil he was. Like the latter, he painted pictures with ancient and mythological subjects. The Messenian General Aristomenus Rescued By A Young Maiden — The Physician Eristratus Diagnosing the Illness of the Young Antiochus, etc. Next he discovered a vocation for historical painting and glorified the god of the day, Napoleon : Napoleon at Tilsitt, Napoleon's Address To the Bavarians, etc. Not an ounce of talent, but many academic honors. In Brazil, he continued his career as official painter in the service of the King and the Court. But his greatest pleasure was to make innumerable sketches and water-colors of the scenes of every day Brazilian life. He was not content with these notes, in pencil and in color, but began to instruct himself, to learn the history of the country, and to study its customs and its topography. The official painter became a historian, geographer, ethnologist and "reporter".

Debret's stay in Rio de Janeiro coincided with the political regeneration of Brazil and ended with the revolution of

1831. He attended the coronation of Juan VI and then, in 1822, that of Dom Pedro who became Emperor of Brazil. When he left the country, Dom Pedro had abdicated. But, more than history or geography, it was ethnology that interested Debret.

How could a man born in the XVIIIth century avoid being attracted by the Indians and their customs? And what a delight to establish that they were just like the civilized Whites — with the same beliefs and ideas, so Debret assures us like the good idealist he was : "To sum up, you will find the elements or the seed of all that the human mind has conceived in the way of philosophical, elevated, admirable or even strange ideas among the savage Indians put into practice simply by instinct or by inspiration." But that does not mean that the savage has nothing to gain from contact with civilization. Debret firmly believed in the benefits of the latter as the following lines testify : "By the effects of civilization, the Indian race should achieve a perceptible amelioration brought about by gradually blending with the Brazilian race, of European origin."

To the reader of 1834, Debret's work provided very valuable information about

Above : a handwriting competition for schoolchildren on Saint Alexis day. The ornaments on this page represent carnaval masks and headpieces.

the Indians of Brazil. He brought them all to life with his pen or brush. Here are the Camacans and the Bogres, both warrior tribes ; the Botocoudos are as savage as one could expect any savage to be ; the Gouaycouroues, who are warriors and farmers, also deal in horses ; the Guaranis are musicians. Debret mentions the "Savages of the Mission of Saint-Joseph" who are musicians like the Guaranis ; he finds them handsome, gay, agile, modest and tatooed. But those who capture his attention most are the Cabocles — the civilized natives. They have been baptised and use hammocks or a mat spread on a wooden frame to serve as a divan. The women often work as laundresses in the city of Rio de Janeiro. They assemble every day to go and do their washing on the banks of the small river which runs under the bridge of Catero, one of the suburbs of the city.

How did the savage Indians become civilized ? "The good-nature of the native", Debret tells us, "succumbed to the blandishments of the European." The wild Indians came in a deputation to Rio to ask the sovereign either for implements to cultivate their land, or for arms so that they could serve as auxiliaries. They lodged with their families in the public work-shops owned by the Government. It was thanks to the civilized Indians that Debret was able to enter into contact with the other Indians in the heart of the Brazilian forest, and these "savages" did not fail to frighten him a little. This is how he describes one of his contacts with them : "During these friendly and most interesting demonstrations, the observant naturalist suddenly feels himself overcome, despite his love of mankind,

by a feeling of sadness at the spectacle of his face reproduced in a savage being in whom the subtlety and perfection of the senses appear only in an aspect apathetic and untamed. He is involuntarily reminded of a wild beast and, just as if he had met one in this jungle, he considers himself lucky to have provoked nothing but a glance of indifference."

The ingenuous charm of his style and of his opinions occurs again in the plates illustrating the three now very rare volumes of the "Picturesque Journey." Turning over their pages, the whole daily life of Brazil in the past century springs to life before our eyes, in all its reality and simple poetry. We witness the departure of a mulatto woman of the prosperous artisan class on her way to the country for Christmas ; we see a government employee strolling with his family and his many servants. Further on he shows the "burning of Judas in effigy, on Holy Saturday, at the moment of the Hallelujah", and then an official ceremony. After the streeets, come houses : we enter the most humble as well as the most prosperous. After dinner, we relax on the veranda with the young Brazilian, in contemplative silence and drift into that "exquisite balancing of the soul, very imperfectly expressed as sweet and dreamy melancholy."

Debret perhaps believed that he was a great painter of historical subjects, but, thanks to the freshness of his vision, he remains for us the charming and poetic observer of a Brazil that is rapidly disappearing with the advent of the skyscraper.